Plans for Peace

Plans for Peace

NEGOTIATION AND THE ARAB-ISRAELI CONFLICT

Karen A. Feste

 PRAEGER

New York
Westport, Connecticut
London

Library of Congress Cataloging-in-Publication Data

Feste, Karen A.
    Plans for peace: negotiation and the Arab–Israeli conflict /
Karen A. Feste.
        p.   cm.
    Includes bibliographical references and index.
    ISBN 0–275–94227–9 (pbk. : alk. paper)
    1. Israel–Arab conflicts.   2. Jewish–Arab relations—1949–
I. Title.
DS119.7.F49   1991b
956.04—dc20   91–37251

British Library Cataloguing in Publication Data is available.

A hardcover edition of *Plans for Peace: Negotiation and the Arab–Israeli
Conflict* is available from the Greenwood Press imprint of Greenwood
Publishing Group, Inc. (ISBN 0–313–26361–2)

Library of Congress Catalog Card Number: 91–37251
ISBN: 0–275–94227–9

First published in 1991

Praeger Publishers, One Madison Avenue, New York, NY 10010
An imprint of Greenwood Publishing Group, Inc.

Printed in the United States of America

The paper used in this book complies with the
Permanent Paper Standard issued by the National
Information Standards Organization (Z39.48–1984)

P

The author and publisher gratefully acknowledge the following for permission to use copyrighted materials:

Lord Caradon, "Security Council Resolution 242," in Caradon, Arthur J. Goldberg, Mohamed H. El-Zayyat, and Abba Eban, *U.N. Security Resolution 242: A Case Study in Diplomatic Ambiguity* (Washington, D.C.: Institute for the Study of Diplomacy, Georgetown University, 1981), 5–6. Copyright 1981 Institute for the Study of Diplomacy. Reprinted by permission.

Middle East Review, Rutgers University, New Brunswick, N.J. Excerpts from Adam M. Garfinkle. "Common Sense about Middle East Diplomacy: Implications for U.S. Policy in the Near Term." *Middle East Review* 17 (Winter 1984–85).

American Arab Affairs, The American Arab Affairs Council, Washington, D.C. Excerpts from Fred J. Khouri. " Major Obstacles to Peace: Ignorance, Myths and Misconceptions." *American Arab Affairs* 16 (Spring 1986).

Atlantic Monthly. Exerpts from Alfred N. Whitehead. "An Appeal to Sanity." *Atlantic Monthly* (1939).

To Little

Contents

Illustrations

Acknowledgements

Thank you to Millie Van Wyke for giving numerous hours of technical care and genuine concern over the language, form, and content of materials that are presented here.

Thank you to Serge Herzog for meticulous effort and good esthetic sense in producing the tables and creating the maps in this book, and

Thank you to Roger Hanson for continuous, solid, long-term advice on academic and professional matters, and who first encouraged my interest in the Middle East.

Introduction

Middle East politics operate in a dynamic arena where old and long-standing issues continue to resurface as significant dimensions in contemporary crises. The decade of the 1990s was ushered in with a host of unresolved political, economic, and demographic problems accompanied by feelings of frustration, deep anger, and despair among many people. From the *intifada* to the Gulf War, once again the place of Israel and the fate of the Palestinians appeared as important aspects within the broader challenge to the global community of devising ways to structure and ensure stability across the entire geographic region.

Protracted hostilities, religious passions, invasions, occupations, and violence have created policy problems for all interested states—those in the immediate vicinity and beyond—forcing them to define their respective principles of national security in the context of balancing levels of political linkage across a multitude of conflict events. The transitional age of the international system, denoted by changing alliance patterns and revised domestic and foreign policy agendas, has effectively weakened the previous framework of bargaining rules that existed in Middle East politics and contributed to an overall sense of uncertainty about the future. Neither a strong, widely respected leader nor an all-embracing ideology that could inspire and guide peaceful political change into a new regional world order has yet emerged.

Within the Palestinian movement and for the Israeli government, questions are being raised about the direction of leadership and the constellation and power of positions advocated by militants and moderates in both camps. Militant sentiments tend to reduce any potential for negotiated solutions, yet experience with violence tends to negate the possibility for growth among moderates. The whirlwind of emotional outcry and seething tensions that dominate the region make it impossible to predict the form of any final settlement. There may be a possibility on the horizon, however, for the international community to move forcefully to resolve the Arab–Israeli conflict, the dispute often identified at the center of any Middle East crisis, the time bomb threatening the whole area.

The Gulf War and the anti-Israeli uprising have seriously affected the nationalist cause and political aspirations for both Jews and Palestinians. The latter group suffered economically to maintain the intifada momentum, and Palestinians sustained financial losses as a result of the Kuwait occupation. On the diplomatic front, maverick alignment with the Iraqi policies of Saddam Hussein compromised the growing support and sympathy for the Palestine Liberation Organization (PLO). Meanwhile, the Israeli policies in the West Bank and Gaza held down Palestinian independence but led to considerable criticism of the Jewish state. The unprovoked Iraqi missile attacks on Tel Aviv, however, evoked sympathy from the world community, including some Arab states, and underscored the role of Israel as a pariah in the conglomeration of Middle East countries. Self-determination in the name of nationalism remains the chief goal for Palestinians; recognition and national security are still primary goals for Israel.

These major unresolved issues continue to appear as agenda items on most Middle East negotiation proposals for settling outstanding claims regardless of the origin of the particular conflict. Advocates of an international peace conference have sought to centralize this theme as the key to any brokered political harmony in the region. There is a strong tendency to collect all political disputes among Middle East actors into a massive, holistic form and to designate the core problem as the Arab–Israeli conflict. Such perceptions influence the outside world and help shape the dominant image that defines the current Middle East political environment. Two recent events in the international arena illustrate how this process works.

First, shortly after the Gulf crisis began in August 1990, Saddam Hussein proposed a linkage between the question of a Palestinian homeland and withdrawal of Iraqi military troops from Kuwait. Trading concessions across political issues had little appeal to the United States or other members of the international community, yet the crossover from one problem to another presented an opportunity to promote a wider Middle East settlement, specifically including negotiation over the Arab–Israeli dispute.

Second, just one month before the outbreak of hostilities in the Persian Gulf, in December 1990—when the world was preoccupied with the escalating conflict stemming from the Iraq–Kuwait–Saudi Arabia crisis—the United Nations Security Council drafted a resolution reflecting the perpetually drawn interconnections, saying it felt that the "convening at an appropriate time of an international peace conference on the Middle East properly structured, with the participation of the parties concerned, would facilitate the achievement of a comprehensive settlement and lasting peace in the Middle East" ("U.S. Joins U.N. Vote against Israel," 1990). After war broke out, France proposed anew that an international peace conference on the Middle East be held after the fighting concluded, and the European community gave its endorsement to the idea.

Throughout the months of military buildup, it seemed impossible that Iraq—an Arab state that enjoyed little official support in the world for its actions against Kuwait, other than the support of the Palestinians—would drift into a major war against the United States, a superpower and Israel's supreme ally. Although the question of military victory was never in doubt, the way a military success translates into a political victory is far less clear. In the Arab world, a decisive loss or a stalemate does not rule out the possibility of diplomatic bargaining over territory.

The tactics of warfare indicate that Saddam Hussein calculated ways to compensate for the extreme disparity in the power balance not only between his country and the United States but also between the Palestinians and the Israelis: by striking Israel, he opened the opportunity for the conflict to spread over other issues in order to achieve an impact on the political situation in Arab countries who had joined the U.S.-led coalition against Iraq. Moreover, this action offered the chance to divide the opposition as a way to pose as the champion of justice for the Arab dispossessed, thereby focusing attention for Palestinians as the victimized party. The policy backfired, however, and instead, moral scores were tallied for Israel as the victimized party when the country exhibited patience and restraint in delaying retaliation to numerous missile attacks at the start of the war. Nonetheless, it is fair to say that both sides can be rightfully regarded as suffering parties in the play of Middle East intrigue.

The tactics of peace negotiations—including the pace of progress, agenda setting, the willingness of players to participate, and overall bargaining strategies—are derived to some extent from interpreting wartime experience and from promoting plans that address the problems of power balance and victimization.

The Middle East is not a tranquil place; power remains precarious, and borders are not respected. Although the Iraqi occupation of Kuwait was foiled, Syria continues to occupy Lebanon, and Israel still occupies the West Bank and Gaza. Only Egypt, among the Arab states, has recognized the state of Israel, and Israel refuses to recognize the self-determination claim of the Palestinians. At the start of 1991, a few legislators in the Israeli Knesset proposed a bill requiring Israel to withdraw from the Gaza strip, marking the first time that lawmakers formally urged Israel to move from the breeding ground of the ongoing revolt that has cost approximately eight hundred Palestinian lives. The proposal suggested Israel withdraw from Gaza after making security arrangements or within two years. The area would be handed over to the United Nations or to a governing body of Palestinians. Both the government of Yitzhak Shamir and the PLO denounced the idea, however.

The people of the Middle East have not been successful in building a stable and settled system of nation-states in the region. Consequently, they often seek the assistance of the Great Powers. Yet, in any negotiated solution, no outside country has been able thus far to impose peace, order, or transition to democracy because political legitimacy remains a regional issue, the rules to resolve political crises are set regionally, and the memories of wrongs are long and bitter on all sides. Wars, however, often bring issues of settlement to the fore. In the Middle East, the structure for settlement is arranged around three general themes: (1) the role of legitimacy, opposition, and nationalist rivalry; (2) the role of outside global powers as negotiation participants; and (3) the role and strategy for dealing with victimized, suffering parties. When the power disequilibrium among antagonists is substantial, the key strategy of the weaker players is to widen the conflict domain to divert main objectives and to foster the idea of interrelationships among all issues. This process pressures the great powers into becoming active participants in conflict and in negotiations, including international peace conferences.

Is it possible to solve the Arab–Israeli conflict through negotiation? The long-standing, resilient Arab–Israeli dispute is an intriguing conflict because no method of resolution has produced a peaceful outcome of any duration. Neither violent means nor negotiation attempts have led to a satisfactory solution for all parties. Instead, the intense feelings that underlie policy objectives for each side have served continuously as a catalyst both for renewed physical fighting and for consideration of the plans, proposals, and prospects for peace.

There is much talk these days about the peace process and the importance of negotiating a settlement. The time is ripe; time is of the essence. Negotiate now, or the moment will be lost and the conflict will go on, perhaps indefinitely and perhaps intolerably. It is far easier to understand *why* the Arabs and the Jews should sit down and discuss their differences than to know *how* they should proceed to reach a successful resolution. What are the precise mechanics of compromise that might work in this case? What overall strategy of negotiation could be followed? What tactics need to be applied by each side to ensure a mutually acceptable outcome?

These are puzzling questions, in spite of the fact that this conflict has been overanalyzed. At this stage there are no mysteries about the origins or progression of hostilities between the parties. New angles for understanding the dynamics of the dispute are hard to uncover. In addition, virtually all types of negotiation have been tried. We seem to know, to understand, and to accept the reasons given for the causes of the conflict and the causes of negotiation failures.

The study of Arab–Israeli relations provides an intriguing and fascinating introduction to international politics. The rich and varied historical circumstances as perceived and interpreted—to be highlighted or ignored by one group or the other—and the entanglement of numerous Great Power policy commitments through time have enriched the complexity of issues that mark the conflict. Together they contribute to the positions currently held by the key participants and add to the emotionally charged views often expressed by interested parties.

This book is ultimately about negotiation potential and reasons for past success and failure as Arabs and Israelis have tried to mend their differences. It is not intended to justify particular positions of the parties, nor, unfortunately, does it conclude with a single elaborate, recommended, or ideal solution. My focus rather is to weave together notions of power politics and perceptions of enemies to show, as these are unchanging or shifting, just what potential for conflict and cooperation emerges. A protracted conflict is by its nature far more difficult to resolve. Is it possible to move away from the details of Arab–Israeli encounters to see patterns that predict success or failure? Are the outcomes of these encounters due to the changes of power balance? Or do these outcomes result from the symmetry or asymmetry of images that parties hold of each other? What allows for flexibility rather than rigidity in positions advocated?

There are many excellent books, written from varying perspectives, about the Arab–Israeli conflict. Some report and explain specific historic events so as to understand conflict origins; others analyze perceptions of key decision-making elites; still others prescribe particular solutions. Treatment ranges from extremely biased and polemical to dispassionate. In fact, this conflict is so high-pitched, enduring, and regularized that almost no one tries to open the field to ask hard questions, such as, what will realistically help to create a broader peace, that is, a real security for the whole region? Only Saunders (1986) has approached this question, mainly from the perspective of a participant negotiator. His numerous lessons are instructive and practical, the guidelines realistic. But his work does not tell the whole story.

My approach is to bring to bear important, dominating perspectives about international politics—the persuasive arguments of power and perception theory—with theoretical and empirical evidence on negotiation and to lock these together with the historical record of solution plans, approaches, and party positions in this unending dispute. This means that a fusion of writings—thoughtful, reasonable pieces centered on the issues of the Arab–Israeli conflict—will be examined in order to convey the flavor of recent thinking on key problems and to see how negotiation, compromise choices, and peaceful arrangements are possible.

This book is designed to provide information about international conflict and contains a highly condensed version of major issues and events surrounding the Arab–Israeli dispute. A first principle in this process is that materials of historical background and argument need to be presented in a manner that minimizes bias toward any side in the dispute. Events must be described in neutral, nonoffensive language, and descriptions are demanded that communicate what happened and give persuasive rationale to indicate the positions adopted by the disputing parties. Although one may give recognition to this principle, it remains a tricky problem in international politics. Mere awareness of the difficulty will not entirely excuse any possible bias that may exist in this analysis. The Arab–Israeli dispute is surely one of the most volatile and deep-seated problems of international politics today, and the passage of time has done little to alleviate the tension of hostility among the parties.

So what is offered here? This is a study about negotiation potential in the Arab–Israeli conflict. There are no stories of analogy, no inside tales, no secrets revealed, no "real" truth. The intention is not to introduce more polemics into this case (there is far too much already) in order to pull the reader to one side or the other. Nor is there an impassioned plea for the parties to negotiate, to compromise their desired goals.

My objectives are modest ones. First, I have chosen to view the dispute as a total structure of conflict and of negotiation and to look again at parts of that structure, namely the frame, the building, and its maintenance. The language here is deliberate. I see the conflict consisting, first, of a basic form—the features that hold it together, namely the issues and political setting, and that provide its shape—which I have labeled the "frame." Once a frame exists, the dynamics of operating to strengthen its foundation fall into place. "Conflict buildup" refers to the policies and actions of the parties that contribute to this process. The maintenance of conflict comes into play as the ultimate clash of attitudes, beliefs about entitlements, and points of view that represent the threshold of conflict, balance between the antagonists. "Sustaining a conflict" usually means keeping the hostile process at a steady pitch, often at a pace where equilibrium points are set and reset in conflict escalation rather than in de-escalation. In a sense, all of these three components are fixed and unalterable.

There is a parallel structure that has developed around negotiation history in this conflict. The frame of negotiation is more fragile; it has not had as much reinforcement as the conflict structure, and it depends on the conflict frame. The building features also exist, reflecting numerous actual start-ups of negotiation talks in formal settings but lacking the intensity of support. Maintenance of a negotiation environment is the weakest link, although the term *peace process* is ever pervasive. In other words, the commitment behind sustaining the conflict far exceeds the commitment behind continuing negotiations.

Why discuss aspects of the conflict in a study devoted to negotiation? For the simple reason that to understand negotiation, we must understand the conflict structure—there is no negotiation without conflict, even though there is conflict without negotiation. The method chosen to examine negotiation is in part historical, in part analytical. The pathway through the conflict structure and through the negotiation structure is not through time, however—it is not chronological. The road from the frame to the building to the sustaining features is followed by enhancing and strengthening that particular direction, be it toward conflict or negotiation. In looking at the historical picture and appraisals of the history of events in the region, I have asked whether there is another way to approach the issue of negotiation. I have wondered also why the multiple negotiation attempts have almost always failed, and I have sought the answer not in the convenient argument of irreconcilable differences between Arabs and Jews who live in the Middle East but in the negotiation approach itself. It is not necessarily true that the cause of any conflict provides the complete key to its resolution. Things that are fixed cannot be changed; that is, some fundamental party goals may not shift, but the strategy in negotiating differences can be altered.

To get into the negotiation possibilities, we need to review and assess what has occurred in negotiation attempts. Thus, following the structural patterns in conflict and negotiation in the Arab–Israeli dispute, several chapters focus on negotiation models and plans pertaining to this conflict. All of the *major* peace plans, beginning with the United Nations (UN) partition resolution of 1947 through the Baker Plan of December 1989, are discussed briefly, along with points of comparison. The Camp David model is examined in detail for negotiation tactics. Comparisons are made across various UN mediation attempts. Two theories of negotiation, positional bargaining and principled bargaining, are considered.

This book is not meant to be controversial; it contains no radical solution schemes. The ideas are fairly simple, in fact, but the suggestions for changing negotiation tactics as well as strategies in a prenegotiation period—in a way more likely to produce a successful outcome—are hard to implement, since we are accustomed to thinking in traditional, confrontational modes—in "positional" terms, in the language of one negotiation theorist. There is a lot of information packed in here about negotiation possibilities, but specific outcomes are not predicted. That is a special feature that remains for the parties to decide.

Maps

The Middle East

The Middle East

British Mandate, 1922

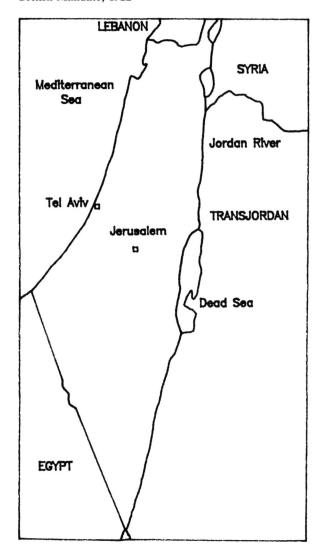

Peel Plan, 1937 (Not Implemented)

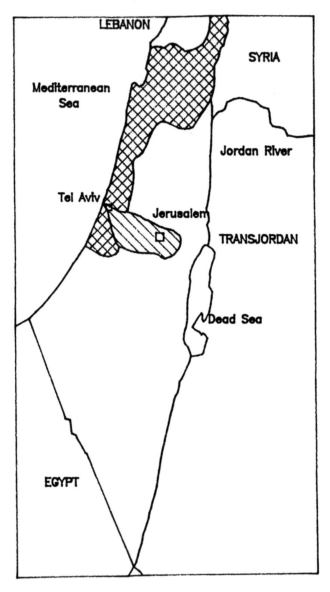

Arab

Jewish

International

UN Plan, 1947 (Not Implemented)

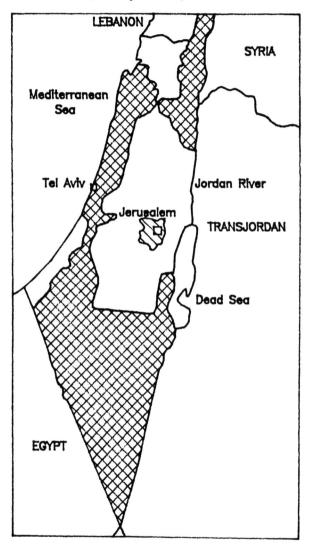

Arab

Jewish

International

Post War, 1949 (Armistice Lines)

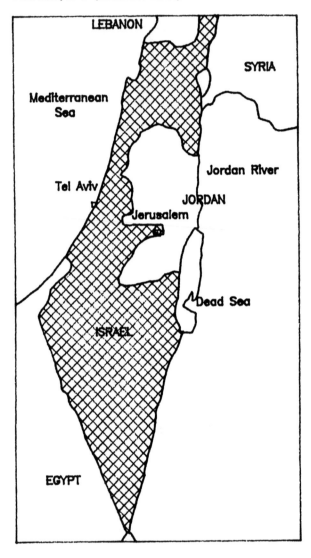

Arab

Jewish

Post War, 1967

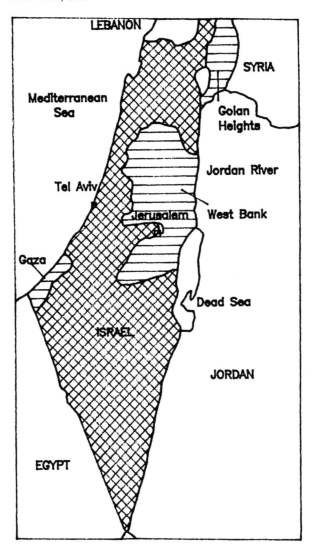

Israeli controlled

Israel

1

The Conflict Frame

INTRODUCTION

In international relations, a low-tension phase means that a disturbance due to some specific conflict will remain geographically local, without arousing emotions elsewhere. In a phase of high tension, vivid emotions dominate and tend to spread across many countries, touching a multitude of foreign-policy topics. Nowhere else is this seen more dramatically than in the Middle East, particularly concerning the Arab–Israeli conflict.

The conflict arose over a small, sensitive piece of territory, along the eastern shores of the Mediterranean Sea between Lebanon and the Sinai Peninsula, known as Palestine. Two distinct ethnic and religious groups—Arabs and Jews— believe that the land within this territory was promised to each of them by the British, who were colonial overlords of the area during the early part of the twentieth century. Hostile relations developed and have persisted as a result of strongly divergent interpretations of history and intense opinions about rights to political freedom and independence. For more than fifty years, two separate ideological expressions—Palestine Nationalism (among Arabs) and Zionism (among Jews)—have clashed in a steady pitch, with the advocates for each side arguing rights, justice, and preferred conditions for a settlement leading to peace. Since the founding of the state of Israel by the Jews in 1948, the feverishness of the conflict has been particularly high. Scores of nations throughout the world have engaged in strong debate about the problem by reassessing grievances, analyzing moral claims, and adopting policies designed to capture their emotional views, to offer suggestions for a practical solution, and to preserve their own national interests. Thus far, no solution has emerged that all the parties find acceptable. Not only have the active participants failed in their efforts to reach accommodation, but outside powers and international mediators have also been unable to locate a strategy for resolving differences in a way that is mutually acceptable to all.

In March 1939, Alfred North Whitehead, writing commentary on world politics for *Atlantic Monthly* in an essay entitled ''An Appeal to Sanity,'' devoted some attention to the problem that came to be known as the Arab–Israeli conflict. He stressed that issues were already complex, that difficult ones faced international relations in the future, and that understanding the claims and positions of all parties was important. With respect to the focus of interests and arguments for controlling the territory of Palestine, he pointed to the significance of the role that multiple cultures have played in the area. ''Many claims converge on Palestine—the Jewish claim in virtue of bygone occupation and of living genius, the Mahometan (Islamic) claim in virtue of age-long occupation and vivid association, and the Christian claim. It must also be remembered that at the end of the Great War (World War I) the British would not have been in command of Palestine except for the Arab revolt against Turkey'' (318).

At the time of World War I, Britain, perhaps as a strategy for securing its own national interest, devised a policy that seems in retrospect to have been bound up in contrasting, inconsistent goals. A 1915 letter to the Arabs stated, ''Great Britain is prepared to recognize and support the independence of the Arabs in all the regions within the limits demanded by the Sherif of Mecca'' (Laqueur, 1970:16). The letter was signed by Sir Henry McMahon, British High Commissioner in Cairo. Two years later, in 1917, the British forwarded to Jewish leaders a letter written by Lord Arthur Balfour the British Foreign Minister, and declared, ''His Majesty's Government views with favor the establishment in Palestine of a national home for the Jewish people and will use their best endeavors to facilitate the achievement of this objective'' (Laqueur, 1970:18). The carrying out of a policy designed to meet two British aims—to establish a national Jewish home in Palestine and simultaneously to secure the rights of the existing Arab population—proved to be a highly complex problem, even though the policy itself expressed the multitude of keen interests that converge on Palestine and the differences that perhaps existed among British decision makers. Although there were examples of cooperative relations between Jews and Arabs at the time, opposing views and feelings of hostility were being established. Today, the Jewish settlement in Palestine, forming the nucleus for the Israeli state, is an accomplished fact; conditions now indicate that the country is not a temporary element in the scheme of international affairs; its longevity and durability point to permanence. However, the Arabs in Palestine are dissatisfied with this arrangement. The nationalist ideals and self-determination goals among the Palestinians have not been realized. In other words, the second part of the declared British policy of colonial days has not been fulfilled.

Whitehead's appraisal that the core difficulty rested with the incompatibility and ultimately the irreconcilability of the two British aims pursued during the interwar period, at a time when the British colonial empire was faltering and the British position in the world was moving away from the pinnacle of power, may indeed be accurate. Yet the international system of today is far removed from that era of history with respect to the political forces that may direct, and the appropriate terms of redress that may set, the peace. The conclusion of his essay is nevertheless timely, for he offered some prophetic advice to the disputing parties and guidance for negotiation. Among his important points were that (1) any fusion of Jewish and Arab interests must be produced by the parties themselves rather than imposed from outside; (2) major powers involved in conflict resolution must remember to serve coordinating rather than imposing functions in seeking political accommodation between opponents; and (3) the essence of success in solving tough political issues in world affairs requires political compromise—that is, an adjustment of differences so that the social life offers the largest spread of satisfactions. Political solutions devoid of compromise are failures from the ideal of statesmanship. In the final analysis, Whitehead warns:

In the adjustment of Jews and Arabs, one-sided bargains are to be dreaded. They spell disaster in the future. The hope of statesmen should be to elicit notions of mutual service and of the interweaving of habits so that the diversity of populations should issue in the fulfillment of the varied subconsciousness claims of life. There is a new world waiting to be born, stretched along the eastern shores of the Mediterranean and the western shores of the Indian Ocean. The condition for its life is the fusion of Mahometan and Jewish populations, each with their own skills and their own memories, and their own ideals. War can protect; it cannot create. Indeed, war adds to the brutality that frustrates creation. The protection of war should be the last resort in the slow progress of mankind towards its far-off ideals. (320).

There are at least three reasons that may explain why this conflict is so intractable and intense. First are the two separate nationalisms. Both are geared toward controlling the historic land of Palestine and have, for a long time, perceived the distribution of the territory as a zero-sum condition. Second is the continuous expansion of political issues that have developed in a local setting involving Israelis and Palestinians into a broader-based, worldwide setting of concern. The dynamics of local-to-global links that have evolved in this protracted dispute include, among other things, an exaggerated, heightened importance of all locally based conflict events, which are elevated into major international crises commanding attention. Third is the steady interest and deep involvement by the Great Powers in the entire Middle East region. This introduces external factors and issues not immediately germane to the dispute and complicates both the conflict dimension and the solution potential. It represents a type of reverse linkage where globally based, Great Power political dynamics become entangled with smaller-field local issues. The two-way crossover of local-global interconnections is related to the factor of nationalist rivalry, the major driving force of the situation, with the following results: competing nationalisms have stretched the duration of the dispute, wars fought by the parties have encouraged outside power participation, and the protracted nature of the dispute has meant that local issues are increasingly treated as international problems. These elements largely frame the conflict picture. Each of the three components is discussed here separately.

NATIONALIST RIVALRY

In the twentieth century, Zionists and Arab Nationalists have argued continuously over their rights to a small piece of land. Whenever immediate conditions in the region change—through violence, new policy directions, or external support—the hard political positions are reintroduced and defended. Each side has responded to the evolving logic. The protracted conflict between the parties has existed for decades, with little sign that the intensity of differences has abated.

The core of the Arab–Israeli problem was foreseen long ago when the British Royal Commission of Enquiry—the Peel Commission—issued its report in 1937 stating that the Arabs and the Jews are two groups of people so different in culture, language, religion, and habits that they cannot live together without one lording it over the other. Such a relationship inevitably fosters humiliation, resentment, and hatred. The commission thus recommended a territorial partition of Palestine as a way to preserve the ethnic identity of each group in a nonthreatening setting. How did the dogma of nationalism, which grew out of ethnic identity, contribute to the conflict?

Intense nationalism is a complex sentiment consisting in part of a frame of mind toward the social order, a distinct philosophy and program of political change including systematic destruction of what is hated and a "positive" replacement, and indignation against outsiders. The emotional tone and its vocabulary often attract people to a national cause, especially when they feel grievances that are rationalized and redirected by the movement. These grievances may repel them into anger and hatred if they believe their privileges, their interests, or their possessions have been assaulted.

The British solution proposed more than fifty years ago was not surprising, since the association between ethnic identity and territorial sovereignty had become widely accepted during the nineteenth century under a doctrinal banner emphasizing race, cultural heritage, or some combination of the two. Attitudes of superpatriotism and a belief in the superiority of one's ethnic group often developed as a result, and the rhetoric of nationalism provided a strong justification for claiming power.

The doctrine and the ethics of intense nationalism are inevitably invested with tensions when the great goals and the order of the future of two parties stand in direct conflict as a zero-sum game. It becomes important in this situation to hold steadfast to the grand scheme and to resist temptations to suspend the relevance of the doctrinaire position for considerations of momentary interest. Threats to discredit the radical stand may occur, but these are to be resisted. On principle, settling for partial gains and becoming assimilated are unacceptable.

Nationalist feelings arise and become intensified as a result of a twofold process of isolation from and contrast with the outside world and cohesion and drawing together within. The appeal to the individual for conscious solidarity with the group is made through the extensive use of propaganda; spiritual and intellectual needs, coupled with emotional and instinctive powers, are built through nationalism. A nationalist ideology is formed in the historical development of the people, with deep myth-like beliefs in the past. Alongside this, a "mission" and a desire for revenge and historical rights, which aim to rectify a past injustice, are developed. Enemy identification also tends to invest historical experience with obligations and commitment to the ideology and the nationalist movement.

The conclusion of World War I signaled a brighter era for self-determination of nations. The prospects for mutual recognition of the aspirations of both Arab nationalism and Zionism were forecast by the leaders of these two liberation movements. Emir Feisal, for example, stated in March 1919: "We Arabs . . . look with deepest sympathy on the Zionist movement. . . . We are working together for a reformed and revised Near East, and our two movements complement one another. The movement is national and not imperialistic" (quoted in Landau, 1971:48). Chaim Weizmann, the president of the World Zionist Organization, stated in 1931, "Cooperation and friendly work with the Arab people must be the cornerstone of all Zionist activities in the land of Israel" (quoted in Jewish Agency for Palestine, 1936:87–89).

These early hopes were shattered. Each side, not surprisingly, blames the other. According to Yonah Alexander (1980:264–65), writing from the Zionist perspective:

[T]he Palestinian Arabs turned all their efforts against the fulfillment of the Zionist vision. This occurred when an extremist minority faction of Palestinian Arabs assumed control over their own people and introduced terrorism as a way of achieving specific political aims: First, to reduce, if not eliminate, Jewish presence in Palestine and to frustrate Zionist designs to establish a distinct state there; second, to reject any efforts of Jewish–Arab coexistence and cooperation; third, to persuade or force the mandatory power to relinquish its policy as expressed in the Balfour Declaration, and finally, to achieve national independence in Palestine under Arab control. These goals were set up at the All-Arab Palestine conference, which met in Jerusalem in January 1919.

Muhammed Hallaj (1988:3–4) gives the Arab point of view as follows:

When the Zionist movement resolved to solve the Jewish problem with the establishment of a Jewish state in Palestine and to set up the World Zionist Organization in 1897 to pursue that objective, it laid down a two-track strategy followed ever since. On the one hand, it believed in and prepared for the inevitability of conflict with the Arabs, while at the same time projecting a benign image that stressed the possible cooperation and peaceful coexistence between Zionist movement and Arab nationalism. Outside of Palestine itself, the Zionists contended that the two nationalist movements were compatible. In reality, the Zionists worked against Arab nationalism throughout the Arab world. The early Zionists saw themselves as colonizers, and historically colonization never happens without resistance by the native population. Moreover, the Zionists made it clear that they had military force in mind when they spoke of the need to impose a fait accompli in Palestine. With the passage of the UN resolution to partition Palestine in 1947, the Zionist colonists would use the resolution to sanction the massive use of violence to impose a Jewish state, to expand its territory and to de-Arabize the country by the eviction of the Palestinians.

Zionism is a form of European nationalism and is true to the spirit of classic nineteenth-century nationalism. The demand for self-determination by European Jews for an independent homeland and for a place in the community of nations was not different from demands made by other people in the European world who sensed that true fulfillment could be achieved only through the establishment of an independent sovereign state reflecting their traditions, customs, and values. What makes Zionism somewhat more dramatic is the selection of the land of ancient Palestine to satisfy the Zionist quest.

The Zionist movement grew out of the work of Theodor Herzl, a Viennese journalist who, in 1896, published *The Jewish State*, a book that called for the granting of a Jewish homeland that would be a refuge from the injustices, prejudices, and anti-Semitism perpetrated on Jews in other societies. He concluded that no matter how patriotic they were, Jews could not escape discrimination and persecution. This theme struck a sympathetic note particularly among East European and Russian Jews, who had already assembled an organization for the purpose of furthering the idea. Called "Lovers of Zion," they planned to create a movement for the return to Zion (the name of the hill in Jerusalem on which King David's palace is believed to have been erected). This group, formed in 1882, was the forerunner of the first World Zionist Congress, which convened in Basel in 1897. The meeting brought together, from around the world, Jews who then drafted the official program, which read: "The aim of Zionism is to create for the Jewish people a home in Palestine secured by public law." Gradually, leaders of the movement managed to settle in the sparsely populated, neglected, resource-poor land. Land was usually purchased from absentee Arab landlords with money raised through philanthropic overtures in the Western world. Immigrants arriving in the early part of the twentieth century established relationship patterns and institutional structures and fomented the ideological basis for the Jewish state, including the kibbutz communities that provided the pioneering spirit, sense of sacrifice, and cooperation that became the hallmark of the later Israeli state.

Zionism was to rescue Jews from their alien status in the world and restore them to "normalcy" within the confines of a Jewish state. If the hostility of the world toward its Jews was a natural phenomenon, then Zionism would remove the provocation. Early Zionist thinkers stirred up a revolution in Jewish thought by suggesting that the crucial dialogue was not between Jews and God but between Jews and the rest of the world. The coming of a new Israel would bestow on the Jews the political liberty and the economic and social justice that the progressives of the nineteenth century had promised to the rest of the world. Yet there was an important difference between Jewish nationalism and the other struggles for self-determination: Jewish identity was not based on an already existing national land or spoken language. Herzl was the leader of a new nation without a homeland; thus his primary goal became to find a place for the Jews to establish their state and the money to finance the exodus. There was not widespread support for the idea in the beginning. Religious Orthodox Jews entirely rejected the notion of a state; some wealthy American Jews found the plan a sentimental theory without a future. But Herzl pushed his scheme, the dream of hundreds of thousands of Russian Jews who viewed political Zionism as a refuge from the vicious anti-Semitism prevailing in their current homeland.

The Balfour Declaration in 1917 was Zionism's first major triumph in the twentieth century, occurring just twenty years after Herzl announced his program at the first Zionist Congress. The British government proclaimed, "His Majesty's Government views with favor the establishment in Palestine of a national home for the Jewish people."

The Arab reawakening of nationalism began to develop at roughly the same time as Zionism. After centuries of subjugation at the hands of the Turks, the Arabs saw an opportunity to retrieve their lost status by assisting the British and the French against the Ottomans in World War I. In return for this support, the Arabs were promised independence, and some envisaged a unified Arab world or a confederation of Arab peoples. Unlike the Zionists, Arab Nationalists formed small and largely ineffective clubs, lacking a charismatic leader like Herzl. Moreover, this group had to contend with more diffuse issues of widespread colonial holdings by both the British and the French governments and to argue for territorial divisions to create individual states. Leadership was also at issue. Palestinian nationalism was connected to this broad set of aims and began to gain momentum directly in response to the growth of Jewish settlements on the land. Antagonism developed between local Palestinian inhabitants and the new settlers, and although riots against the Zionist community aroused passion and hatred, nothing occurred to advance political consciousness and the creation of specific institutions to instill national identity among the Arabs of this region. It was only after the creation of the state of Israel in 1948 that such a consciousness began to emerge.

The modern leader of the Pan-Arab movement, Gamal Abdul Nasser, came on the scene in the late 1950s, stressing unity, military prowess, and physical struggle to achieve the goals of the Arab world—identity, dignity, and national purpose. His compassionate speeches had a large influence on Palestinians, who by this time stood alone as a stateless people. Under Nasser's direction, the Palestine Liberation Organization (PLO) was formed in 1964 with the aim of establishing a sovereign state under Arab control on the land occupied by the Zionists.

Following the partition of Palestine, thousands of Arabs were displaced. Many took up life in dreary camps organized under the auspices of the United Nations, camps that grew into permanent communities in the Gaza Strip (administered by Egypt), on the West Bank (administered by Jordan), and Lebanon. Conditions of squalor, high unemployment, and few opportunities for economic and social advancement for these people fostered attitudes of resentment that eventually were incorporated into the development of self-identity and nationalism. For the next twenty years, this group of people, identified as Palestinians in their countries of exile, lacked any effective leadership or specific territory in which they exercised political representation. Jordan agreed to grant citizenship to the Palestinians (as a way to broaden the country's population base), and subsequently Palestinians were represented in the Jordanian parliament and achieved some high governmental posts. The nationalist-minded Palestinians have regarded this arrangement as an intrusion into their defined right to self-determination.

Only after the 1967 Six-Day War, in which large numbers of Palestinians were displaced and others came under Israeli rule, with the occupation of the West Bank and Gaza, did Palestinian nationalism surface in a tangible and formidable way. The curious fate of the West Bank area and Gaza is that these regions were to have formed part of the original Palestinian state if the UN partition plan had been accepted and implemented. Israeli occupation of the territories exacerbated the refugee problem, since the majority of the Palestinians who had retreated from their homes in the 1948 war now lived in these areas.

By 1968, a National Covenant had been written outlining the precise goals of the organization: to remove the Zionists; to allow the return of Palestinian refugees; and to create a homeland for them. The organization reflected increased confidence and militancy by stating that "armed struggle is the only way to liberate Palestine and that the partition of Palestine in 1947 and the establishment of the state of Israel are entirely illegal." Some of these goals, articulated through a formal, institutionalized organization, were very similar to the ones expressed by the Zionists seventy years earlier. The Palestinians too needed a leader, a refugee problem, and a strong sense of persecution and injustice in order to develop the intense attachment to nationalist goals. These elements also provided the basis for acquiring sympathy and support across the international community.

There are other parallels in the roots of these two nationalist movements. Each responded to the developing currents of ideology within their regions of origin. Political development in European movements in this direction occurred in the last half of the nineteenth century and continued up through World War I; Third World nationalist feelings experienced heightened intensity in the 1950s and the 1960s. Each nationalist movement stresses the role of an enemy outsider as a causal agent for ensuring group cohesiveness. The Zionists emphasize the growth of anti-Semitism in European society; the Palestinians focus on the Zionist agitators. Each argues that the sole escape from continued persecution and minority feeling is separation and sovereignty. Indeed, the only real difference between the ideology of the Zionists and the Palestinian Arab Nationalists at this level is one of timing. The Palestinians are at least two generations behind in terms of establishing strong, solid roots of nationalist fervor.

The Palestinian Declaration of Independence, issued in 1988, precisely forty years after the Zionists had proclaimed independence and the creation of the state of Israel, surely represents a milestone in the unfolding conditions of the dispute. The single-purpose documents prepared by each side to justify claims for self-determination and sovereignty are strikingly similar, not only in the range of themes addressed but also in the specific set of grievances and natural rights that identify the parties and give rationale to their respective claims for independence in the "much too promised" homeland. The symmetry of entitlements and demands is remarkable, and the similarity in the developmental sequence of the two respective nationalist movements is clear, albeit under different timetables.

The arguments commonly stressed by the protagonists to explain the origins and reasons for the dispute show very different causal chains, however. The line of blame for current conditions in the Arab Palestinian community is as follows: European colonialism is responsible for creating the state of Israel, which has led to numerous wars between Zionists and Arabs, which has encouraged the Israelis to expand their power base and behave as imperialists, which results in intransigence and an unwillingness to accommodate the local Arab community, which means there is no justice for Palestinians. Consequently, the extreme feelings of frustration and relative deprivation naturally evolve into aggressive behavior that has included acts of terrorism. This becomes one of the few open routes to eventual justice.

The causal linkages expressed from the Zionist perspective run somewhat differently: Historical anti-Semitism and harsh discrimination against the Jewish people in European communities led to the development of Jewish nationalism in the form of Zionist ideology. In its extreme, this policy resulted in the Holocaust of European Jews during World War II, which underlined the necessity of a safe place where Jews could live in peace. The creation of the state of Israel resulted in wars with neighboring Arabs, who would not accommodate the tiny minority in their midst. This meant that Israel had to invest in its security; a strong military policy became necessary for self-protection in order to maintain justice.

The chain of argument differs, yet there is symmetry in that both parties conclude their position by stressing the necessity and perhaps inevitability of a conflict-oriented stand to allow justice to prevail. The logic of intense nationalist ideology is evident in each case; yet this points also to the danger of future instability in the region.

This conflict situation basically involves a clash of ideological systems, where entire belief structures play a major role in shaping the nature of the conflict process itself. Hubert Blalock, in *Power and Conflict: Toward a General Theory* (1989), links the causes of conflict to a series of ideological dimensions, among them oversimplification of issues, manipulated and exaggerated expectations, the uniqueness or specialness of a belief structure and corresponding insulation from alternative belief systems, ethnocentrism, and rigid dichotomization of issue positions. Strong, basic, stripped-down ideologies operate with a small number of goals arranged hierarchically where the means to achieve them are unambiguous. This enhances cohesion.

In the presence of an enemy, the potency of an ideological belief system intensifies, building group cohesion. For example, the enemy is likely to be blamed for a large number of offenses, past and present, and to be characterized in extremely negative ways. Distrust of the opposing party is reinforced by carefully contrived unfavorable stereotypes, and internal enemies are anticipated where deviants are accused and punished as disloyal. Motives are oversimplified. Since the opponent cannot be trusted, one's own potentially illegitimate behaviors are seen as necessarily defensive or preemptive measures. The expected costs of defeat by opponents are exaggerated.

Finally, as Blalock writes: "Beliefs about the supernatural can practically always be modified so as to reinforce a highly compatible system of social controls and to alter subjective probabilities of success. Not only will God punish those who defect and reward those who make extreme sacrifices, but He will sustain us in our greatest need and ultimately assure our victory" (1989:138).

Belief systems cannot be created quickly, nor are they altered easily. Because nationalism is an ideology, it becomes important to understand, in the context of the Arab–Israeli dispute, what kinds of ideological dimensions or features seem most conducive to belligerency and to rapid and effective mobilization for conflict. Sometimes ideological simplicity provides unambiguous interpretations of others' actions and clear guidelines for response. A rigid belief system, for example, places sharp lines between right and wrong, correct and incorrect ways of behaving, and stresses superiority of one's own group practices over those of others.

An ability to construct a history consisting of a glorious past and a set of heroic figures and martyrs, along with a catalog of past injustices inflicted at the hands of enemies, helps preserve an ethnocentric cultural emphasis. Ironically, a long history of martyrdom and grievances against powerful enemy groups often serves to produce the very kind of ethnocentric belief system that perpetuates such conflicts into the present (139). An important objective in transmitting such beliefs is to extol the virtues of extreme sacrifice, militarism, and unquestioned loyalty in case the future provides an opportunity to avenge these wrongs (142). Either myths or accurate historical records may convince members that the costs of suffering a defeat by the enemy would be considerably higher than the costs of maintaining conflict. At the same time, it is the flexibility of belief systems that permits their ready adaptation to objective changes that are likely to occur during the course of a conflict (145).

The prospects for dispute resolution in this environment are not good. A long history of grievances against an opponent may make an initial consensus on conflict more likely and may reinforce those ideological features that simplistically tend to place the blame for nearly all unfavorable events on the opposing party. This tends to undermine efforts by moderates to discourage the engagement in conflict and also makes it more difficult to terminate a conflict once the costs begin to mount (208).

Trust of the opponent becomes a critical variable here. A party believed to be the cause for a long list of grievances can hardly be expected to behave favorably in the future, regardless of promises to alter attitudes and actions. Neither the rigidity nor, ironically, the flexibility of belief systems seems to help in this regard. To maintain group cohesion and to reinterpret inconsistent or confusing facts so as to keep order and stability, a group needs rigidity and possibly flexibility for change. However, either direction appears to work against moving toward cooperation with an enemy. Thus, although the two nationalisms of Zionism and Palestinian self-determination were absolutely essential for building individual group policies, establishing legitimate claims, and securing a set of rights and privileges, such ideological force serves to undermine efforts at collaborative conflict resolution. Sheer nationalist rivalry intervenes as a major obstacle as local problems are magnified into central events on a broader stage of world politics in an effort to maintain ideological justification and cohesion. The way this dynamic affects the Arab–Israeli conflict is discussed below.

LOCAL-TO-GLOBAL LINKAGE

Due to the difference in timing in the development of the two nationalisms, the Arab–Israeli conflict has been extended over a long period and taken on certain characteristics. This dispute has been labeled a "protracted social conflict" (Azar, Jureidini, and McLaurin, 1978; Azar, 1979; Azar and Cohen, 1979, Azar, 1983). In such disputes, structural relationships between parties along ethnic, cultural, linguistic, or economic lines are in disequilibrium, which precipitates recurring hostile behavior and creates a complicated causal network that makes these conflicts very difficult to solve. Tension reduction among conflicts of a long-standing nature seems to resist even the most persistent efforts of well-intentioned mediators; when it is achieved on one level of the dispute, hostile feelings in other, related areas will flare up. This characteristic leads to inertia when it comes to problem solving.

The frequency and the intensity of the periodic eruptions of protracted social conflicts fluctuate, and under these conditions of hostile interactions, interspersed with sporadic outbreaks of war, there are no clear or distinct termination points. This contributes to the spread of conflict thinking and hostile feelings into all aspects of social life. Because these conflicts involve whole societies, their stakes are very high, and the issues become the determining criteria in the definition of national identity, social solidarity, and national security.

According to Edward Azar, these conflicts are not terminated in a final sense by explicit decisions, although cessation of overt violence—usually achieved through cease-fire agreements following war—may defuse tensions somewhat. Rather, "they tend to linger, gradually cool down, become transformed, or wither away" (Azar, 1983:89). Attempts to resolve these disputes or even to contain them become complicated precisely because protracted social conflicts are not specific events at distinct points in time; they are processes. Protracted social conflicts such as the Arab–Israeli dispute do not allow for alterations in the fundamental grievances of the parties that initially set the stage for hostile interactions; this serves to reinforce and to intensify mutual images of deception while simultaneously reducing the chances for dealing with settlement issues in a nonviolent way. In other words, the very nature of these conflicts only increases the anxieties of the parties and fosters tension and conflict-maintenance strategies.

One of the structural determinants of hostile behavior noted by Azar in defining protracted social conflict relevant to the Arab–Israeli dispute is group identity formation. Group identity, or ethnicity, is an acute awareness of a bond among people of similar culture, language, religion, belief, and life perspectives. Shared perceptions encompass core values and issues defining the social existence and leave an indelible mark of identity on all heirs. Ethnic groups help an individual structure reality and provide security from the uncertain and often hostile outside world. In this sense, ethnicity is a crucial ingredient of protracted social conflict.

When both parties to a conflict attribute malevolent motivations to each other, self-fulfilling prophecies create a vicious circle where intercommunal hatred passing from one generation to another, through primary socialization, fosters individual group identity and also mutual hatred. Eruptions of violence appear "disjointed and discrete" because they are sparked by the continuing presence of cultural identification and intercommunal antagonism (Azar, 1983:91). The ethnic imagery held by each group becomes more solidified as outside threats are perceived.

New outbreaks of the conflict might erupt over a whole range of interactions that take place at a neighborhood level and that constitute daily life, and the resulting interconnected nature of various factors—political, ethnic, and religious, among others—is what makes protracted social conflicts so difficult to resolve, according to Azar. It is impossible to isolate each issue and deal with it separately because each issue of the conflict is linked to others at a number of different levels and in different ways, depending on the perceptions of various parties. Even new elements introduced into the conflict or the conflict-resolution arena compound complexity because they tend to become linked with every other factor previously defining the issue setting. As a result, resolutions on any given issue or sector of the dispute are not viewed as absolute or final.

There are exaggerated connections between minor local issues and major international concerns. Boundaries dividing local, national, regional, and international dimensions are blurred. Political initiatives generated by states within the area or by regional radical or reactionary groups are even undertaken specifically to judge the response of the outside world and to reap the potential benefits of self-interest rather than to settle matters on an internal basis. Recognizing the dispute as a protracted social conflict heightens the intractability of prospects for a resolution of issues and also indicates why outside powers have often been drawn into the fray. The role of global actors and their effect on local conflict conditions are examined next.

GLOBAL-TO-LOCAL LINKAGE

The Middle East region has been thoroughly ensnared in major power international politics for several hundred years. Such a distinctive political experience continuing from generation to generation has left its mark on regional political attitudes and actions, leading to a special international relations game, argues L. C. Brown (1984:3). The game consists of old rules that have been in effect for more than two hundred years and that structure the conflict arena and settlement prospects (Brown, 1984:15–18).

1. *The Great Power Involvement Rule.* The Great Powers play out their own rivalries and national security goals in the Middle East, leading them to view regional players in terms of extraregional alignments. This rule minimizes the advancement of any specific regional interests.

2. *The Alliance Rule.* Making and breaking alliances tend to be comprehensive procedures in which outsiders are brought into the picture and all issues are interrelated. Diplomatic initiatives in the Middle East set in motion a realignment of all the players into a new configuration. This interrelatedness of politics restricts the ability of a single state to impose its will or set in motion major new orientations.

3. *The Negotiating Rule.* Middle East actors tend to favor certain actions and political style, such as (a) an unwillingness to accept any changes in the status quo as a preliminary bargaining position; (b) a disinclination to divide conflict or bargaining situations into major and minor issues or to establish priorities in sequence of resolution or by substantive areas; (c) an emphasis on the political mentality in which one player gains only through a commensurate loss by another; and (d) a preference for conducting delicate political bargaining through the use of mediators and third parties, who often become intimately involved in the issues of conflict and serve as guarantors of arrangements reached between the regional parties.

The Middle East, as the most penetrated area in today's world (measured by the intensity of outside interest, involvement, and economic domination), exists in continuous confrontation with a dominant external political system. According to Brown, the roots of this arrangement can be found in the "Eastern Question," which refers to the period when European powers slowly dismantled the Ottoman Empire, roughly from the late eighteenth century until the end of World War I.

The Eastern Question developed into an elaborate, multiplayer diplomatic game and produced the modern Middle Eastern pattern of politics: intense interrelationships between two unequal power systems, the tangled ties between East and West (Brown, 1984:21). The Middle East served Europe as a convenient arena for handling rivalry among Europeans, rivalries that could be fought out with little risk, making the region a kind of environment of sublimated but carefully regulated European conflict. Political integrity of the entire Middle East depended on European attention (32).

One consequence of the Eastern Question mentality is that European statesmen (and later the superpowers) accepted the notion that Great Power rivalry is responsible for developments among regional political actors, who are regarded as puppets (197). This linkage has evolved into the present day with evidence to support the Eastern Question logic: ideas of "communist meddling," Soviet-inspired insurrection, or U.S. imperialism have emerged in line with the puppeteer theme. Such reasoning implies that Middle Eastern problems can easily be resolved by reducing the problem to a single cause, that of the outside meddler (199). Such an explanation seeks out a single, evil-minded manipulator and denies political autonomy to other states of the region; regional troubles are caused by machinations of superpowers.

Current attitudes about the Arab–Israeli conflict origins do link political developments to the presumed behind-the-scenes actions of a Great Power, according to Brown (1984:234):

An interesting twentieth century example of such thinking is the persistent Zionist assumption that Britain was "really" supporting the Palestinian Arabs and trying to abandon its commitment to the Jewish National Home, matched by the equally persistent Arab assumption that Britain "really" remained committed to Zionism throughout the Mandate period in order to keep the Arabs divided and weak. Neither side has found it easy to accept that the British political establishment was divided on the issue, awkwardly searching a way to reconcile the irreconcilable.

Middle East actors tend to exaggerate both the power and the consistency of purpose of the presumed outside manipulator. The myth of the master controller shifts responsibility away from the local scene. It seems as if no one recognizes or appreciates the influential power that is available to even the weak players in the Eastern Question game.

CONCLUSION

Although the politics of Middle Eastern international relations may appear to have coherence on the basis of this analysis, this is not a comforting thought. There are high costs for maintaining this elaborate network of two-way local-global linkages within the nationalist rivalry that operates between Israelis and Palestinians. Persistent intergroup violence and intensified national security concerns curtail possibilities for negotiation and at the same time retard political and economic development that would allow movement away from strongly held ideological positions.

A strain in either nationalist belief system could develop if incompatible needs of the members of the groups become polarized and undermine the purpose for initiating and engaging in conflict. The Zionists and the Palestinians both depend heavily on group sympathizers who do not reside in the local, disputed area. Yet these diaspora affiliates have a limited number of interests and concerns that overlap those of the people living in the local community, in part due to the differences in economic positions and personal safety needs. Gaps between broad ideological aspirations and basic needs of daily life exist in both groups. If translated to levels of need for group attachment, the incompatibility of interests could surface and assume some importance, thereby weakening the ideological strength of cohesion among Jews or Arabs. At the moment, however, this seems unlikely.

Similarly, any compromise resolution designed to terminate the Arab–Israeli conflict is a remote possibility, since it would depend heavily on mechanisms for building up trust between the opposing parties. In conflicts, each party depicts the opponent as completely untrustworthy; negative stereotypes that reinforce a suspicious orientation will be highlighted. Thus the very beliefs that motivate members to support the conflict will make it difficult for anyone to take initial steps toward reconciliation. Even if steps were taken, there are no assurances that, having a similarly distrustful orientation, the opposing party would not take advantage of the temporarily vulnerable position of the first party. Thus a conflict, once initiated, becomes very difficult to terminate until both parties have become totally exhausted or until one is the clear winner. Because of the support of intractable ideological props, a conflict that may initially have been perceived as rather minor and easily mediated is likely to run its course and to result in far more damage to both parties than was originally anticipated by either (Blalock, 1989:146).

After a prolonged conflict, genuine peace will probably require a lengthy period of calm for building up trust. But the basic trust necessary for a more cooperative environment may never emerge, so that any peace becomes tentative and may perhaps be only a brief interval between periods of overt conflict.

There is little evidence that an outside superpower can successfully organize and dominate politics in the Middle East in a way that will produce minimal conflict in the future. Nor is it true that any state within the area has successfully established regional prominence. Still, the attempts at outside control and manipulation are instructive.

Six of the Arab–Israeli wars—1948, 1956, 1967, 1969–70, 1973, and 1982— were stopped by international diplomatic intervention. Yet efforts to bring about permanent settlement beyond a cease-fire have not been successful. Why? The local–global linkage points to the multilateral nature of the confrontation, suggesting that many issues require attention simultaneously to find a peaceful settlement. The global–local connection highlights the involvement and interests of Great Power outsiders, interests that only partially overlap with the goals of the regional powers. This two-tiered linkage has also exacerbated the conflict by feeding the ideology of both Zionism and Arab Nationalism. Each side has appealed to world public opinion in important ways. The Zionists were successful in getting the UN General Assembly to vote for the partition of Palestine in

1947, leading to the creation of Israel. In 1974, the PLO leader, Yasir Arafat, was triumphantly received as a speaker before the same UN forum, and the PLO was granted observer status in that international body.

Environmental conditions and the structure of politics in the Middle East allow the linkage theme to perpetuate. Although the original idea behind linkage politics may have been born with the interdependent world, in affairs of the Middle East it works as a two-way manipulation between large and small powers both as a penetrative process and as a reactive process (Rosenau, 1969). The linkage is not systematically accountable, that is, tracing specific policies in one system to unique reactions in another may prove to be difficult. It is rather the relevancy, the perception, and the use of ideology manipulation that sharpen the picture, that highlight and emphasize the unified struggle. Linkage refers to the shrinking world of interconnections and to the expanding world of interconnections, to the set of blurred boundaries for issue consideration and analysis. Not a causal device, it draws global–local links to offer some assumptions about the meaning of the cause of conflict continuance. It is a device that, if frequently used, builds walls and makes conflict resolution more difficult.

From the inside-out vantage point, the protracted Arab–Israeli dispute means that the urban politics phenomena of rock-throwing and police-action responses occurring in localized arenas, directly involving Israelis and Palestinians, assume far broader significance at the international level and incorporate aspects of Arab identity, anti-Semitism, and even global power, thereby encouraging outside interest, support, or mere reaction.

From the outside-in perspective, the logic of the Eastern Question political environment means that events as different or distant as the migration of Soviet Jews from the Soviet Union and the Iraqi invasion of Kuwait are readily seen as part of the Arab–Israeli conflict and seem to revolve around the fate of Jews and Zionism and the future of Palestinian Nationalism.

The continually reinforced web of mutual needs involving the primary local actors and the primary movers of the international system (the Great Powers) operates in a symbiotic two-way style of manipulation. The consequence of these factors, coupled with the ideology of group solidarity, too often has been violence, self-righteousness, and intensified nationalism to control the land in question.

As Niccolò Machiavelli stated long ago in *The Discourses* (Book 3, Chapter 4), ''How difficult and dangerous it is to deprive anyone of a kingdom and leave him his life, even though you try to conciliate him by benefits . . . (thus) . . . a warning to all princes that they will never be so safe so long as those live whom they have deprived of their possessions; . . . and . . . it should remind every potentate that old injuries can never be cancelled by new benefits, and the less so when the benefits are small in proportion to the injury inflicted.'' Although he was writing in the context of saving government systems, the words are equally relevant to the Israeli–Palestinian dispute. Without advocating the principles of realism to terminate the conflict, it is clear that this Machiavellian legacy is part of Middle Eastern politics.

2

Conflict Buildup

INTRODUCTION

One of the unique issues of world politics concerns which groups are entitled to be independent states. Does a particular cluster of individuals legitimately constitute a cohesive entity? The struggle to achieve and maintain individual identity becomes a special characteristic of international politics and is closely bound up with the struggle for territory. For a group to achieve nationhood, exclusive land claims are made on particular territories. Not surprisingly, conflicts often result when territorial rights are staked for the same piece of land by more than one group. Such disputes may eventually be "resolved" by partition plans, based on well-intentioned principles of fairness and justice to divide the territory and distribute a section to each claimant. These plans may appear to be reasonable compromises; unfortunately, they are rarely desired and usually unacceptable, since most conflicts of this type involve at least one party who wants to win the whole territory at stake. Partitions thus tend to be unstable in that they are regarded as provisional and unjust. Forcing parties to share the possession of some disputed property in international relations, as well as the terms and conditions of the partitions, is accomplished mainly by the driving influence of power factors and shows the dominance of realpolitik solutions to pressing problems.

After decades of confrontation between Arabs and Israelis, the issues surrounding the status and future of the Palestinian people remain the greatest obstacle to resolving the central conflict. How is it possible to reconcile Israel's sovereignty and security with the national aspirations of the Palestinian people and the interests of their Arab supporters? Although it may not be necessarily true that finding a homeland for the Palestinians and establishing a full or semi-sovereign system of self-governance will guarantee a stable Middle East and ensure an end to all the rivalries and current levels of conflict, an unresolved Palestinian issue will surely contribute to regional instability and fuel an endless conflict between Israel and its Arab neighbors.

The problem is tied in to the national consciousness and self-identity of both Israelis and Palestinians. The essence of conflict buildup is that the layering of issues over a long period of time—points of disagreement, rallying concerns, policy suggestions, accusations of intransigence, and aggressive moves by the parties—complicates the dispute because defining lines between individual areas of conflict issues become blurred, eventually melting into a far bigger holistic mass of political obstacles that are more difficult to dislodge. The value of the stakes in dispute may change as the conflict and participants are gradually entrenched into firmer, opposing positions through their own mutually reinforcing hostile actions or through anger at feeling victimized by the enemy. The entrenchment in turn serves to sharpen self-identity and cohesiveness among the members of each group, in effect hardening their ideological commitment and reducing the potential for agreement.

To understand the contemporary picture of conflict buildup, we should look at the past. An outline of key political developments before the UN partition resolution of 1947 is covered here, followed by a brief chronology of major periods of violent conflict and a description of some of the main factors leading to the current definition of policy by Palestinians and Israelis alike. It will be seen that the notable feature in defining this conflict is that each step results in further frustration, tension, and thus deadlock.

PREPARTITION POLITICS

Palestine began its four centuries under Ottoman domination in 1516. During the first three centuries of Turkish rule, the area was isolated from outside influences. This period came to an end with Napoleon's effort to carve a Middle Eastern empire in 1798. After the French withdrawal in 1801, Egypt came under the rule of the Ottoman general, Muhammad Ali, who created an independent government in that country. In 1831 his armies occupied Palestine, and for nine years he and his son, Ibrahim, ruled the Holy Land. Their tolerant administration opened the country to Western influences and enabled Christian missionaries to establish many schools, which accelerated the process of modernization. When the British, Austrians, and Russians came to the aid of the sultan, in 1840, after an attack by Muhammed Ali into Syria, the Arabian peninsula, and parts of the Ottoman Empire, the Egyptians were forced to withdraw, and Palestine was returned to Ottoman control. Later the country witnessed an increase in foreign settlements and colonies established by the French, Russians, and Germans. By far the most important (in spite of their initial numerical insignificance) were the Zionist agricultural settlements, which foreshadowed later Zionist efforts to establish a Jewish state in Palestine. These earliest settlements originated with Russian Jews in 1882. In 1896 the Austrian journalist Theodor Herzl issued *Der*

Judenstaat, advocating an autonomous Jewish state. Two years later he went to Palestine to investigate the possibilities and to seek the help of the German Emperor Wilhelm II, who was then making his pilgrimage to the Holy Land.

By the end of the nineteenth century, Baron Rothschild had begun a program to subsidize the development of these agricultural settlements by Jews in Palestine. More than twenty existed by 1900. Political and nationalist manifestations appeared. The Ottomans tried to prohibit the immigration of foreign Jews into Palestine, but the inflow continued. In 1914, Palestine's population was about 650,000; about 10 percent were Jews, some 75 percent were Muslims, and at least 10 percent were Christians.

During World War I, Turkish and German armies occupied the area until Jerusalem was captured by British forces under the command of General Edmund Allenby in December 1917. The rest of the area was occupied by the British by October 1918. Palestine was hit hard by World War I. Contradictory Allied negotiations conducted during the war had not clearly excluded Palestine from the territories pledged to the Arabs; at the same time, proposals had been put forth to establish an international status for Palestine, and other promises had favored the establishment in Palestine of a National Home for the Jewish people. The Arabs maintained that Palestine was included in an area that Britain had promised independence through the exchange of correspondence between Sir Henry McMahon, the high commissioner of Egypt, and Husayn ibn 'Ali, then sharif of Mecca, from July to October 1915. Yet, by May 1916, Britain, France, and Russia had reached a secret agreement (Sykes-Picot) in which the bulk of Palestine was to be internationalized. And in November 1917, Arthur Balfour, the British secretary of state for foreign affairs, addressed a letter to Lord Rothschild promising British support for the National Home for the Jews in Palestine on the understanding that "nothing shall be done which may prejudice the civil and religious rights of existing non-Jewish communities in Palestine" (Laqueur, 1970:18).

After the war, Britain wanted to secure international approval for the continued occupation of Palestine in a manner consistent with its wartime commitments. A British military administration was set up after the capture of Jerusalem, and a general international framework existed for Britain in Article 22 of the Covenant of the League of Nations signed in July 1919. This article recognized the provisional independence of the former Ottoman Arab provinces, subject to the assistance of a mandatory power. In July 1919, a general congress at Damascus, which included Palestinian delegates, passed a resolution electing Faisal, the son of Husayn ibn 'Ali (now king of Hejaz), the king of united Syria including Palestine and rejected the Balfour Declaration. King Faisal was deposed by the French in July 1920.

Meanwhile, the Paris Peace Conference held after the war agreed to the establishment of a Palestinian state, and Great Britain was assigned the mandatory power by the San Remo Conference of 1920. The terms of the mandate directed Britain to assist in the building of the Jewish National Home. Accordingly, provisions were made in 1920 for the entry of one-thousand Jewish immigrants per month. Undoubtedly this policy affected the atmosphere in Palestine, causing violent clashes between Jews and Arabs. But the capital and skilled labor influx led to the development of prosperous agricultural districts and improved education, health, and general living standards to the advantage of the entire population.

President Woodrow Wilson, who had endorsed the Balfour Declaration, dispatched the American-sponsored King-Crane Commission to the former Arab provinces of the Ottoman Empire to ascertain the inhabitants' wishes regarding the postwar settlement of their territories. The commission report, disclosed in December 1922, challenged the propriety of creating a Jewish homeland in the face of major Arab opposition (more than 70 percent of the Arabs surveyed were anti-Zionist). Hostility between the groups was growing. Already in April 1920, riots in Palestine had resulted in Jewish and Arab casualties. The cause of this uprising was attributed to Arab disappointment at the nonfulfillment of promises of independence and to their fear of economic and political subjection to the Zionists.

Further violence ensued in May 1921 between Jews and Arabs in Palestine, prompting the British to issue a White Paper in July 1922, with its interpretation of the concept of the Jewish National Home. The intention was not that Palestine as a whole should be converted for this purpose but that such a home should be established within Palestine. Immigration would not exceed the economic absorptive capacity of the country, and steps would be taken to set up a legislative council. These proposals were rejected by the Arabs in principle and because Jewish immigration with a political objective was to be regulated by an economic criterion. A few months later, Transjordan, although included in the British mandate of Palestine, was excluded from the scope of the Balfour Declaration.

The council of the League of Nations, meanwhile, had approved in July 1922 the mandates for Syria and Lebanon for the French, and Palestine and Iraq for Great Britain. The preamble incorporated the Balfour Declaration and stressed the Jewish historical connection with Palestine. Article 2 made the mandatory power responsible for placing the country under such "political, administrative and economic conditions as will secure the establishment of the Jewish national home . . . and the development of self-governing institutions and also for safeguarding the civil and religious rights of all the inhabitants of Palestine, irrespective of race and religion" (Laqueur, 1970:35). Article 4 allowed for the establishment of a Jewish agency to advise and cooperate with the administration of Palestine in matters affecting the Jewish National Home. Article 6 required that Palestine, "while ensuring that the rights and position of other sections of the population are not prejudiced," under suitable conditions facilitate Jewish immigration and settlement on the land (36). These arrangements were formalized by the Treaty of Lausanne with Turkey in September 1923. About this time, the newly formed British administration tried to win Arab cooperation by offering a legislative council and an Arab agency to parallel the Jewish agency, but these offers were rejected because they fell short of national demands. For the remainder of this decade, there were sporadic clashes of violence in Palestine.

In the early 1930s representatives from more than twenty Muslim countries gathered in Jerusalem to discuss the danger of Zionism. They also proclaimed a boycott of Zionist and British goods. By 1933, however, the Nazi ascension to power in Germany gave a great impetus to Jewish immigration. In 1936 the Arabs called for a general strike, which was maintained for six months. The movement grew and assumed the dimensions of a national revolt, which continued into 1939. The Peel report of inquiry, publishing its findings in July 1937, attributed the revolt to the Arab desire for independence and fear of the Jewish National Home. It declared the mandate unworkable and Britain's obligations to Arabs and Jews mutually irreconcilable. The report advised that, should the mandate continue, political, social and psychological factors, in addition to economic factors, must be taken into consideration in regulating Jewish immigration. The Peel Commission report summarized the cause of the dispute in this way:

An irrepressible conflict has arisen between two national communities within the narrow bounds of one small country. About 1,000,000 Arabs are in strife, open or latent, with some 400,000 Jews. There is no common ground between them. The Arab community is predominantly Asiatic in character, the Jewish community predominantly European. They differ in religion and in language. Their cultural and social life, their ways of thought and conduct, are as incompatible as their national aspirations. These last are the greatest bar to peace. Arabs and Jews might possibly learn to live and work together in Palestine if they would make a genuine effort to reconcile and combine their national ideals and so build up in time a joint or dual nationality. But this they cannot do. (Report of the Palestine Royal Commission [Peel Commission] in Laqueur, 1970:57).

The commission recommended partitioning the area into a zone for the Zionists and a zone for the Arabs. The Zionist attitude to partition was ambivalent at the time; the Arabs were quite displeased by the idea of a forcible transfer of their country. A British statement of policy announced the impracticability of partition and called for a roundtable conference in London.

The 1939 London conference produced no agreement among the parties—British, Arabs, and Jews—so in May of that year the British made a unilateral statement of policy in a White Paper, based on the assumption that the pledge for the Jewish National Home had already been substantially fulfilled and that indefinite Jewish immigration and transfer of Arab land to Jews were contrary to the spirit of Article 22 of the Covenant of the League of Nations and to British obligations to the Arabs under the mandate. Jewish immigration would be subject to Arab acquiescence, land transfer would be allowed only in certain areas of Palestine, and an independent Palestinian state would be considered within ten years. The policy favored some of the Arab positions, although the Arabs were not entirely satisfied with the statement since they wanted a stronger British commitment to independence for Palestine. The Zionists were opposed to the policy. The outbreak of war in Europe in September 1939 prevented the council of the League of Nations from discussing the British White Paper.

During World War II, the Zionists found themselves in the paradoxical position of fighting the British White Paper and at the same time rallying to Britain's side against the common enemy. Both Jews and Arabs had enlisted in British forces during the war. The end of the war saw the Jewish community in Palestine vastly strengthened; equally important was the support won by the Zionists in the United States, where they had concentrated their efforts after 1939. In 1942, at a conference in New York City, the Biltmore Plan demanded unrestricted immigration, a Jewish army, and the establishment of Palestine as a Jewish commonwealth. But by May 1945, the Covenant of the League of Arab States had been drawn up, with an annex emphasizing the Arab character of Palestine. That December, the Arab League declared a boycott of Zionist goods. The pattern of the postwar struggle for Palestine was emerging.

In November 1945, an Anglo-American commission of inquiry was formed at the initiation of the British in an effort to secure U.S. coresponsibility for a Palestine policy. The commission recommended continuation of Jewish immigration and repeal of the land regulations of the White Paper of 1939. Although it recommended continuing the mandate, the commission stipulated a plan of provincial autonomy for Arabs and Jews. Zionist pressure in Palestine was intensified by the unauthorized immigration of European Jewish refugees. Attacks between British and Zionist forces occurred; the Arabs passed resolutions threatening British and U.S. interests in the Middle East if Arab rights in Palestine were disregarded.

Early in 1947, after another conference with the parties, Britain decided to refer the Palestinian question to the United Nations. In a majority report on August 31, 1947, a UN commission of inquiry recommended the partition of the country into Arab and Jewish states. The substance of the report was adopted by the General Assembly in a resolution on November 29 of that year. There were thirty-eight votes in favor (cast by nearly all European states and some Latin American countries), thirteen votes against (cast by Arab member countries, Greece, Turkey, India, and Cuba), and ten abstentions (Britain, Yugoslavia, China, Ethiopia, and several Latin American states). After the war, the Zionist cause gained tremendous sympathy due to the Holocaust. In the plan, roughly 55 percent of the land of Palestine was allotted to the Jewish state; 45 percent to the Arabs. The Zionists welcomed the partition plan because it offered recognition of a Jewish state; the Arabs rejected it. Britain was unwilling to implement a policy that was not acceptable to both sides and thus refused to share the administration with the UN Palestine Commission, which was to supervise the transitional period. Britain left the area on May 15, 1948.

Soon after the resolution, communal fighting broke out in Palestine, and in December 1947 the Arab League pledged support to the Palestinian Arabs and organized a force of volunteers. The Zionists mounted successful offensive attacks, and the Arabs of Palestine, badly led and ill equipped, collapsed. Thousands of refugees from Palestine streamed into neighboring Arab countries. On the departure of the British, units of the regular armies of Syria, Transjordan, Iraq, and Egypt crossed the frontiers of Palestine. Full-scale war developed, establishing a long-term trend for settling grievances in the Arab–Israeli dispute.

VIOLENCE HISTORY

Continuous conflicts have occurred between the Jews and the Arabs in the Middle East since the partition plan. Once the state of Israel was formally proclaimed, hostile relations intensified. There have been nine major periods of violent conflict in which Israeli and Palestinian forces either faced each other directly or faced another Arab state in opposition. Problems that originally were primarily political and ideological have developed into military issues of tactics and strategy with economic ramifications. No one has been able to effect a stable, long-term solution. Temporary settlements have been difficult and unsatisfactory for the conflicting parties. At various points, major powers in the international system, including the United Nations, have played a central role in attempting to negotiate arrangements on a number of problems. Each successive military encounter has solidified the positions held by the opposing sides in the conflict, making solutions more difficult and more complex but, nonetheless, very important to the stability of the region and also critical for the larger international system. A brief synopsis of each conflict follows.

MAJOR CONFLICTS

The 1948 War: May 15, 1948–January 7, 1949

Open warfare began on the day the Jews declared the independence of the state of Israel. The Arabs, despite numerical strength many times that of the Zionists, were soundly defeated. Torn by internal rivalries and unable to agree on common objectives, Arab forces never succeeded in placing their armies under effective joint command. The Zionists, however, showed greater cohesion. Their war effort was augmented by an influx of men and aid from abroad. The Zionist military strategy was to acquire control over all territory allocated to the Jewish state by the partition plan and to secure the main roads linking Jewish settlements throughout the area. After the shooting stopped, Egypt, Lebanon, Jordan (then called Transjordan) and Syria eventually signed separate armistice agreements with Israel. (Iraq refused to sign an armistice agreement and simply withdrew its troops from the area.) Through fighting, Israel had acquired close to one-third more territory than had been designated for the Zionists under the UN partition plan. No Palestinian state ever emerged. The remaining territory under Arab control was eventually annexed by neighboring states. Jordan assumed jurisdiction over the West Bank of the Jordan River, and Egypt took the Gaza Strip. Jerusalem was divided between Israel and Jordan.

UN armistice commissions were established to police the frontiers, and demilitarized zones were set up to divide Israel from bordering Arab states. The United Nations Relief Works Agency (UNRWA) for Palestinian refugees was organized to assist Palestinian Arabs who had fled or been driven from their homes. Somewhere between three-hundred-thousand and seven-hundred-thousand Palestinian Arabs who had lived in the area taken over by Israel became refugees; most of them resettled in the West Bank and Gaza while others scattered in Lebanon, Jordan, and Syria (Congressional Quarterly, *The Middle East,* 1990:13, 1981:16).

The defeated Arab states still refused to accept the existence of the Jewish state; the Palestinians had been forced to give their land to the Zionists either through battle or by the dictates of the United Nations. In the end, the primary goal of building an Arab-Palestinian state had been lost. Israel perceived itself to be in a weak geostrategic position, fearing future attacks by enemy neighbors, and began building a strong military organization. This posed a threat to Arab countries and thus started the escalating spiral of mutual perceptions of hostility. The end of the war was unstable, since neither side was satisfied with the outcome.

The Suez War: October 29, 1956–November 7, 1956

Another major military confrontation took place in October 1956. President Gamal Abdul Nasser of Egypt, a charismatic, reformist leader, had nationalized the Suez Canal Company in July of that year after the evacuation of British forces from the canal zone, in accordance with a 1954 agreement. He wanted to invest the total revenue from the canal in the Aswan High Dam project, which was at the center of his plan for social reform and economic progress. In 1955 Nasser had broken ranks with the West and signed a major military agreement with the Soviet Union whereby that country would supply armaments to Egypt.

A short time after the nationalization of the Suez Canal Company, the British government, along with the French, decided to use force to recover the canal and force Nasser out of his position. (Both nations were heavy users of the canal and held the majority of stocks in the company, and the waterway provided the shortest route to their oil supplies in the Persian Gulf.) The two countries began planning for joint military action, secretly enlisting Israel's participation in the plan.

Led by the Palestinian Arabs who had been displaced by the war in 1948, border raids from the Gaza area into Israeli territory were increasing, and Israel was ready to retaliate. On October 29, Israel launched an attack into the Sinai Peninsula of Egypt. British and French aircraft also attacked Egypt, on October 30. By November 7, when a cease-fire was put into effect, British and French forces had secured control of the canal, and Israel occupied nearly the entire area of the Sinai. However, intense international pressure from the United States and the Soviet Union forced Britain and France to withdraw their troops, which departed in December 1956. Israeli units were removed from the Sinai in March 1957, following a U.S. threat to impose economic sanctions if Israel failed to comply.

After the crisis, the United Nations placed an emergency force, known as the United Nations Emergency Force (UNEF), in the Suez to guard the area and to prevent future hostilities. This force was composed of 6,000 officers and troops from ten member states, increased from an initial 2,500 in October and November. Host-country consent, however, is necessary for UNEF entry. Israel did not permit the UN-created emergency force on its territory, but troops were placed on Egyptian soil in the Sinai with the understanding that withdrawal of consent for stationing the troops would require the departure of UNEF from Egypt. By May 1957, UN troops were in position along the Gaza frontier and at the southernmost tip of the peninsula, Sharm el-Sheikh, the entrance of the Gulf of Aqaba. Israel gained free passage through the gulf (but warned that withdrawal of UN troops would constitute an act of war), and the operation of the Suez Canal resumed. Ships from all states except Israel were allowed to use the waterway.

Although the battle resulted in no territorial redistribution and no concessions for the Palestinians, the war contributed both to increased Arab hostility toward Israel and to increased concern within Israel over its own national security.

The 1967 War: June 5, 1967–June 10, 1967

By 1967, numerous terror and counterterror activities were taking place between the Israelis and the Palestinians, the latter having been organized as the Palestine Liberation Organization (PLO) since 1964. This group later formally declared that the land distribution could be resolved only by the force of arms. Border clashes between Israel and Lebanon and Syria were increasing, and troop buildups on Israeli borders were in evidence on both sides. On May 16, 1967, Nasser requested that the UNEF be withdrawn from the Suez area. UN Secretary-General U Thant concluded that Egypt had the right to ask for UNEF withdrawal so that it could move its troops up to the border, as Israel had been doing. Once UNEF withdrawal was complete, the Israelis were denied further access to shipping through the Gulf of Aqaba. Fearing an attack on three fronts, Israel launched a preemptive strike on the Arabs on June 5, 1967. Thus began another conflict—known as the Six-Day War, or the June War.

The Arabs insist they did not intend to attack Israel but were trying to prepare for the Israeli blow, which in fact did come. Nasser, in announcing the reinstituted blockade against Israeli shipping through the Gulf of Aqaba, may have planned to use this as a bargaining position, but Israel interpreted the action as aggression. The Israelis were seized by the fear that they would be attacked from all sides by an enemy who was determined to eliminate them.

The military confrontation in 1967 was clearly a case of decisive victory for the Israelis, whose military forces moved in three directions. In battles with

Egypt, they acquired a complete takeover of the Sinai Peninsula and the Gaza Strip. The Suez Canal was closed afterward and was not reopened again by Egypt until June 1975. In battles with Jordan, the Israelis won control of the entire West Bank region of the Jordan River and the old city sections of Jerusalem. And in battle with Syria, they achieved territorial control over the Golan Heights area. A truce went into effect on June 10, although periodic clashes continued.

As war victor, Israel claimed it had now achieved a viable geostrategic position, taking into account the new borders established by the recently conquered territories, and had enhanced its national security. Since fears among Arabs about Jewish expansionist activities had been confirmed, security for Arab states was correspondingly threatened.

Along with the territories taken, Israel assumed possession of refugee camps that had been set up for the Palestinians. Thousands of Palestinian inhabitants on these lands were brought under Israeli rule, under Israeli occupation. The new authorities governing the Palestinians decided to remain in the conquered territory, insisting on negotiated peace agreements with Arab neighbor countries as the condition for land returns.

This round of fighting complicated the issues. The fight was against formal Arab countries directly, not Palestinians. The acquired lands had previously been governed by three different nation-states. Some of the land taken was beyond mandated Palestine—neither the Sinai Peninsula nor the Golan Heights was inhabited by Palestinians. Terrain and population patterns across these areas varied tremendously, from desert to small mountains to land rich in agricultural production, from sparsely settled regions of the Sinai to the densely populated West Bank. Superpower involvement was brought into the conflict. Because the United States was the major arms supplier to Israel, Egypt broke relations with the United States. Because the Soviet Union was the major supplier to Egypt, the Soviet Union severed diplomatic ties with Israel.

In November, the superpowers and others joined together to pass a resolution in the UN Security Council, Resolution 242, that urged Israel to withdraw from the lands conquered by force and pressed the Arab states to recognize the existence of Israel as the means to terminate the state of belligerency of parties in the Middle East. Although this land-for-peace exchange suggested a route of nonviolent conflict resolution, it did not halt the pattern of violence.

The War of Attrition: March 8, 1969–August 8, 1970

In an effort to break the Israeli resolve and to force the withdrawal of troops from the Sinai, Nasser launched an alternative military plan in the spring of 1969. Known as the "war of attrition," the strategy called for an extended conflict of sporadic fighting, which was designed to wear down Israeli resistance by inflicting unacceptable casualties. Almost daily, Egyptian–Israeli artillery duels occurred across the Suez Canal. Palestinians and Israelis engaged in raids that affected not only Israeli territory but also the Jordanian, Syrian, and Lebanese frontiers.

With the situation highly volatile and with scattered border clashes continuing, U.S. Secretary of State William Rogers submitted a proposal for a cease-fire and called for a resumption of UN mediation efforts. The parties agreed to a ninety-day cease-fire, beginning August 8, and conditionally accepted the U.S. formula for peace negotiations that included the Egyptian recognition of Israeli sovereignty and the Israeli withdrawal from occupied lands and that required the Jordanian government to control Palestinian commando activities that were organized within its borders and were launched against Israel. The Palestine Liberation Organization, Syria, and Iraq rejected the plan. In Israel, several cabinet members resigned over the government's acceptance of the peace formula.

In September 1970, Israel announced it was withdrawing from the peace talks. That same month Nasser died suddenly from a massive heart attack. The outcome of this round of fighting, including the Rogers plan for resolving the dispute, did not reduce tensions but polarized internal differences on the two sides.

The Jordanian Civil War: September 1, 1970–September 27, 1970

After the 1967 war, guerilla commandos of the Palestinian resistant movement, the fedayeen (part of the PLO), expanded their activities within Jordan, Syria, and Lebanon. (Jordan suffered heavy losses in the war and an influx of thousands of additional Palestinian refugees.) With headquarters in Amman, they used the country as a basis for their assaults on Israeli targets. The purpose of these actions was to recapture their homeland from Israeli control. By 1970, the PLO sought to establish political dominance within the Palestinian refugee community in Jordan and ultimately in all of Jordan. Particularly strong activity was aimed at the overthrow of King Hussein so that war against Israel could be stepped up. The PLO became a state within a state, threatening the survival of the Hashemite dynasty. Tensions led to sporadic fighting.

In September 1970, fighting erupted between the Jordanian army and the PLO. One Palestinian group hijacked three commercial planes belonging to the United States, Britain, and Switzerland, flew the planes and four-hundred hostages to an airstrip outside Amman, and after several days, blew up the planes. The hostages were later released in exchange for fedayeen members held prisoner in West Germany, Britain, and Switzerland. On September 27, following a cease-fire, a fourteen-point agreement was signed to end hostilities in Jordan. The plan called for King Hussein to retain his position, but Arab leaders also pledged to support the Palestinian struggle against Israel.

Although some fighting continued into 1971, King Hussein had strengthened his position and ordered the fedayeen out of Amman. The Jordanian army crushed the last guerrilla strongholds, and the Palestinians threatened reprisals for this action. Members of the Black September PLO organization claimed responsibility for the assassination of the Jordanian prime minister in November 1971 and for an unsuccessful attempt on the life of Jordan's ambassador to Britain. Hashemite rule was preserved in Jordan, but the regime had come to be viewed as an enemy of the Palestinian movement. PLO headquarters moved to Beirut.

The 1973 War: October 6, 1973–October 22, 1973

By 1971 Anwar Sadat, the new Egyptian leader, had begun plans for another war against the Israelis, since from his perspective it did not appear that the issue of territorial possession could be resolved through diplomacy. Military buildup was a priority; the money was supplied through Libyan oil wealth, and sophisticated arms were sent from the Soviet Union to both Egypt and Syria.

This war—known as the "Yom Kippur War" or the "Ramadan War"—broke out when Egyptian and Syrian troops advanced into the Sinai Peninsula and the Golan Heights in a surprise attack. The Arab forces were able temporarily to dictate the conditions of battle. Despite the Arabs' early success in striking Israeli-occupied territory, however, the Israeli forces subsequently took charge by breaking through the Egyptian lines as far as the western bank of the Suez Canal and advancing to within twenty miles of the Syrian capital of Damascus. The Arabs, who had fought with conspicuously more success than in 1967, were still defeated, though the Israelis suffered heavy losses, when a cease-fire resolution by the UN Security Council was implemented on October 24.

Still, fighting continued. Sadat called on the superpowers to commit troops to support the cease-fire. Shortly thereafter, U.S. armed forces were placed on worldwide alert in response to the possibility of a unilateral move by the Soviet Union to move troops into the Middle East. The crisis was defused when agreement was reached to establish a more broadly based international peacekeeping force.

This war, after extended negotiations, led first to the Disengagement of Forces Agreements brokered by Henry Kissinger, the American secretary of state (1973–75), and to the gradual withdrawal of troops from the Sinai. It also set the stage for the Camp David Accords of 1978, providing for the complete withdrawal from the Sinai, which was finished in April 1982. Thus ended the Egyptian–Israeli belligerency, where military might and land-for-peace exchange provided the formula for reaching agreement. Yet the result of this round of fighting touched only one aspect of the overall dispute and hardly the central core. The war outcome, however serious, dealt with a political–military dispute rather than with the direct and opposing ideologies that form the basis of the nationalist rivalry between Israelis and Palestinians. The Sinai territory was never a part of Palestine, nor did refugees occupy the area.

The Lebanon Civil War: April 13, 1975–

After the PLO was forced from Jordan in 1970, its chief training ground, principal supply depot, and most advantageous position from which to strike at Israel was in Lebanon. By an Arab-brokered agreement in 1969, PLO activity in southern Lebanon was sanctioned as long as the Palestinians respected Lebanese sovereignty. This broke down, and violence that erupted in Beirut between the Christian Lebanese Phalange and commandos of the PLO in April 1975 sparked the onset of a long, drawn-out war. The conflict turned into a power struggle that became increasingly complicated by the eventual participation of historic rival groups of an assortment of Muslim and Christian communities in Lebanon, intensifying and prolonging the civil war.

By 1976, Syria intervened. Palestinians were in key positions and were reluctant to permit the PLO free reign in Lebanon; the two sides were soon engaged in bloody battle. The civil war began to subside by November of that year, but intermittent, often intense, fighting continued throughout the 1980s. In 1978, after an attack by PLO commandos on an Israeli beach, a major Israeli invasion into southern Lebanon was launched with twenty-thousand troops. The purpose was to clear an area along the Israeli northern frontier to serve as a security zone. Soon after, the United Nations Interim Force in Lebanon (UNIFIL) was organized and stationed in the south to keep the PLO and the Israelis from attacking one another. Violence, however, continued, involving many groups and essentially dissolving the previous character of the state of Lebanon despite various cease-fire accords and peace-agreement attempts.

The War in Lebanon: June 6, 1982–June 10, 1985

On June 6, 1982, the Israeli government invaded southern Lebanon. Heavy air attacks were launched against PLO targets in Beirut and throughout the country. The PLO militia reacted to Israeli fire by attacking Israeli settlements in northern Galilee. Syria was involved too, since it had thirty-thousand troops stationed in Lebanon at the time. Israel and Syria agreed to participate in a cease-fire that went into effect on June 11, although Israel made it clear that the cease-fire did not apply to the PLO forces.

Fighting continued until mid-July, and through the efforts of U.S. Ambassador Philip Habib and the Lebanese government, it was agreed that eight-thousand PLO fighters would be evacuated from Lebanon and dispersed to other Arab countries (none bordering Israel). By September, the evacuation had been completed under the supervision of a multinational force composed of U.S. Marines and French and Italian troops. Shortly thereafter, the new president-elect of Lebanon, Bashir Gemayel, was killed in a bomb explosion, which set off a new wave of instability. With Israeli control over West Beirut, Christian Phalangist forces entered two Palestinian refugee camps, Shatilla and Sabra, and massacred hundreds of defenseless men, women, and children.

In May 1983, an Israeli–Lebanese agreement was reached, calling for the withdrawal of all foreign forces from Lebanese soil and for arrangements to normalize relations between the two countries. Provisions were made for a mechanism that would guarantee Israel against the re-creation of a Palestinian base in southern Lebanon. The United States was also the target of attack when more than 250 U.S. Marines temporarily stationed in Beirut lost their lives in a bomb explosion in September 1983. Still the fighting continued, involving a variety of Christian militia groups, Palestinians, Syrians, Lebanese Muslim organizations, and Israelis. The Israelis began a phased withdrawal in the early months of 1985; by July, most of the troops were gone except for a "security zone" force in the south of Lebanon.

The conflict was long and did not lead to stability inside Lebanon. The PLO was dispersed but not eliminated as an actor in the dispute. Once again, the Israelis "won" the war technically but gained nothing politically; in addition, there was much dissension about the war effort within Israel itself. The Palestinians seemed to acquire at least some public sympathy when they were forced to evacuate from Lebanon, but they lost the battle militarily. This war did not create the conditions for a settlement or a negotiation involving the principal parties.

The Intifada: December 9, 1987–

On December 9, 1987, Palestinians in the Gaza Strip confronted Israeli soldiers with rocks and Molotov cocktails in response to an accident involving an Israeli army truck that had killed four Arabs the previous day. So began the intifada. Israeli soldiers killed one Palestinian and wounded about fifteen others. The unrest spread to the West Bank. Israeli efforts to suppress protests in the occupied territories failed as the quick and sudden explosion of Palestinian anger turned into a sustained uprising. Later that month, the Palestinians residing in the territories held a general strike. In January 1988, Israel announced its decision to deport Palestinians accused of inciting riots in the occupied lands and to combat the uprising with force and beatings. By the end of 1990, nearly eight-hundred Palestinians had lost their lives in the three-year-old uprising.

The intifada was a reaction to Israeli efforts to control life in the occupied territories. The Israeli government had expropriated available land in the territories, built Jewish settlements, controlled the area water and electricity, destroyed the houses of families who resisted, and arrested and detained Arabs arbitrarily. Although violent resistance to the occupation was not new, the massive, popular upheaval in the territories and the inability of Israeli authorities to contain it, despite curfews, school closings, beatings, and rubber bullets, showed a tremendous tolerance among the Palestinians to sustain their cause.

The movement has intensified the Palestinian goal to achieve an independent state, increased the economic and moral cost of occupation for Israel, caused Jordan to renounce legal and administrative links to the occupied West Bank territory (which Jordan annexed in 1950 and lost in the 1967 war), and pushed major political concessions by Arafat in December 1988 to affirm the principle of partition, accept the existence of the state of Israel, and renounce terrorism. But the Israeli government has remained adamantly opposed to the idea of a Palestinian state and continues to occupy the area of Palestinian inhabitants.

POSTPARTITION POLITICS

After winning the war in 1948, Israel became a modern miracle. Jews migrated to Israel and went to work; the population tripled. Supported by massive donations from individual Jews, American aid, and German reparation payments, the country was quickly transformed into an enclave of dynamic purpose, building power and irrigation plants, modern cities, and industries. For more than a decade, its gross national product grew by at least 10 percent. By the mid–1960s, Israel boasted a standard of living almost equivalent to that of Western Europe. The miracle was not confined to the Jewish homeland. Israel had created a new image of the Jews all over the world, an image of a working and intellectual people who can fight with heroism.

After the war of 1967, most of the Palestinian Arabs did not flee from the land conquered by Israel. Thus, the Jewish state assumed responsibility for the West Bank and Gaza refugees who had left their homes twenty years earlier. On the West Bank, more than a half million Arabs remained. Their desire was to stay until they could fight again and take back the land. As for the Israelis, the 1967 war reopened a tremendous burden the Jewish state had inherited: the captured territory offered no ready assets; the area was crowded and short of water; and nearly half the people living there were dependent on international aid and government-funded relief. A Jewish nation of roughly 2.5 million ruled an Arab population of over 1 million, made up of West Bankers, Gazans, and the Palestinian minority that had stayed in Israel after 1948.

The future and status of Palestine and the people living there have been open questions since the establishment of the British mandate over the territory at the end of the First World War. However, it was not until the late 1950s, with the political renaissance of the Palestine movement, that the new realities resulting from the 1948 war began to be grasped. The Palestinians adopted a position of total rejection of partition solutions and dreamed of ''return'' and the expulsion of the occupiers from the land. With the creation of the PLO, there were at first calls for the destruction of the Jewish state and, later, the idea of a secular state in part of Palestine where Muslims, Christians, and Jews could coexist, but by the end of the 1980s, Palestinians had moved to de facto acceptance of Israel.

After the Camp David accords of 1979, the PLO aim was not to destroy Israel but to establish an independent Palestinian state on land from which the Israelis would withdraw. The West Bank and Gaza were the main focus of the Israeli–Palestinian confrontation. The Israeli government, however, stepped up Jewish settlement and introduced the autonomy plan. After the disappearance of a Palestinian armed presence from southern Lebanon, the idea of an armed struggle was called into question. Among other things, problems arose between the Palestinian masses inside the occupied territories and the PLO leadership on the outside. Only the intifada has brought focus back to the Palestinian struggle and reunited groups inside and beyond the occupied territories.

The punitive measures taken against Palestinian armed resistance in the West Bank have been formidable and have fueled hatred of the occupier. In this struggle, the Palestinian inhabitants of the West Bank and Gaza are alone, face-to-face with the Israelis, which has helped strengthen the national identity and anger on both sides. Moreover, a new generation of Arabs and Jews has come of age knowing only an occupied West Bank and Gaza Strip. Polarization between them widened as the politics of frustration was vented. The passage of time became an obstacle against workable compromise, and physical violence—not discourse—became the accepted norm for dispute resolution.

After the 1967 war, the parties to the conflict perpetuated the idea that peace depended on Israel's willingness to return the occupied territories. Israel had the main card—the land; therefore, Israel alone could make the concessions that any solution entailed. However, years of occupation created significant changes in Israel's attitude toward the issue. The days of waiting for the Arabs to agree to negotiations had disappeared. Israelis became fully aware of what Judea and Samaria meant to Jews, whereas the symbolism of the West Bank to Palestinians became more pronounced.

Part of the legacy of the decade or so following the 1967 war was that the Arabs and the Israelis effectively changed their roles in readiness and willingness to negotiate and compromise with the enemy. In September 1967, at a summit meeting in Khartoum, the Arabs issued an outright rejection of compromise with Israel. The communique delivered at the end was symbolized by a series of "no"s—no peace with Israel, no negotiations with Israel, no recognition of Israel.

Arab Summit Conference Communique Excerpt,
Khartoum, Sudan,
September 1, 1967

3—The Arab heads of state have agreed to unite their political efforts on the international and diplomatic level to eliminate the effects of the aggression and to ensure the withdrawal of the aggressive Israeli forces from the Arab lands which have been occupied since the 5 June aggression. This will be done within the framework of the main principles to which the Arab states adhere, namely: no peace with Israel, no recognition of Israel, no negotiations with it, and adherence to the rights of the Palestinian people in their country (Moore, *Documents*, 1974:788).

Since the mid–1970s, the Israelis have adopted the same stance regarding the Palestinians: no negotiations with the PLO, no Palestinian state, no self-determination for the Palestinians. The result has been a dispute in which first one side, then the other, laid down preconditions that preempted any meaningful discussion. Near the end of the decade, on December 14, 1988, the PLO leader Yasir Arafat explicitly recognized Israel's right to exist, renounced terrorism, and accepted UN Resolution 242. His statement prompted the United States to open a dialogue with the PLO.

What has Arafat gained by meeting the demand the international community has stressed for so long? The rewards are by no means guaranteed. The talks of negotiation have still not made significant headway. The general concept of peace and territorial compromise has been laid out explicitly; the diplomatic concessions needed from both sides have yet to occur. From the mid–1970s onward, Arafat accepted the principle that a homeland on the West Bank and Gaza was the only realistic prospect. In doing so, the PLO effectively acknowledged that 20 percent of Palestine would have to suffice. He maintained that Israel was responsible for the stalemate by refusing to negotiate on those terms and insisted that time is on the side of the Palestinians. The reality suggests otherwise: Israel has built enough settlements to guarantee security and a permanent home for the Jewish people.

By 1990 the PLO had gained sympathy and recognition around the world. As many states maintain diplomatic relations with the organization as with Israel; it is the only nongovernmental body to gain observer status at the United Nations, securing a platform from which it initiates anti-Israeli resolutions in the General Assembly. Yet, the PLO has been unable to translate this support into concrete results. No piece of Palestine has been liberated from the occupiers.

More than twenty years after the 1967 war, there was a powerful case to be made for believing that Israel's occupation of the promised land would continue, in spite of the intifada. No Israeli government was ever likely to enjoy a clear mandate for the exchange of territory for peace. The future tension meant neither formal peace nor formal war but a solution based on a tacit understanding, not a negotiated armistice. A loose, unspoken understanding between Israel and the Palestinians offered the nearest thing to a settlement, short of any territorial return. This would condemn Israelis and Palestinians to a conflict without end.

The Palestinian intifada brought both new dangers to Middle East politics and renewed opportunities for negotiations. This process may result in a stalemate, or the Palestinians may choose to begin armed struggle again as part of their resistance campaign. Another stage of violence would be necessary to regain the opportunity for political negotiations. Thus, the significance of understanding the meaning, rationale, justifications, and functions of bargaining and prenegotiation strategies between Israelis and Palestinians looms large in the last decade of the twentieth century.

CONCLUSION

Through violence and politics, the Israelis and the Palestinians have entrenched their nationalist rivalry by continuing conflicts and developing ideological conditioning. Each group still seeks a legitimate place in the scheme of Middle East regional configurations. Themes of acceptance, security, and sovereignty are constant. Since 1967, a special superior-subordinate relationship has existed under the confines of occupation by Israel of Palestinian-inhabited lands, which has fueled hostility and perceptions of grievances. Superpower interest via negotiation attempts and huge foreign-aid packages in military assistance have become commonplace, enabling the sides to play out the dispute through military encounters and basic expressions of power assertion.

However different their strategies, Israelis and Palestinians have very actively pursued their mutually incompatible goals and maintained the central core of

their differences throughout time. Nationalist rivalry remains strong, and ideological positions are held intensely by each side. Both parties have been successful
in organizing resistance movements as a way to strengthen self-identity, although
the confrontational tactics practiced by them are different. Both persist in the
application of military solutions (conventional or unconventional) to achieve
their objectives. Each has made attempts to destroy the foundation core of its
enemy by trying to break down the ideological commitment or forcing dispersion
of supporters.

The Zionists are decidedly stronger and operate from a permanent, land-settled
power base. The weaker Palestinians have moved around a lot—from mandated
Palestine to Jordan to Lebanon to the West Bank—to build their power base.
Neither side shows strong signs of willingness to retreat from basic goals. The
notion of exchanging land for peace has emerged as an operating principle to
govern reconciliation possibilities of the rivalry problem. Although it appears to
be acceptable at an abstract level to the parties in this dispute, implementing the
steps to negotiate such a policy into a workable program has failed to attract the
interest or dedication that would be required to overcome the obstacles and to
scrape away the deeply held mutual perceptions of animosity formed by conflict
buildup.

3

Sustaining Conflict

BACKGROUND

Ideological cohesion and intensified nationalism develop not only out of direct experience in conflict participation but also through perspectives created to interpret such experience. To understand how the Arab–Israeli conflict has been maintained, one should examine some of the views about rights and entitlement to statehood, based primarily on concepts of ethnic identity and suffering advanced by Zionists and Palestinian Nationalists alike. Each of the two political movements produced a major document of political freedom expression in its Declaration of Independence. Although these statements were issued forty years apart—the Zionist position was presented in May 1948, whereas the PLO declaration appeared in November 1988—it is remarkable how the two nationalisms rely on very similar arguments of emotional appeal to justify their beliefs of entitlement to the land of Palestine for the purpose of creating an individual nation-state.

Some early, important manifestos formalizing nationalist aspirations were issued by the Zionists during the Basel Conference of 1897 and by the Palestinians in Jerusalem in 1964 (and as amended by the National Covenant of the PLO in 1968). Although the tones are quite different, the messages are essentially the same. Each pledges a commitment to mobilize material and intellectual forces in the cause of nationalist aspirations and indicates a readiness to take action in order to achieve these goals. The Palestinian statement is more forceful, more confrontational, than the one prepared by the Zionists. This is undoubtedly because the Palestinians face an organization whose nationalist spirit and emotional appeals are quite developed. The early Jewish settlers, by contrast, dealt with Arab opponents who, at the time, had not coalesced into a solid, patriotic unit.

ZIONIST MANIFESTO
(Basel Conference, 1897)

The aim of Zionism is to create for the Jewish people a home in Palestine secured by public law.

The Congress contemplates the following means to the attainment of this end:

1. The promotion, on suitable lines, of the colonization of Palestine by Jewish agricultural and industrial workers.
2. The organization and binding together of the whole of Jewry by means of appropriate institutions, local and international, in accordance with the laws of each country.
3. The strengthening and fostering of Jewish national sentiment and consciousness.
4. Preparatory steps toward obtaining government consent, where necessary, to the attainment of the aim of Zionism. (Laqueur, 1970:11–12)

PALESTINIAN MANIFESTO
(From the National Covenant, 1968)

In the name of God, the Magnificent, the Compassionate,

Believing in the right of the Palestine Arab People to a sacred homeland Palestine and affirming the inevitability of the battle to liberate the usurped part from it, and its determination to bring out its effective revolutionary entity and the mobilization of the capabilities and potentialities and its material, and spiritual forces:

And in realization of the will and determination of our people to wage the battle of liberating its homeland forcefully and vigorously in harmony with its role as the effective and fighting vanguard of the sacred march,

And in realization of a genuine and dear national aspiration embodied in the resolutions of the League of Arab States, and the First Arab Summit Conference.

And depending upon God the Almighty and in the name of the First Arab Palestine Congress held in . . . Jerusalem May 28, 1964 . . . the Palestine Liberation Organization is proclaimed as a mobilizing leadership of the forces of the Palestine Arab people to wage the battle of liberation, as a shield for the rights and aspirations of the people of Palestine and as a road to victory (*The Middle East and North Africa*, 1990:85–86).

How these original statements were translated into specific nationalist philosophies that led to the significant next step, the Declaration of Independence issued by each party, can also be explored in a search for parallel developments and themes. Both Zionism and Palestinian Nationalism are marked by a mainline group that developed originally to plant the basic philosophy of ethnic affiliation (rights and claims to a territory) and by a radical-revisionist movement that functioned as a challenge to the goals and leadership of the first-formed group. The revisionists concentrated on tactics for achieving objectives more swiftly. Violent means are accepted as legitimate justifications to reach the noble end— an independent nation-state. Whereas the original movement showed an idealism and emphasized the forces of order and possibilities for reasonable accommodation as the path toward realizing the final objectives, radical-revisionists are impatient and, mindful that individuals and existing governments respond more readily to events of a violent nature, see violence as a useful pressure technique to produce change. The forces of conflict are more significant as operating norms for these latter-formed groups.

For the Zionist movement, shortly after the Balfour Declaration, internal ideological disputes began to surface about the purpose and basis of a "national home" for the Jewish people. Chaim Weizmann, the first chair of the mainstream, World Zionist Congress, believed that the British would eventually support the Zionist presence and that the Arabs would be won over by European technical expertise and culture. The strategy for securing Jewish presence in Palestine during the early years was to purchase land step-by-step from Arab landowners. Not until World War II—and the information that the Jewish communities of Europe were being systematically destroyed in the Holocaust—did mainstream Zionism take a clear stand on statehood, adopting the policy explicitly in 1942.

Vladimer Ze'ev Jabotinsky, a Zionist revisionist, dreamed of mass immigration of European Jews to Palestine to present the colonial British and the Arabs with a fait accompli of a Jewish state. Since this group believed the Arabs were bound to resent the presence of the Jews, they advocated building an iron wall of Jewish military might around Palestine. The revisionists dismissed gradualist approaches and the plodding pragmatism of mainstream Zionism. Their forces stepped up terrorist attacks against the British and Arab inhabitants, and Zionist lobbying for statehood was carried out around the world. The violence jeopardized the mainstream's efforts to rally international support for Zionist causes, but at the same time the relentless attacks against the enemies in Palestine probably sped the process toward Jewish statehood.

Palestinian Nationalism reflecting the mainstream—the philosophy of the PLO and Arafat as derived from Al Fatah—rejects Marxist or Maoist leanings, has strong Islamic links, and believes that discussion of divisive social, politico-ideological issues should be avoided until victory is won. It also opposes a pronounced orientation of the Palestinian movement toward any Arab state or bloc and emphasizes political independence. Officially it stands for the establishment of a democratic, secular, multireligious state after destruction of the Zionist entity. A major revisionist organization, the Popular Front for the Liberation of Palestine (PFLP), led by Dr. George Habash, coalesced in 1969 out of the radical Arab Nationalist Movement. It combines militant nationalism and unrestrained, terrorist modes of operation with a neo-Marxist ideology, advocates guerrilla war, and opposes any political solution to the Arab–Israeli conflict. The group was responsible for hijacking foreign civilian airlines during the 1970s, which mainstream Arafat supporters opposed. The PFLP boycotted the PLO meetings from the early 1970s continuously through 1987, at which point a reconciliation was forged with the Al-Fatah Arafat camp. It advocates violence and armed struggle to achieve the goal of statehood.

A major point of difference between the two groups is the victimization and persecution each has experienced. Both Jews and Palestinian Arabs have suffered powerlessness and deprivation of liberty, but only the Jews suffered genocide. Many people on each side have been victims of expulsion, displacement, and war. They have found themselves scattered and rejected in their immediate surroundings and excluded from full participation in the countries where they have settled; both have experienced the phenomenon of refugee status for a significant proportion of their population.

In essence, Jewish and Palestinian identities are now intricately bound together, but there is an aversion on both sides to the idea of a symmetry of claims. For once the symmetry is accepted, the other side is also a legitimate national movement, and feelings about rights and self-legitimacy will be diminished. This recognition is very threatening in terms of nationalist ideology. War is the means throughout history by which people have established their right to territory and nationhood. Nationalist ideology may be conceived and popularized by politicians, but real transformation occurs when the people are directly confronted with threats to their existence and their ability to live peacefully. A declaration of independence cannot forge this intensity of commitment to the cause, but such a statement of intent usually follows the buildup of nationalist feeling coupled with violent obstacles to achieving that end. In fact, this is precisely what happened in the historical turn of events leading up to both the Israeli Declaration of Independence in May 1948 and the Palestinian Declaration of Independence in November 1988.

NATIONALIST THEMES

Given the parallels of nationalist developments in both groups, one should carefully examine the specific language and themes that appear in the two documents. Each of the statements contains thirteen identical themes, appearing virtually in the same order. The statements range from a broad assertion of the unique link between the respective people and this land, to the catastrophe of victimization each group has suffered, to an appeal to the Almighty to trust in the cause. It is worthwhile directly quoting the relevant passages under each theme.

Civilization on the Land

Israeli Declaration of Independence, May 1948, paragraph 1:

Eretz-Israel was the birthplace of the Jewish people. Here their spiritual, religious and political identity was shaped. Here they first attained to statehood, created cultural values of national and universal significance and gave to the world the eternal Book of books.

Palestinian Declaration of Independence, November 1988, paragraph 1:

On the same terrain as God's apostolic missions to mankind and in the land of Palestine was the Palestinian Arab people brought forth. There it grew and developed, and there it created its unique human and national mode of existence in an organic, indissoluble and unbroken relationship among people, land and history.

Love for the Land

Israeli Declaration of Independence, May 1948, paragraph 3:

Impelled by this historic and traditional attachment, Jews strove in every successive generation to re-establish themselves in their ancient homeland. In recent decades they returned in their masses. Pioneers, ma'pilim and defenders, they made deserts bloom, revived the Hebrew language, built villages and towns, and created a thriving community, controlling its own economy and culture, loving peace but knowing how to defend itself, bringing the blessings of progress to all the country's inhabitants, and aspiring towards independent nationhood.

Palestinian Declaration of Independence, November 1988, paragraphs 3 and 4:

Nourished by many strains of civilization and a multitude of cultures and finding inspiration in the texts of its spiritual and historical heritage, the Palestinian Arab people has, throughout history, continued to develop its identity in an integral unity of land and people and in the footsteps of the prophets throughout this Holy Land, the invocation of praise for the Creator high atop every minaret while hymns of mercy and peace have rung out with the bells of every church and temple.

From generation unto generation, the Palestinian Arab people has not ceased its valiant defense of its homeland, and the successive rebellions of our people have been a heroic embodiment of its desire for national independence.

Rights to the Land

Israeli Declaration of Independence, May 1948, paragraph 5:

This right was recognized in the Balfour Declaration of the 2nd November, 1917, and reaffirmed in the Mandate of the League of Nations which, in particular, gave international sanction to the historic connection between the Jewish people and Eretz-Israel and to the right of the Jewish people to rebuild its National Home.

Palestinian Declaration of Independence, November 1988, paragraph 6:

The deep injury already done the Palestinian people was therefore aggravated when a painful differentiation was made; a people deprived of independence, and one whose homeland was subjected to a new kind of foreign occupation, was exposed to an attempt to give general currency to the falsehood that Palestine was "a land without a people." Despite this falsification of history, the international community, in Article 22 of the Covenant of the League of Nations of 1919 and in the Lausanne Treaty of 1923, recognized that the Palestinian Arab people was no different from the other Arab peoples detached from the Ottoman State and was a free and independent people.

Suffering

Israeli Declaration of Independence, May 1948, paragraphs 6, 7 and 8:

The catastrophe which recently befell the Jewish people—the massacre of millions of Jews in Europe—was another clear demonstration of the urgency of solving the problem of its homelessness by reestablishing in Eretz-Israel the Jewish State, which would open the gates of the homeland wide to every Jew and confer upon the Jewish people the status of a fully-privileged member of the comity of nations.

Survivors of the Nazi holocaust in Europe, as well as Jews from other parts of the world, continued to migrate to Eretz-Israel, undaunted by difficulties, restrictions and dangers, and never ceased to assert their right to a life of dignity, freedom and honest toil in their national homeland.

In the Second World War, the Jewish community of this country contributed its full share to the struggle of the freedom and peace-loving nations against the forces of Nazi wickedness and, by the blood of its soldiers and its war effort, gained the right to be reckoned among the peoples who founded the United Nations.

Palestinian Declaration of Independence, November 1988, paragraphs 7 and 8:

Despite the historical injustice done to the Palestinian Arab people in its displacement and in being deprived of the right to self-determination following the adoption of General Assembly Resolution 181 (II) of 1947, which partitioned Palestine into an Arab and a Jewish State, that Resolution nevertheless continues to attach conditions to international legitimacy that guarantee the Palestinian Arab people the right to sovereignty and national independence.

Political Independence

Israeli Declaration of Independence, May 1948, paragraph 2:

After being forcibly exiled from their land, the people kept faith with it through their Dispersion and never ceased to pray and hope for their return to it and for the restoration in it of their political freedom.

Palestinian Declaration of Independence, November 1988, paragraph 2:

With epic tenaciousness in terms of place and time, the people of Palestine fashioned its national identity. Its steadfast endurance in its own defense rose to preternatural levels, for despite the ambitions, covetousness and armed invasions which deprived that people of an opportunity to achieve political independence, and which were prompted by the allure of this ancient land and its crucial position on the intersecting boundaries of powerful nations and civilizations, it was the constancy with which the people adhered to the land that gave that land its identity and which imbued its people with the national spirit.

Rights to Independence on the Land

Israeli Declaration of Independence, May 1948, paragraphs 9 and 10:

On the 29th November 1947, the United Nations General Assembly passed a resolution calling for the establishment of a Jewish State in Eretz-Israel; the General Assembly required the inhabitants of Eretz-Israel to take such steps as were necessary on their part for the implementation of that resolution. This recognition by the United Nations of the right of the Jewish people to establish their State is irrevocable.

This right is the natural right of the Jewish people to be masters of their own fate, like all other nations, in their own sovereign State.

Palestinian Declaration of Independence, November 1988, paragraphs 9, 10 and 11:

In the heart of its homeland and on its periphery, in its places of exile near and far, the Palestinian Arab people has not lost its unwavering faith in its right to return nor its firm belief in its right to independence. Occupation, carnage and displacement have been unable to dispossess the Palestinians of their consciousness and their identity—their epic struggle has endured, and the formation of their national character has continued with the growing escalation of the struggle. The national will has established its political framework; and that is the Palestine Liberation Organization, the sole, legitimate representative of the Palestinian people, as recognized by the international community and represented in the United Nations and its institutions and in other international and regional organizations. Founding itself on a belief in inalienable rights, on the Arab national consensus and on international legitimacy, the Palestine Liberation Organization has assumed leadership in the battles of a great people fused in an exemplary national unity and in a legendary and steadfast resistance to carnage and encirclement within its homeland and outside. To the Arab national consciousness and to that of the entire world, the epic of the Palestinian resistance has manifested itself as one of the most conspicuous national liberation movements of the age.

The great popular uprising now mounting in the Occupied Territories, together with the legendary steadfastness of the camps within and outside the homeland, have raised mankind's grasp of the true nature of the Palestinian issue and of Palestinian national rights to a level higher than that of full and mature comprehension, have brought down the final curtain on an entire epoch of falsification and conscientious indifference and have beleaguered the official Israeli mentality, prone as it is to appeal to arguments based on mythology and to resort to intimidation in its denial of Palestinian existence.

With the Uprising, with the escalation of the revolutionary struggle and with the accumulation of revolutionary experience whenever the struggle is in progress, the Palestinian conjuncture reaches a sharp historical turning point. The Palestinian Arab people asserts once more its inalienable rights and its demand to exercise those rights in its Palestinian homeland.

The Establishment of the State

Israeli Declaration of Independence, May 1948, paragraph 11:

Accordingly we, members of the People's Council, representative of the Jewish community of Eretz-Israel and of the Zionist Movement, are here assembled on the day of the termination of the British Mandate over Eretz-Israel and, by virtue of our natural and historic right and on the strength of the resolution of the United Nations General Assembly, hereby declare the establishment of a Jewish state in Eretz-Israel, to be known as the State of Israel.

Palestinian Declaration of Independence, November 1988, paragraphs 12,
13, 14, and 15:

By virtue of the natural, historical and legal right of the Palestinian Arab people to its homeland, Palestine, and of the sacrifices of its succeeding generations in defense of the freedom and independence of that homeland.

Pursuant to the resolutions of the Arab Summit Conferences and on the basis of the international legitimacy embodied in the resolutions of the United Nations since 1947, and

Through the exercise by the Palestinian Arab people of its right to self-determination, political independence and sovereignty over its territory:

The Palestinian National Council hereby declares, in the Name of God and on behalf of the Palestinian Arab people, the establishment of the State of Palestine in the land of Palestine with its capital at Jerusalem.

Organization and Purpose of the State

Israeli Declaration of Independence, May 1948, paragraph 13:

The State of Israel will be open for Jewish immigration and for the Ingathering of the Exiles; it will foster the development of the country for the benefit of all its inhabitants; it will be based on freedom, justice and peace as envisaged by the prophets of Israel; it will ensure complete equality of social and political rights to all its inhabitants irrespective of religion, race or sex; it will guarantee freedom of religion, conscience, language, education and culture; it will safeguard the Holy Places of all religions; and it will be faithful to the principles of the Charter of the United Nations.

Palestinian Declaration of Independence, November 1988, paragraph 16:

The State of Palestine shall be for Palestinians, wherever they may be, therein to develop their national and cultural identity and therein to enjoy full equality of rights. Their religious and political beliefs and human dignity shall therein be safeguarded under a democratic parliamentary system based on freedom of opinion and the freedom to form parties, on the heed of the majority for minority rights and the respect of minorities for majority decisions, on social justice and equality, and on non-discrimination in civil rights on grounds of race, religion or color or as between men and women, under a Constitution ensuring the rule of law and an independent judiciary and on the basis of true fidelity to the age-old spiritual and cultural heritage of Palestine with respect to mutual tolerance, coexistence and magnanimity among religions.

Commitment to UN Principles

Israeli Declaration of Independence, May 1948, paragraph 14:

The State of Israel is prepared to cooperate with the agencies and representatives of the United Nations in implementing the resolution of the General Assembly of the 29th

November 1947, and will take steps to bring about the economic union of the whole of Eretz-Israel.

Palestinian Declaration of Independence, November 1988, paragraph 18:

The State of Palestine declares its commitment to the purposes and principles of the United Nations, to the Universal Declaration of Human Rights and to the policy and principles of non-alignment.

Commitment to Peace

Israeli Declaration of Independence, May 1948, paragraphs 16 and 17:

We appeal—in the very midst of the onslaught launched against us now for months—to the Arab inhabitants of the State of Israel to preserve peace and participate in the upbuilding of the State on the basis of full and equal citizenship and due representation in all its provisional and permanent institutions.

We extend our hand to all neighbouring states and their peoples in an offer of peace and good neighbourliness, and appeal to them to establish bonds of cooperation and mutual help with the sovereign Jewish people settled in its own land. The State of Israel is prepared to do its share in a common effort for the advancement of the entire Middle East.

Palestinian Declaration of Independence, November 1988, paragraph 19:

The State of Palestine, in declaring that it is a peace-loving State committed to the principles of peaceful coexistence, shall strive, together with all other States and peoples, for the achievement of a lasting peace based on justice and respect for rights, under which the human potential for constructive activity may flourish, mutual competition may center on life-sustaining innovation and there is no fear for the future, since the future bears only assurance for those who have acted justly or made amends to justice.

Appeal to the International Community

Israeli Declaration of Independence, May 1948, paragraph 15:

We appeal to the United Nations to assist the Jewish people in the building-up of its State and to receive the State of Israel into the comity of nations.

Palestinian Declaration of Independence, November 1988, paragraphs 17 and 20:

The State of Palestine shall be an Arab State and shall be an integral part of the Arab nation, of its heritage and civilization and of its present endeavor for the achievement of the goals of liberation, development, democracy and unity. In affirming its commitment to the Pact of the League of Arab States and its concern for the strengthening of joint Arab action, the State of Palestine calls upon the members of the Arab nation for their assistance in achieving its de facto emergence by mobilizing their capacities and intensifying the efforts made to bring the Israeli occupation to an end.

In the context of its struggle to bring peace to a land of peace and love, the State of Palestine calls upon the United Nations, which bears a special responsibility toward Palestinian Arab people and its homeland, and upon the peace-loving States and peoples of the world and those that cherish freedom to assist it in achieving its goals, in bringing the plight of its people to an end, in ensuring the safety and security of that people and in endeavoring to end the Israeli occupation of Palestinian territory.

Appeal to the Diaspora

Israeli Declaration of Independence, May 1948, paragraph 18:

We appeal to the Jewish people throughout the Diaspora to rally round the Jews of Eretz-Israel in the tasks of immigration and upbuilding and to stand by them in the great struggle for the realization of the age-old dream—the redemption of Israel.

Palestinian Declaration of Independence, November 1988, paragraph 22:

On this momentous day, the fifteenth day of November 1988, as we stand on the threshold of a new era, we bow our heads in deference and humility to the departed souls of our martyrs and the martyrs of the Arab nation who, by virtue of the pure blood shed by them, have lit the glimmer of this auspicious dawn and who have died so that the homeland might live. We lift up our hearts so that they may be filled with light from the radiance of the hallowed Uprising, of the epic resistance of those in the camps, in the dispersion and in exile, and of those who have borne the banner of freedom; our children, our elders and our youth; our prisoners, detainees and wounded based on the hallowed soil and in every camp, village and city; the valiant Palestinian women, the guardians of our life and our survival and keepers of our eternal flame. To the spirits of our righteous martyrs, to the masses of our Palestinian Arab people and our Arab nation and to all free and honorable men, we give our solemn pledge to continue the struggle for an end to the occupation and the establishment of sovereignty and independence. We call upon our great people to rally to the Palestinian flag, to take pride in it and to defend it so that it shall remain forever a symbol of our freedom and dignity in a homeland that shall be forever free and the abode of a people of free men.

Appeal to God

Israeli Declaration of Independence, May 1948, paragraph 19:

Placing our trust in the Almighty, we affix our signatures to this proclamation at this session of the Provisional Council of State, on the soil of the homeland, in the city of Tel-Aviv, on this Sabbath Eve, the 5th day of Iyar, 5708, (the fourteenth of May, 1948).

Palestinian Declaration of Independence, November 1988, paragraph 23:

Almighty God has spoken the truth.

The only provision appearing in the Palestinian document and not in the Israeli statement is the pledge to resolve regional problems by peaceful means. This shows a definite break from the philosophy of the National Covenant. Paragraph 21 reads:

The State of Palestine further declares, in that connection, that it believes in the solution of international and regional problems by peaceful means in accordance with the Charter of the United Nations and the resolutions adopted by it, and that, without prejudice to its natural right to defend itself, it rejects the threat or use of force, violence and intimidation against its territorial integrity and political independence or those of any other State.

There are both common and unique features that appear in these declarations of independence. The desire for political freedom for recognized ethnic groups to form a separate nation-state is hardly an unusual request and is well-known in twentieth-century politics. Moreover, the appeal for God's support, in exchange for the promise of peace in the international environment, represents aspects of a general strategy for wider acceptance of a group's nationalist aspirations. These ideas form the bulk of the themes contained in the documents of the two parties.

A few special clauses of political expression have also been written into these official statements, however. First is the strong claims placed on that particular piece of territory, Palestine. Both Zionists and Palestinians proclaim a unique link between their people and that land, and each justifies this link as a historic, cultural, loving attachment. Obviously, these arguments are introduced because the land in question is in dispute; each side thus must make higher, nobler claims for occupancy, and both have resorted to legitimizing their respective positions by appealing to the continuous thread of individual ethnic history and its civilization development. Cultures are respected for their civilization contributions and earn the right to further enhancement by establishing a separate ethnic identity. Both Zionists and Palestinians have captured this basic idea in their nationalism documents.

A second feature of these declarations is the appeal each group makes to the global community not only for acceptance into the world system of nations but also for the rights and promises issued to them by the League of Nations. The Zionists and the Palestinians draw the local–global linkage, which is meant to enlarge the ideological stage and gather outside interest in and responsibility for their plight. This stamps the nationalist claims with a particular Middle East flavor.

Each group has pointed to its victimization and has used the dynamics of suffering to create sympathy and to bring attention to its nationalist cause. The declarations of independence issued by the Zionists and by the Palestinians, however, are upbeat statements overall and are directed toward creating the impression that the two groups possess the right combination of commitment, ethnic identity and cohesiveness, and moral order suitable for self-governance. It is the strength of these beliefs that brings the parties into conflict and at the same time draws them closer in building a negotiation environment.

Nationalism consists of direct sentimental ties between individuals to the nation or ethnic group and to its symbols, possessions, prestige, and history. It is a generous spirit of identification with the sufferings of a group, a love of compatriots. It simultaneously promotes solidarity alongside hatred and suspicion as it seeks to define people inside the group as trustworthy and outsiders as untrustworthy enemies. The creation and growth of nationalist feelings and the evolution of a nationalist ideology may be related to the development of political ideas generally within an ethnic group that has its source in a pattern of change resulting from particular goal-directed causes. Nationalist feelings and ideology may be influenced by the nature of the traditional political system, the sequences in which new groups enter politics, the values and skills of political leaders, and the relation between the expansion of political participation and the development of political institutions. The political evolution of a society is influenced by its external as well as its domestic environment and may take the form of importation of ideas, models, techniques, resources, and institutions from other societies, or reactions by groups within the society against the threat of foreign intervention or rule (Huntington and Dominquez, 1975:13).

Radical nationalism implies an excess of concentration or focus on the pursuit of ideas, where a militant assertion of sovereign and unqualified supremacy of rights replaces expediency and pragmatism. This approach lacks flexibility and contains no element of compromise or accommodation. It is absolutist. The objective of illustrating the parallel tracks of nationalist argument presented by the Zionists and the Palestinians is to show how ideological devices sustain the conflict by intensifying the identical claims in a zero-sum way. This may be a good strategy to develop nationalism, but it is not suitable for international negotiation in situations of nationalist rivalry.

CONCLUSION

The Zionists and the Palestinian Arab Nationalists began intense articulation of goals more than a half century apart. But it took violence, victimization, and suffering for both groups to accelerate the process, leading toward a declaration of independence. In the Israeli case, only fifteen years passed between the onset of the major refugee problem and persecution (the beginning of the Nazi era in Europe in 1933) and the establishment of statehood, immediately following the independence declaration, in 1948. For the Palestinians, if the main refugee–human displacement problem is dated from the 1967 War, rather than 1948 (since the 1960s also brought the aspirations of nationalism into focus with the founding and charter of the PLO), then roughly two decades passed before their own independence declaration was proclaimed. By this logic, the issue would

Table 1
Some Key Events in Zionist and Palestinian Nationalist Movements

EVENT	ZIONISTS	PALESTINIANS
Institution:		
National organization founded	August, 1897	May, 1964
Philosophy:		
Important Manifesto issued	Herzl, *The Jewish State*, 1896	PLO, *The National Covenant*, 1968
Issues of Suffering:		
The refugee problem	1933-1945	1948 and 1967
The oppressors	The Nazis	The Israelis
The persecution period	The Holocaust (1933-1945)	The Intifada (1987-)
Resolution:		
Declaration of Independence	May, 1948	November, 1988
Statehood	May, 1948	?

seem to be not *whether* there will be a sovereign Palestinian state but *when* it will be formed, with the prediction that it will be sooner rather than later.

In table 1, the timings of key events of the nationalist movements of the Zionists and the Palestinians are compared (see table 1). The table makes the two nationalist developments appear more symmetric than is actually the case. One very important difference between them is that the Jewish people left the environments of persecution, namely Russia and countries of Eastern Europe in addition to areas under Nazi occupation, and their former oppressors and sought self-identity and independence in a new land, in an alien environment. The Zionists were not dependent on their persecutors to grant them territorial rights over land. However, the Palestinians must work directly with the Israelis to achieve the final step of statehood. The parallel developments break down at this stage, which is an important departure in the evolution of significant events toward reaching nationalist goals. The question now becomes: what happens in such colonial-controlled states when massive revolt against outside rule develops? How freedom is acquired for the subjugated peoples out of this context, and what level of protracted violence is necessary to achieve that end, vary from case to case. Thus, the precise end in this struggle is hard to predict.

4

The Negotiation Frame

ISSUES

Either peaceful or violent resolution of conflict may lead to an outcome of territorial conquest, withdrawal, or a compromise settlement representing something other than these two extremes. In the Arab–Israeli dispute, violent means have been used by each side to pursue an outcome of conquest time and again. However, this form of solution has not ended the dispute but has led only to temporary stalemate in the wake of passionate feelings of nationalism evident on both sides.

Political negotiation is concerned with compromise and passive settlement, where both sides agree to a partial modification of their initial objectives, positions, demands, or actions. The crucial point in achieving a solution to conflict through compromise arrangements is that before the sides can begin discussing the substantive terms of a negotiated settlement, both have to realize and accept the idea that the price of dispute perpetuation outweighs the costs of reducing demands or altering a diplomatic or military position. It is almost impossible to predict at what point a compromise is possible, since it depends on unique factors such as skill of bargainers, capabilities they can mobilize to offer rewards or make threats, desire to reach agreement, diplomatic pressure from outside, and degrees of need, dependence, and responsiveness. Analyzing the evolution of the Arab–Israeli conflict, noting both permanent features and the changes that have occurred since its inception, would strongly suggest that no single, all-inclusive theory or formula exists to account for the periodic eruptions of violence or the moments of relative quiet.

Is a solution possible that simultaneously provides for a full, unconditional recognition by relevant Arab states of Israel's right to exist in peace with secure and recognized boundaries and for a clear Israeli policy stand and promise to relinquish the Palestinian-dominated territories now held under Israeli control? A number of conditions would be required for constructive progress toward a gradual resolution of the conflict, according to Haim Shaked (1984:203). First, the parties must share a vital interest in the promotion of peace and must act with urgency to create such an arrangement. Second, the solution must be fully acceptable to all of the local actors. Third, the most appropriate framework for negotiations should be sought relating to the parties directly involved.

Whether the Arab–Israeli conflict turns into an eternal war or partial solutions and arrangements are crystallized into a new peaceful situation will be a function of bargaining and communication and the basic underlying cause of the conflict. If the resolution of conflict depends on effective communication, it can come only from the parties themselves. Processes are required that alter perceptions and promote the points of view of the parties and not of third parties. The process of resolution of conflict is essentially the process of testing whether the information is received as it was transmitted and whether what was transmitted was sent deliberately and contained accurate information (Burton 1969:55). Establishing tests to evaluate the accuracy of information received presents problems: initiatives by one party are inhibited by fear that they will be perceived as a confession of weakness or of defeat if they indicate a willingness to negotiate, which might imply a willingness to compromise (Burton 1969:56). This problem is especially acute in the Arab–Israeli conflict due to the nationalist rivalry that encourages distrust of outsiders and enemies.

The issues and positioning relevant for bargaining are set by the conflict frame of nationalist rivalry, the conflict buildup violence record, and conflict-sustaining devices, including the growth and intensification of nationalist aspirations across several generations of Zionists and Palestinians. The actual path of negotiation as a social process can be marked by similar points seen in the growth of nationalism, points that may enhance the probability of negotiated conflict resolution: a set of specific *issues* incorporating human suffering and obstruction of fundamental goals of security and preservation; the creation and use of *institutions* designed to help parties achieve their objectives; a *philosophy* reflecting attitudes and posturing toward resolution of the problem; and *previous experience* in negotiated settlement.

The negotiation frame for the Arab–Israeli conflict springs primarily from two factors. First, the institutional element is intended to provide a management mechanism for conflict resolution and to encourage consultation, negotiation, and the exploration of alternatives. The main organization in this role has been the United Nations. The second factor is the attitudes toward compromise expressed by the parties to the dispute. This refers to the emotional and psychological outlook of the disputants and represents a philosophical amalgamation of rights and entitlements due each party. Recognizing the context of issues that divide the Israelis and the Palestinians, this chapter focuses on these two elements by analyzing selected instances in the environment of prepartition and postpartition politics. The UN management mechanism is examined by looking at the contents and tone of the report and recommendations made by the Special Committee that recommended the partition solution in 1947. The philosophy of compromise is described through the contemporary debate on negotiation strategies and issues in which different interpretations are advocated by the opponents.

MANAGEMENT MECHANISM

One of the earliest, and later the most common, institutions used in attempts to regulate and solve the Arab–Israeli conflict is the United Nations. The policy positions adopted by the central groups in the Arab–Israeli conflict were first formalized and presented as extensive arguments to the UN Special Committee set up early in 1947 to investigate the dispute before the 1947 partition resolution was introduced to the General Assembly the following November. To understand the nature of the conflicting interests and understand how the negotiation orientation, basis, and argument were formed, we should examine portions of the actual UN report. Each group was invited to outline and justify its own case. Many points remain relevant today; in fact, the themes that have been extracted as a way to contrast positions adopted by each side echo the two major elements in this conflict: that national rivalry dictates each party will assert its absolute rights to the land of Palestine, and that major power outsiders through the local–global linkages are central players in the conflict. When these ideas combine with the vagueness or confusion attributed to earlier solution attempts and the expectation of inevitable conflicts foreseen in the report, it becomes quite clear how accurately such themes parallel the conflict-sustaining mechanisms of the respective declarations of independence prepared by the Zionists and the Palestinian Arabs.

In the prepartition period, the issue before the United Nations was how to assure the establishment of a Jewish national home and simultaneously provide for the development of self-governing institutions among the local Arabs. According to the *Report of the UN Special Committee on Palestine*, September 3, 1947, UN Doc A/364 (Moore, *Documents*, 1974:262):

There has been great controversy as to whether the obligations relating to the National Home and self-governing institutions were equal in weight, and also as to whether they were consistent with each other. Opinions have been expressed that between these two obligations the Mandate recognizes no primacy in order of importance and no priority in order of execution, and that they were in no sense irreconcilable. According to other opinions, however, the primary purpose of the Mandate, as expressed in its preamble and in its articles, was to promote the establishment of a Jewish National Home, to which the obligations of developing self-governing institutions was subordinated.

The practical significance of the controversy was that, if the country were to be placed under such political conditions as would secure the development of self-governing institutions, these same conditions would in fact destroy the Jewish National Home. It would appear that, although difficulties were anticipated, when the Mandate was confirmed it was not clearly contemplated that these two obligations would prove mutually incompatible. In practice, however, they proved to be so.

A summary of key points made in favor of each case presented by the disputants to the UN Special Committee is listed below.

Rights to the Land (Nationalist Rivalry)

The Zionist Case:

1. The issues of the Jewish state and unrestricted Jewish immigration into Palestine are inextricably interwoven.
2. A Jewish state is needed to assure a refuge for Jewish immigrants from the displaced persons camps and from other places in Europe and elsewhere.
3. A Jewish state needs immigrants to confront the preponderance of Arabs over Jews in Palestine.
4. There are biblical and historical sources that attach the Jewish people to the land of Palestine.
5. The British, through the Balfour Declaration of 1917 and the Mandate for Palestine, promised a Jewish national home.

The Palestinian Arab Case:

1. An Arab numerical majority in the ratio of two to one exists in the present population of Palestine.
2. The Arabs have been in continuous possession of the land for many centuries.
3. The Arab majority has a natural right to remain in undisputed possession of the land.
4. The Arab community wishes to safeguard its national existence from foreign intruders without interference in its own political, economic, and cultural development.
5. General promises and pledges for an independent state were made to the Arab people during World War I by the British.

British Support (Local-Global Linkage)

The Zionist Case:

1. The British, as Mandatory Power in Palestine, were entrusted to secure a Jewish National Home by immigration and settlement of Jews on the land.
2. The pledges to the Jews in the Balfour Declaration and the Mandate are international commitments to the Jewish people as a whole.
3. The Mandate was to be terminated only when the establishment of the Jewish national home had been fulfilled—when it could stand alone, free from Arab domination.

The Palestinian Arab Case:

1. Promises and pledges of Arab freedom and independence were among the main factors inspiring the Arabs to revolt against the Ottoman Empire and to ally themselves with Britain and other allies during World War I. Britain is under contractual obligation to accept and uphold its promise.

2. The Mandate for Palestine, incorporating the Balfour Declaration, is illegal.

3. The Mandate is inconsistent with Article 22 of the League of Nations Covenant, which stipulated that certain communities could be provisionally recognized as independent nations subject to limited administrative advice and assistance of a mandatory power until they were able to stand alone. The Mandate for Palestine omitted provisional recognition and gave Britain full powers of administration.

The conclusions drawn by the UN Special Committee incorporated a number of points pushed by the Zionists and the Palestinian Arabs. The most significant features included:

1. The desire of Arab people to safeguard their national existence is recognized.

2. The desire of Jewish people to safeguard their national existence is recognized.

3. The meaning of "national home" is not clear: it has no known legal connotation and no precedents in international law for its interpretation. The vagueness of wording in the Balfour Declaration seems to have been intentional; the word seems to be more restrictive than "state."

4. There is no unequivocal agreement that Palestine was pledged independence by Great Britain: British and Arab experts examining key correspondence from World War I were not able to give one exact, straightforward interpretation about specific territories included and excluded from the independence pledge.

5. Violence will continue if the parties are not separated; neither side feels secure in trying to accomplish its goals.

6. Partitioning the Palestine territory into two individual states, one for Jews and one for Palestinian Arabs, is recommended.

The negotiation solution presented by the UN Special Committee reflects the legitimacy of the themes that subsequently appeared in the Israeli and the Palestinian declarations of independence, themes such as land rights, ethnic preservation, suffering, and the role of an outside power. In other words, the central ideas of the *conflict frame*, namely nationalist rivalry and local–global linkages, along with the themes developed to sustain the emotional pitch of ideological positions of nationalism formed the core and structured the parameters for finding a negotiation solution and thereby formulated the major element in the *negotiation frame* for the Arab–Israeli dispute. The strategy represents a "split the difference" approach to compromise, which meant finding some middle ground between the conflicting claims to the land of Palestine.

Although the committee was willing to grant that vagueness, confusion, and interpretation difficulties were an important part in the role played by outsiders in this dispute, specifically that obligations and promises of Great Britain and the League of Nations were not always easy to understand when it came to the responsibilities of the Middle East inhabitants, the UN members chose to give the nationalist rivalry issue more prominence and forced the role of global actors into the background. Were these promises compatible or mutually exclusive? Were they of equal standing? These issues were not sorted out but were put aside. The tone of the UN management mechanism in this negotiation picture was to highlight the key claims of the opponents and to discover a middle ground that was intended to provide partial satisfaction for Zionists and Palestinian Arabs alike. This did not produce a settlement, however. "Split the difference" was an unstable approach.

ATTITUDES TOWARD COMPROMISE

In contemporary times—with the evolution of the conflict, the articulation of demands, and the presentation of numerous peace plans—there have been some shifts in the cases argued by Israelis and Arabs. An article written by Adam M. Garfinkle in 1984–85, " 'Common Sense' about Middle East Diplomacy; Implications for U.S. Policy in the Near Term," lists points that support the Israeli position; another article, written by Fred J. Khouri in 1986, "Major Obstacles to Peace: Ignorance, Myths, and Misconceptions," discusses positions that are generally regarded as more sympathetic toward the Arabs. The issues identified by each of them are nearly identical, although the positions they advocate are somewhat different. It is worth looking at these points to evaluate the sharpest areas of divergence and, in addition, to note possible openings for agreements. Issues addressed by Garfinkle and Khouri again reflect the national rivalry theme, local–global linkages, and negotiation strategy. Each also addresses the problem of confusion over the core truth about the Arab–Israeli conflict. As Khouri states, echoing a theme carried over from the UN partition report, ignorance and misconception of critical aspects of the dispute are major obstacles to peace in the Middle East. The stands of the two sides are illustrated here by drawing out relevant portions of text from the two articles.

Rights to the Land (Nationalist Rivalry)

Perspective Supporting Israel:

The recognition by Israel of Palestinian Arab national rights, even if simultaneous with the Palestinian recognition of Israel's legitimacy, is not necessarily a harbinger of a just settlement. It may instead be a harbinger for the solution of the Palestinian national problem at the cost of recreating the Jewish national problem. (Garfinkle, 1984/85:25)

There are many who claim that more Arabs today than ever before, including Palestinians, accept Israel's existence and that Israeli recognition of Palestinian national rights would cause a veritable avalanche of Arab moderation. But in many parts of the world political concessions are viewed not as an indicator of a willingness for pragmatic compromise but as an indication of weakness and decaying willpower. (Garfinkle, 1984/85:25)

That the PLO's status has been gained by default—a consequence of Israeli occupation policies since 1967 more than anything else—is also irrelevant. What is not irrelevant is that Israel cannot be expected to parley with an organization whose *raison d'etre* is Israel's destruction. (Garfinkle, 1984/85:26)

There is a great deal of difference between "accepting Israel" as a fact of life—which an increasing number of Arabs do—and "accepting Israel" as a legitimate expression of Jewish national rights to even part of Palestine—which almost no Arabs do. The latter kind of acceptance is a matter of principle, the former is a function of the transient balance of power. (Garfinkle, 1984/85:25)

Between 1949 and 1967, when the Arab states successfully contained the Palestinian national movement and when there was no question about Israeli "occupied territory," there was also no peace. And though it is seldom spoken of in public, there is still considerable latent and not-so-latent anti-Semitism in the world. So the frustration of Palestinian nationalism is only half the problem at best, the protection of Jewish national rights in the longer term being an issue of equal significance. (Garfinkle, 1984/85:26).

Perspective Supporting Palestinians:

It has been repeatedly contended by many Israelis and others that the PLO is a terrorist organization which unequivocally denies the right of Israel to exist as a nation and which has as its ultimate goal the destruction of the present state of Israel. (Khouri, 1986:56)

However, after the [1973] war, the views of the more pragmatic PLO leaders began to change. The resolutions of the Palestine National Council (PNC) stopped referring to the "liberation of Palestine" through "armed struggle" and to the establishment of a "secular, democratic state" of Palestine . . . accepting the establishment of a Palestinian state in only those areas to be evacuated by Israel in accordance with Security Council Resolution 242. (Khouri, 1986:56)

By giving up their more extreme aspirations and tactics, the moderate Palestinians were able to win wider political and popular support throughout the world, and this progress encouraged moderate leaders and their followers to continue on this path in the hope that it would ultimately pay off. However, this path did not lessen Israel's opposition to the PLO and a Palestinian state. Leaders repeatedly insisted that they would never deal with the PLO, even if it openly accepted the state of Israel, and would never accept a Palestinian state, even in return for peace with the Arabs. . . . Since this path gave no sign of ever paying off because of Israel's uncompromising position, increasing numbers of even moderate Palestinians became convinced that the only option left to them was armed struggle. (Khouri, 1986:57)

Over the years, the readiness of moderate PLO leaders to accept a peace settlement as long as it provided for their right of national self-determination in at least part of Palestine has been expressed in many ways. (Khouri, 1986:57)

Negotiating Strategy: Land for Peace

Perspective Supporting Israel:

As to the matter of an Israeli territorial withdrawal, it is true that no stable and formal peace on Israel's eastern frontier is imaginable that does not require renewed Arab sovereignty over major parts of the West Bank (and perhaps Gaza). . . . It is true that any "returned" territory probably cannot revert to the exact political condition that obtained before the June 1967 War, i.e., to exclusive Jordanian sovereignty. . . . Withdrawal does not necessarily and cannot practically mean total withdrawal, as posited by the common knowledge. . . . There must be withdrawal in order for there to be peace, but the withdrawal cannot be total, and there is a nearly wall-to-wall consensus in Israel against returning to the exact lines of June 5, 1967. There must be Palestinian participation in the governing of whatever is returned, but it must be something less than exclusive Palestinian sovereignty and it cannot ignore Jordan's interests. (Garfinkle, 1984/85:26)

Perspective Supporting Palestinians:

A total—or nearly total—Israeli withdrawal is essential to promoting not only peace and stability in the Middle East but also Israel's own long-term security interests as well. (Khouri, 1986:42)

It must be stressed that whereas Resolution 242 affirmed the right of every state in the area—and not only Israel—"to live . . . within secure borders," whatever added security Israel might achieve by holding on to the Golan Heights would be achieved only at the price of greater insecurity for Syria. (Khouri, 1986:44)

Moreover, the very concept of attaining perfect and everlasting security, whether through the expansion of borders or through other traditional means, has been one of mankind's greatest and most persistent delusions. Since the other states will not accept permanent insecurity, they will do everything they can to rectify the balance of power in their own favor—leading to never-ending arms races and instability and ultimately to armed conflicts. (Khouri, 1986:44)

Negotiation Strategy: Comprehensive or Incremental Approach

Perspective Supporting Israel:

The argument against the incremental step-by-step strategy for peace and for the comprehensive, all-at-once package deal approach . . . [which] advocates a "comprehensive" approach, is not really a negotiation at all; it is a euphemism for a superpower *Diktat*. For a *negotiated* comprehensive settlement to succeed, Israel must agree freely to make concessions not only to the pragmatists, like Jordan, but to the rejectionist ideologues like Syria and the PLO. Only strong Israeli faith in a foolproof package of international guarantees could produce acceptance of such a settlement that would expose it to so many risks. But there is no such package. Moreover, the comprehensive negotiations approach makes the incredible assumption that all the major actors involved—including Syria and the PLO—want peace even if they have to compromise and negotiate directly with Israel to get it. It also presumes a more or less unified Arab position. In practice, the comprehensive approach allows the most extreme and recalcitrant elements to sabotage any progress whatsoever.

The charge that step-by-step agreements divide the Arabs and make each step harder reverses the truth. The step-by-step approach is not the source of contemporary divisions among the Arabs; it is the division among the Arabs that is the source and *raison d'etre* of the step-by-step approach. The step-by-step process does not make each *successive* step harder; it makes possible any steps at all. (Garfinkle, 1984/85:29).

The contention that Israel has no incentive to make peace owing to its great power is a malicious half-truth. Israel is strong today by many measures. But Israel was not always so strong militarily, and the local power balance is subject to swift change owing to the advance of modern military technology and the eagerness of the world's arms merchants. Moreover, Israel's increased strength is roughly proportional to its increased dependence on the United States. (Garfinkle, 1984/85:27)

If Israel is strong enough not to need peace, then how does one explain the withdrawal from Sinai? Why do its people so ardently desire peace? And why does at least half its electorate favor peace even at the expense of land? (Garfinkle, 1984/85:27)

Perspective Supporting Palestinians:

Following the 1973 war . . . Henry Kissinger initiated a step-by-step diplomacy aimed at dealing with the conflict piecemeal—primarily because he hoped that this would enable us to bypass the Soviet Union and establish the United States as the key diplomatic broker; to put off indefinitely dealing with the Palestinian issue; to buy time for Israel so she could improve her bargaining position; and to convince the Arabs that they had no realistic alternative to negotiating directly with Israel and mostly on Israeli terms. But this step-by-step approach had no sense of long-term purpose or goal. (Khouri, 1986:40)

After the initial 1974 Egyptian–Israeli and Syrian–Israeli disengagement agreements had helped to stabilize the military situation, some American officials and experts opposed the continuation of the piecemeal process because they believed that making progress on one issue could end up making it even more difficult than ever before to deal later with broader and more vital goals. Disregarding this view, Kissinger, in September 1975, negotiated a second Egyptian–Israeli agreement which, while achieving some gains, had long-term harmful consequences, especially because it required the United States to provide Israel with such vast and long-term economic, military and political commitments that American leverage over her to obtain future concessions on far more vital territorial and political issues (such as the Palestinian issue) was seriously undermined and Israel was left with much less incentive than before to soften her stand. Thus, the second Egyptian–Israeli accord ultimately did more to impair than to improve the climate and chances for an overall settlement. (Khouri, 1986:40)

The Camp David accords and an Egyptian–Israeli peace treaty ended up dealing with only one major aspect of the overall Arab–Israeli problem, providing no effective ties to progress on other important Arab–Israeli differences, splitting and weakening the Arabs while further strengthening Israel's bargaining position—thereby making it more difficult than ever to promote progress on all of the other unresolved Arab–Palestinian–Israeli issues . . . consequently making it easier for Israel to ignore the Palestinian question and to reject any further territorial concessions. (Khouri, 1986:41)

Therefore, under existing circumstances the step-by-step approach, because it has so many inherent defects, cannot bring real, durable peace to the Middle East. Only a fair, comprehensive settlement which deals effectively with all major aspects of the Arab–Palestinian–Israeli problem can have a chance of doing this. (Khouri, 1986:42)

United States Support (Local–Global Linkages)

Perspective Supporting Israel:

U.S. mediation *is* a necessary but *not a sufficient condition* for progress. There must be a local inclination to progress, or at least not a strong disinclination. The application of strong U.S. pressure at unpropitious moments is both counterproductive to the peace process and damaging politically to any U.S. administration stricken with such illusions of omnipotence. For the United States, the Arab–Israeli conflict is an irritant but not a mortal threat. For the local states, it *is* a mortal threat, and no amount of superpower pressure can make Israel or Jordan or Syria do anything that runs against its sense of survival. (Garfinkle, 1984/85:30)

The Soviet Union should be excluded from Middle East negotiations—public and private—unless and until its general attitude toward international order and law changes in such a way as to willingly tolerate ideological diversity and to respect the interests of other powers. Since this is improbable, the United States should assume that Soviet policy will be obstructive unless it has firm evidence to the contrary. (Garfinkle, 1984/85:30)

Although there is little hope of imminent indigenous movement toward peace, this does not mean that the best U.S. policy is one of benign neglect. An active and ambitious diplomacy does not have to be an open diplomacy whose main objective is a formal treaty of peace. Even in the absence of local movement toward peace, the United States can help lay the groundwork for peace in advance of the day when local conditions change for the better. The United States has in the past been successful at quiet diplomacy; U.S. aid in helping Israel and Syria reach an understanding about their respective security concerns in Lebanon in 1976 is a case in point. But such diplomacy has never been given highest priority and, as such, the scope of its ambitions has been modest. Since it is far better to succeed at modest tasks than to fail at grand ones, the United States should consider the benefits of a strategy of building a quiet peace. (Garfinkle, 1984/85:31–32)

The so-called Jewish lobby *is* strong in the United States. It tries to influence policy and sometimes it succeeds. The same is true of the Greek lobby, the AMA, the AFL-CIO, the "peace lobby," and many other groups. And like these other issue-oriented pressure groups, the Jewish lobby is patriotically American by its own lights. What is wrong with that? The arguments that pro-Israeli groups make about the strategic value of Israel to the United States may be correct or incorrect, but their right to make them is not open to question as long as the United States remains a free society. Moreover, there is good reason for government decision-makers to accept many of the arguments of the pro-Israel lobby, whatever their feelings about religion or about Jews. (Garfinkle, 1984/85:27–28)

But the proposition that the Arabs are more important than the Israelis is without substance. The Arab countries are politically distinct and are often, if not always, in contention with one another. Israel is the only true democracy in the Middle East and the only country in the Middle East for whom the United States is truly a friend of the spirit, not merely a friend of convenience. It is true that the foreign policies of democracies tend to be less capricious and less subject to erratic shifts than those of dictatorships, but that is not the only reason we ought to and do prefer to consort with them. (Garfinkle, 1984/85:28)

Perspective Supporting Palestinians:

Far too little effort has been made to evaluate how effective our large-scale and virtually unconditional economic, political and military support of Israel and her policies has actually been in combating Soviet penetration and promoting real American interests in the Middle East. Even the most pro-Western Arabs regard the Soviet threat to be more remote and less dangerous to them than the threats from regional neighbors, especially Israel. . . . Besides, the more we armed Israel, the more convinced even moderate Arabs became that the United States was primarily concerned about Israel's security and the attainment of her political and territorial objectives and the more dependent key Arab states became on Soviet military and political assistance—thereby, in some critical ways, making Israel more of a liability than an asset in preventing the spread of Soviet influence in the Middle East. (Khouri, 1986:47)

The "strategic partner myth" encourages Israel to hold on to occupied territories and the United States to support her aggressive and expansionist Israeli policies in the name of preserving "presumably critical strategic benefits." . . . This claim is "not only unsound but . . . a menace to U.S. interests." The Arab world, because of its vast size and strategic location, would be far more valuable to the United States in providing bases for deterring or engaging Soviet armed forces not only in the Gulf area but elsewhere in the Middle East as well. (Khouri, 1986:50)

It has been frequently contended that the United States should not apply pressures on Israel since they would be counterproductive, that Israel would only toughen her position and be even less forthcoming. However, it should be obvious by now that the Arabs and Israelis are not capable of bringing about peace on their own, regardless of the process used, and that Israel is not prepared on her own to make even those concessions we feel are essential for peace. (Khouri, 1986:62)

In fact, if the Arabs today were in a position of superior strength vis-a-vis Israel, they would be prepared to negotiate directly while Israel would understandably be the party to object to it. In brief, if both sides insist on negotiating only from a position of superior strength, there will never be any negotiations because there will always be the weaker party—no matter who it is—who will object. (Khouri, 1986:38)

Direct negotiations between parties where a big disparity of power exists between them, as in the case of the Arabs and Israel, and where the stronger party's main objective in the negotiations is to obtain treaty terms most favorable to her, would be the worst way to try to resolve the Arab-Israel problem. (Khouri, 1986:38)

The Arabs, as the weaker party, understandably oppose direct negotiations, at least until they can rectify the imbalance in their favor. However, the Arabs and even the moderate Palestinians led by Yassir Arafat have been prepared to negotiate within an international conference, where UN resolutions acceptable to them would play a role, and Arab weaknesses could be partly overcome by attending and negotiating as a single party in the presence of the major powers, who could help counterbalance the existing advantage in Israel's favor. (Khouri, 1986:39)

Positive attitudes toward compromise by disputants may enhance the chance of a negotiated settlement. But the philosophy of compromise is seen in rather harsh terms through this contrived "paper debate" presentation. Themes from the conflict frame remain intact—both nationalist rivalry, expressed here as an ideology toward an enemy, and the role to be assumed by a main outside power, in this case the United States, are significant aspects of the perspectives on negotiation today. Neither party seems to be able to relinquish basic goals.

The posturing for the Israeli case views the situation as a zero-sum condition: Any gains for the Palestinians would present a corresponding loss for the Zionists. The Palestinians have structured their arguments in a less zero-sum fashion: mutual gains are envisioned. Yet, it is important to remember that Israel represents the far stronger party in this dispute and would be in a position of having to give up something. The weaker party can more easily put forth an argument of mutual gains for everyone, since it stands to lose little, relatively speaking.

Lacking trust in the opponent, each side holds fast to confrontational ideological positions and seems inflexible in its stand toward negotiation or compromise. Part of this rigidity is perhaps due to the power imbalances between Israel and Palestinians. Still, it is true that postpartition politics continue to operate in the negotiation arena, heavily influenced by the conflict frame set in the Arab–Israeli dispute. Current attitudes toward compromise do not suggest much encouragement toward settlement possibilities, although some points highlighted by Garfinkle and Khouri may not be that relevant in the 1990s.

CONCLUSION

Fears, distorted perceptions, and traditional social hatreds growing from conflicts whose origins lie in expansive demands and in the incompatibility of recognizable objectives have long-term effects. The perpetuation of the conflict by widespread and deep-seated animosity between Israelis and Arabs is not based exclusively on concrete objectives, as implied in the incompatible territorial claims to the same piece of land. The land itself serves as a symbol of a more complicated, intense relationship between the parties, suggesting that neither a negotiation process nor a particular conflict resolution decision would lead automatically (or logically) to a reconciliation.

The frame of negotiations in the Arab–Israeli dispute is far more fragile than the conflict-sustaining structure. The negotiation frame lacks the solidness of commitment. There seems to be no escalation of resolve, and nothing matches distrust and tension—hallmarks in the ideological-based debate—to contribute to the peace ledger. Mostly, the negotiation frame is held together by obstacles to peace rather than by positive factors that would encourage resolution development.

Negotiation difficulties point directly to the national rivalry question in the following way: Since both parties maintain an inflexible position on the distribution of land (each lays claim to the same piece of territory, although the overlap of claims has been revised throughout the years), and since both harbor their differences on this issue to make it central in the dispute, two principles facilitating conflict resolution are violated. Issues that are perceived to be important to subordinate well-being and that do not lend themselves to many satisfactory alternatives are less likely to be resolved than are those characterized by less centrality and rigidity. Moreover, there is not a long history of a cooperative atmosphere, another factor conducive to a sturdy negotiation frame. In fact, the use of violent means to attain peaceful ends generally increases the chances that such methods will be used again and decreases the probability that stability will ultimately be achieved.

Another aspect in the negotiation frame in the Arab–Israeli conflict is the significance of the power balance. Conditions have altered over time; in effect, the Zionists and the Palestinians have exchanged positions on the balancing scale. At the time of the UN Partition Plan in 1947, the Jews had no land and were far outnumbered by Arabs; today, the rough populations of Israelis and Palestinians (a far narrower designation of this particular Arab group than existed before) are not that far apart, and Israel occupies land inhabited by Palestinians. It means that each side has served in the "weaker" position, and each has played the role of the "stronger" player, either by self-perception or through actual capabilities. The problem here is that power asymmetry makes negotiation more challenging. First of all, disputes tend to expand when the parties involved are of much different strengths. Weaker parties can augment their strength by defining the core of a dispute so that it involves a larger share of an audience or by linking core issues with others that have more public appeal. Once disputes begin to escalate sharply, it is necessary for each party to recruit from a wider group in an attempt to reach the original goals.

A final component in the shaky frame that structures the negotiation general history and setup is the miscommunication, misunderstood assumptions, and confusion that everyone seems to agree has been part of the situation. Although this factor is tied in with individual estimates of power and weakness, unanticipated consequences and varying expectations among all concerned—including Israelis, Palestinians, outside Great Powers, and the United Nations—it cannot be excluded as a significant element in the negotiation atmosphere that over time has inhibited progress toward peaceful resolution of issues.

A few signs lend support for the rickety negotiation frame; that is, evidence exists favoring resolution possibilities over this old dispute. The continuing involvement of an outside Great Power, which has not only offered support to each side but has also served as a sounding board for parties to air complaints and has structured compromise negotiation plans, can be considered as a type of management mechanism designed to help regulate conflict intensity. Great Britain, and later the United States, have served in this role, in effect providing ongoing institutional third-party mediation support.

Furthermore, the fact that the parties are discussing the mechanical style of negotiating (Should there be a step-by-step approach or a comprehensive strategy? Should the format be bilateral talks or an international conference?), rather than debating the issue of whether to negotiate differences at all, has to be entered as a positive sign. At this point, neither side is ignorant of the other in terms of expectations, objectives, or commitment, which also clears the way for negotiation potential. Finally, the land-for-peace theme, which was not included in the issue constellation until the end of the 1967 war, presents a bargaining opportunity that offers a somewhat broader view than the traditional zero-sum assumptions of winners and losers in this conflict. Whereas the attitudes of both sides toward negotiating their differences is somewhat less than enthusiastic and more aptly characterized as begrudging acceptance of the idea, the frame still has some substantial parts that prevent the situation from being a hopeless paralysis.

5

Negotiation Buildup

INTRODUCTION

What is the best way for Arabs and Israelis to deal with their differences? Negotiation is a basic means for meeting objectives through bargaining in oral-communication settings and for reaching an agreement when two parties have some interests that are shared and others that are opposed. Although negotiation has been a frequent topic in considerations for solving this dispute, the party positions are far apart, and standard strategies for bargaining have usually not produced satisfactory results.

Getting to Yes: Negotiating Agreement without Giving In, by Roger Fisher and William Ury, is a popular, widely read study that outlines opposing strategies for conflict resolution. One approach is called *positional bargaining*, a more traditional orientation, which may be pursued through ''hard'' or ''soft'' negotiating tactics. For a variety of reasons, this strategy fails to achieve amicable settlement between disputing parties. The other approach, strongly advocated by Fisher and Ury, is *principled negotiation*, which combines hard and soft aspects of bargaining behavior into a new style that maximizes the chance for a solid, mutually agreeable settlement.

In this chapter, the two different orientations toward negotiation in the Arab–Israeli dispute are brought to light. After a review of negotiating principles presented by Fisher and Ury, the basic approach adopted by Israeli and Palestinian decision makers in peace plans will be described, and a variety of international peace proposals that have been offered to settle this conflict will be introduced to show the evolution of policy positions and how positional bargaining works. Finally, several recent studies on the peace process will be evaluated, providing a few recommendations for principled negotiation.

NEGOTIATING STRATEGIES

Positional bargaining essentially means that antagonists begin the bargaining encounter from their respective positions of polar edges in desired policy outcomes, which highlight their differences. The purpose of bargaining is to get each side to move carefully and cautiously toward the center of the bargaining space. The hallmark of positional negotiation strategy is that each side emphasizes its power base and holds firm to its initial position in policy preference.

According to Fisher and Ury (1983:4), people routinely engage in positional bargaining: each side takes a position, argues for it, and makes concessions to reach a compromise. The authors believe that any method of negotiation may be fairly judged by three criteria: it should produce a wise agreement (if agreement is possible); it should be efficient; and it should improve (or at least not damage) the relationship between the parties. A wise agreement is defined as one that meets the legitimate interest of each side, resolves conflicting interests fairly, has durability, and takes community interests into account. The most common form of negotiation depends on successively taking and then giving up positions.

But positional bargaining is unlikely to lead to harmonious, intelligent agreement for the following reason. In bargaining for positions, negotiators get locked in and fully committed to a single policy stance. As more attention is focused on positions and on the gap between the parties on specific issues, rather than on underlying commonalities of the disputants, any agreement reached may reflect a technical approach that merely splits the difference between final policy demands rather than a solution that addresses legitimate interests of the parties. Such a result tends to be less than satisfactory to both sides.

Fisher and Ury (1983:6) state that bargaining for positions creates incentives that stall settlement, since each side will try to improve the chance for a favorable settlement by opening with an extreme position and yielding only small concessions to maintain the negotiation process. Arguing over positions is inefficient because extreme starting positions and small concessions require enormous time and effort to discover whether agreement is possible.

Moreover, arguing over positions endangers an ongoing relationship: The process becomes a contest of will; each side tries to force the other to alter its policy stand. Mutual hostility develops as each party perceives itself as bending to the rigid demands of the other side while its own legitimate concerns are not recognized. This is a high cost for hard positional bargaining, state Fisher and Ury (1983:6–7).

As an alternative, the soft negotiating game emphasizes the importance of building and maintaining a relationship. The standard moves are to make offers and concessions, to trust the other side, and to yield when necessary to avoid confrontation. This makes agreement more likely, but it may be unwise. Pursuing a soft form of positional bargaining increases vulnerability to a hard bargainer, one who insists on concessions and employs threats. The outcome of the negotiating game will be biased in favor of the hard player.

There are other problems in the positional bargaining style of negotiation. Policymakers may refrain from accepting a settlement proposal simply because they wish to avoid the appearance of backing down, giving in, or compromising. Often, face-saving devices that allow negotiators to reconcile agreement principles with their own self-image are very important. In bitter disputes, the stakes are high and feelings are threatened. Emotion can have a sharp, negative effect and terminate the negotiation process. In the Arab–Israeli conflict, the parties have developed strong, passionate sentiments that affect negotiation over most issues, even the concrete practical problems. Any discussion becomes difficult because each group perceives its own survival as the central, underlying concern. Feelings and commitment to particular positions become inextricably connected and reduce the possibility for finding a suitable settlement.

Principled negotiation rests on an entirely different set of premises. Here parties bargain from the point of their overlapping interests and common agreement. The antagonists begin at a central focal point and then branch out to widen their settlement. In negotiations of this type, parties are more likely to develop mutual *trust*, generate a series of *creative ideas* to solve the problems existing between them, and produce *principles as precedents* in their bargaining strategy. Although this is perhaps more difficult to accomplish, since the common interests will be seen as narrower and evaluated less intensely than the party differences, the mutual exchange and sharing of views is a positive psychological inducement for two enemy sides to venture into agreement on other issues.

The authors advocate a focus on interests, not positions, to emphasize the importance of enhancing party *trust*. The difference between these two perspectives is crucial. Fisher and Ury cite an example from the Egyptian–Israeli peace treaty at Camp David in 1978 to show how valuable it is to discover real interests that exist underneath advocated policy positions. Israel controlled the Sinai Peninsula and insisted on keeping some of this territory for security reasons. Egypt wanted all of the Sinai land returned to Egyptian sovereignty. Various maps of possible boundary lines were drawn to divide the Sinai between Egypt and Israel, but such compromising was wholly unacceptable to Egypt, and relinquishing everything was equally unacceptable to Israel. However, focusing on their interests, specifically Israeli security and Egyptian sovereignty, instead of on their policy positions, allowed them to develop a solution: return the Sinai to Egyptian control and demilitarize large areas. "The Egyptian flag would fly everywhere, but Egyptian tanks would be nowhere." Reconciling interests rather than positions worked, according to Fisher and Ury (1983:43).

Behind opposing positions lie many more mutual interests than conflicting ones. "We tend to assume that because the other side's positions are opposed to ours, their interests must also be opposed," Fisher and Ury assert (1983:43). A policy position is likely to be concrete and explicit, but the interests underlying it may well be unexpressed and intangible. How does one understand the interests involved in a negotiation? Examining each position taken by the opponent, thinking about the other side's choices, and figuring out where the opponent's mind is at the moment helps to construct the other side's presently perceived choice. Each side will have multiple interests, yet the most dominant interests are basic human needs: security, economic well-being, a sense of belonging, recognition, control over one's life. Negotiations are not likely to make much progress as long as one side believes that the fulfillment of its basic human needs is being threatened by the other (Fisher and Ury, 1983:50). "If you want the other side to take your interests into account, explain to them what those interests are," Fisher and Ury recommend (1983:51).

Interests need to be acknowledged as part of the problem. Additionally, looking to the future to satisfy interests is a better approach than dwelling on the past (Fisher and Ury, 1983:54). They advise parties to be concrete but flexible, suggesting that it is wise to keep one's interests in mind, short of committing to a specific position. Often the wisest solutions develop from strongly advocating one's interests, which helps stimulate creativity to invent acceptable options.

In most negotiations, four major obstacles inhibit the process of constructing a series of options: (1) judging prematurely, (2) searching for a single answer, (3) assuming a fixed pie, and (4) thinking that "solving their problem is their problem." Usually, negotiators try to narrow the gap between positions, not broaden the options available. Yet to reach an agreement, parties need solutions that appeal to both sides. Emotional involvement makes this process difficult, and Fisher and Ury urge detachment so that wise ways to meet the interests of both sides can be thought up (1983:62).

To generate *creative ideas*, the two sides need to separate the act of inventing ideas from the act of judging them. The intent is to broaden the alternatives rather than to look for a single answer and to search for mutual gains. Since judgment hinders imagination, it is important to distinguish the creative act from the critical one. Invest first and decide later by postponing all criticism and evaluation of ideas, assert Fisher and Ury (1983:62). The task of multiplying the number of possible agreements involves thinking of "weaker" versions in case a sought-for agreement proves beyond reach. Stronger agreements are characterized as substantive, permanent, comprehensive, final, and unconditional. Weaker agreements are procedural, provisional, partial, in principle, and contingent (Fisher and Ury, 1983:72).

The scope of a proposed agreement may also be changed in ways that parties find more acceptable by fractionating problems into smaller, more manageable units or, alternatively, by enlarging the subject matter to make cooperation more attractive to settlement. When a third party enters into negotiations, for example, there may be an incentive to form a settlement if the outsider promises a payment of substantial financial assistance to each of the parties (Fisher and Ury, 1983:72–73).

A final component of principled negotiations involves the development and use of objective criteria as a basis for agreement, criteria that enhance the possibility of developing *principles as precedents*. Fair standards and fair procedures are very important, and at a minimum, these need to be legitimate and practical and apply to both sides, say Fisher and Ury (1983:88–89). Understanding which standards are most appropriate and how they should be applied and yielding only to principle, not pressure, will more likely produce proposed options that reflect mutual interests. But Fisher and Ury warn:

[S]ome people begin by announcing that their position is an issue of principle and refuse even to consider the other side's case. "It's a matter of principle" becomes a battle cry in a holy war over ideology. Practical differences escalate into principled ones, further locking in the negotiators rather than freeing them.

This is emphatically *not* what is meant by principled negotiation. Insisting that an agreement be based on objective criteria does not mean insisting that it be based solely on the criterion *you* advance. One standard of legitimacy does not preclude the existence of others. (1983:93)

The relative negotiating power of two parties depends primarily on how attractive each side considers the option of not reaching an agreement. If both sides have attractive alternatives to negotiated settlement, the best outcome of the negotiations for both parties may well be not to reach agreement (Fisher and Ury, 1983:104–5). Knowing one's best alternative to a negotiated agreement—the standard against which any proposed agreement should be measured—is the only way to protect against accepting terms that are too unfavorable and rejecting terms that would be in one's interest to accept. Not having developed any alternative to a negotiated solution, parties will be unduly pessimistic about what will happen if negotiations break off.

Interests (*trust*), options (*creative ideas*), and objective standards (*principle as precedent* form the structure of a useful negotiation game, but these work only when everyone plays by the rules. Often one side may try to discuss interests while the opponent, concerned only with maximizing its own gains, attacks the proposals. Fisher and Ury offer these ideas for focusing attention on the merits of the proposals: if one side pushes hard, the other side should not respond by rejecting the proposal (if that happens, players are in a positional bargaining game); rather than resisting, the two should explore interests, invent options for mutual gain, and searching for independent standards. Here they suggest that a third party may be useful (Fisher and Ury, (1983:113).

In the end, the main message is that negotiating parties should not attack one another's position but should look underneath in a search for commonalities to build trust as a way to seek out principles for arriving at a solution. The goal throughout this process is to reach a "yesable proposition," which is a proposal for settlement where each side's response with the single word *yes* would be sufficient, realistic, and operational (Fisher and Ury, 1983:82).

ISRAELI AND PALESTINIAN OBJECTIVES

Most prenegotiation efforts in the Arab–Israeli conflict illustrate positional bargaining, which is criticized by Fisher and Ury. Each party specifies a series of policy objectives, and as will be obvious, many of these conflict with the wishes of the other side. Basic Israeli and Palestinian aims and their general orientations toward accommodation are described here. This is followed by a series of international peace plans that have been proposed to resolve the dispute. These proposals are also examples of positional negotiation, for they combine individual policy points advocated by the government of Israel or the Palestinian Arabs, but they do not bring together differences in the creative-agreement bargaining strategy of principled negotiation. Yet it is of some significance that such a large number of specific proposals have been developed. Surely proposal generation represents a prelude to peace.

The key issues in the Arab–Israeli dispute have remained much the same since Israel was established in 1948, although there have been modifications in the parameters of a peace settlement. These changes are related to the balance of power between Israel and the Arab states; they correspond with Israel's growth from a minor, weak nation to the most dominant military power of the region.

The Israeli Position

Since the beginning of the conflict, most Zionists have perceived the key issues as ideological. The goal was Arab recognition of a Jewish state and its right to a secure existence in Palestine. Official government policies and peace proposals have emphasized that the key to peace is not through concessions by Israel but through Arab acceptance of the Jewish state. It is believed that a weak Israel would never be accepted but rather would open the opportunity for conquest. Thus, Israeli power is absolutely central, regardless of compromise strategies and tactics. The Israeli government argues that concessions will not soften Arab hostility or lead to peace. For this reason, official peace proposals stress Israel's security position in relation to its Arab neighbors.

Before 1948, Israel was weak militarily and in no position to insist that it control all of mandatory Palestine. Therefore, the UN partition plan was accepted. As a result of military victory in 1948–49, Israelis held additional territory, and for all practical purposes, the partition plan was dead. The major questions shifted to substantive matters, including Israel's borders, the fate of Jerusalem, and the rights of Arab refugees who had fled Israeli-held territory. The Israelis argue that these substantive matters are direct results of Arab refusal to accept the Jewish state.

On the issue of Palestinian refugees, between 1949 and 1967, Israel consistently argued that return of the refugees would undermine national security and dilute the Jewish character of the state. The government offered only token concessions, reuniting within Israel those Arab families separated by the 1948 war, unfreezing Arab bank accounts, and laying the groundwork for evaluation of Arab property so that a formula for compensation *might* be devised in the future.

Victory in the 1967 war radically altered the parameters of Israel's peace plans. A new conception of secure borders emerged (based on the Jordan River rather than the armistice lines) under the concept of strategic depth; the idea of exchanging land for peace was born. Since 1967, the West Bank question—encompassing the issue of Jerusalem, the problem of the refugees, the dilemmas of Palestinian nationalism and the Palestinian national rights, and relations with Jordan—has overshadowed all issues in peace plan developments. The importance of the area became greater after the 1979 peace treaty and Sinai's return to Egypt.

The position of the Israeli government is that the West Bank (Judea and Samaria) is an integral part of Israel and not negotiable in a peace settlement. It is Israeli land, liberated from Jordan in the 1967 war and need not be annexed because it already belongs to the Jewish state. By international law and historic right, the area is a part of Israel. The best plans for the Arab inhabitants of the West Bank, according to the Israelis, were outlined in the autonomy proposals in September 1978 at Camp David. This would include terminating the Israeli military government in the West Bank and replacing it with administrative autonomy by and for Arab inhabitants. Primary responsibility for security and public order would remain with Israel, but other issues of social affairs, transportation, housing, etc. would rest with an Arab administrative council. West Bank and Gaza citizens would be offered the right to choose either Israeli or Jordanian citizenship. Residents of Israel would be entitled to acquire land and settle in West Bank and Gaza, and Arabs in these areas would be entitled the same rights in Israel.

The idea of autonomy was to apply to Arab residents of the West Bank but not to the territory, a notion derived from Jewish experience in Eastern Europe during the nineteenth and twentieth centuries. The term *autonomy* was then coined to designate a theory and conception of Jewish nationalism in the diaspora in which personal autonomy would be granted to Jewish communities living within the Tsarist and Austro-Hungarian empires (Lapidoth, 1983:36; Beliny, 1986:18–19). The basic objective of "personal autonomy" was to preserve the religious, legal, social, and cultural self-sufficiency of the Jewish community within the sovereign (non-Jewish) state or its subdivisions. The notion of autonomy is based on the premise that the Arab population will govern itself with as little interference as possible from Israeli authorities, but that all strategic points in the West Bank will remain under Israeli control. A ring of Jewish settlements would be required around the Arab-inhabited regions, with military bases and outposts controlled by the Jewish settlers.

Israel totally rejects a Palestinian state or the separation of Jerusalem from Israeli sovereignty, arguing that it would be a security threat to Israel. Autonomy is a price Israel is paying to gain peace. The Israeli government does not recognize the PLO or any other organization based on the Palestinian Covenant that denies Israel's right to exist as a state.

Some Israelis have argued that it would be no more difficult to evacuate the West Bank and Gaza as part of a peace settlement than it was to evacuate Sinai.

Security arguments are used to justify the evacuation of the remaining occupied territories, but they are overridden by common perceptions that see Gaza, the West Bank, and the Golan Heights as threats to Israel if returned to Arab hands, even if demilitarized. Jerusalem is especially difficult because of its historic and religious connotations. Many Jewish settlements have been set up in the West Bank, and a generation of Israelis has grown up thinking of Judea and Samaria as integral parts of the Jewish state. There is a reluctance to make specific proposals unless the Arab states alter basic attitudes toward Israel.

Many Israelis cling to the belief that the Arabs will never make peace, so there is little use in taking initiatives. Although peace is a lofty aspiration of nearly all Israelis, security has far greater priority and is seen as the key to peace.

The Palestinian Position

Before the state of Israel was established in 1948, few voices in the Palestinian community argued for any kind of permanent reconciliation with local Zionists. The vast majority considered Jewish immigration into Palestine as threatening and intrinsically hostile: the debates were not about whether or how to forge a settlement with the Zionists but about how to combat them. Mistakenly considering the regional balances of force to be in their favor, the Palestinian leaders opposed the UN partition plan, holding out for the establishment of a Palestinian Arab state in the entire mandate area.

The defeat in 1948 and the mass exodus of Palestinians from regions taken over by Zionists were not followed by any other leadership for nearly two decades. Palestinian society in the diaspora was demoralized and angry; no one could think of proposing creative solutions to coexistence with Israel. Moreover, from 1948 to 1967, the Palestinians' future became the almost exclusive preserve of the rulers of various Arab states, who often manipulated such Palestinians for their own purposes. (Nasser, for example, claiming support for the Palestinian cause, argued that Arab unity was a prerequisite for the liberation of Palestine.)

Following the 1967 war, an authentic Palestinian leadership emerged among the diaspora Palestinians, who started groping for a solution, which accounted for the reality of the substantial Jewish population in their former homeland. One plan was to foment a broad popular uprising against the Israeli occupation by the residents of the West Bank and Gaza. Another plan was the rapid escalation of guerrilla activity directed into Israeli territory.

In 1968 there arose a new breed of Palestinian activist who has dominated the nationalist movement ever since. The first plan was committed to the goal of establishing a single, unitary state in all of Israel/Palestine, in which Jews and Arabs would live together under a secular system. Six years later, in 1974, when this goal appeared unattainable, these activists formulated the idea of working for the interim goal of a two-state solution. Under this formula, a Palestinian Arab ministate would be established in the West Bank and Gaza alongside Israel, which would withdraw to its 1948 borders. In 1983 and 1984, a number of Palestinian leaders spoke openly of the possibility of this state entering into some kind of confederation with Jordan.

The PLO charter of 1968 said, "Armed struggle is the only way to liberate Palestine." In 1974, further revision of the political strategy was announced: "The PLO will struggle by every means, the foremost of which is armed struggle, to liberate Palestinian land and to establish the people's national, independent and fighting sovereignty on every part of Palestinian land to be liberated. This requires the creation of further changes in the balance of power in favor of our people and their struggle." And in March 1977, the reference was made more explicit: to establish an independent, national state on the soil of the homeland.

The major strategy of the PLO was that by establishing a firm claim to Palestinian sovereignty over the West Bank and Gaza, the PLO could participate in peace talks. The ministate idea received tremendous backing from the West Bank and Gaza Palestinians, who were living under Israeli occupation. From 1974 and 1978, there was some internal PLO opposition to the ministate concept, under the argument that this would liquidate the Palestinian refugee claims to return to their former homes and properties inside Israel. Thus the PLO continued to reject UN Resolution 242, which had always been based on the fact that the resolution made no mention of the Palestinian question in political terms, referring instead only to a just settlement of the refugee problem. The resolution was finally accepted in December 1988, even though it falls short of noting one of the key goals in Palestinian nationalism, namely the creation of an independent state. This resolution has always been explicitly defined as one of the basic principles according to which any reconvened talks should be held.

Palestinians living in the West Bank and Gaza would naturally continue to live in the area defined as the ministate. But most refugees still have outstanding claims for their homes and properties within 1948 Israel, and the long-standing choice is still to allow them to return or to receive compensation from Israel. The balance of the diaspora refugees cannot realistically return to Israel, because of Israeli objections, nor to the Palestinian ministate, because of absorptive capacity. Refugees still need the options of compensation and Palestinian citizenship.

The concept of Palestinian sovereignty could be designed to allay legitimate fears of Israel on a reasonable basis, argues the PLO. The state could declare its nonaligned status in the defense and military fields, yet not be demilitarized. It could be a UN member, along with the Arab League, and have its own foreign policy. There would be some intimate linking with Jordan, to be decided in an evolving manner of joint agreements.

In 1983, the Palestinian National Congress decided to continue talks with Jordan, begun in 1977, and encourage the idea that future relations with that country should be founded on the basis of a confederation between two independent states. Later, they adopted the position that an international conference should be commenced to resolve the Arab–Israeli conflict, advocating that the PLO attend the conference on an equal basis with the other parties. PLO leaders refuse to accept the notion of autonomy, since it would apply to the people of the occupied territories rather than touching on any questions of sovereignty over the land. Palestinians reject any plan that does not guarantee their rights to repatriation, self-determination, and establishment of an independent Palestinian state.

POSITIONAL BARGAINING

Beginning with the UN General Assembly Resolution on Partitioning Palestine, in 1947, there have been numerous proposals to resolve the conflict between Arabs and Israelis. Particularly since the 1967 War, plans that centered on trading land for peace have been popular. Twenty-two major peace proposals are compared here—in terms of origin, content, and direction—as another strong indicator of the positional bargaining approach. Of these selected plans, three developed out of the United Nations (in addition to General Assembly Resolution 181 on partition, the Security Council passed Resolutions 242 and 338); three were created by the United States (the Reagan, Shultz, and Baker plans); two emerged from joint superpower actions (the Geneva Peace Conference in 1973 and the joint statement by the United States and the Soviet Union in 1977); five originated from Arab state initiatives (summit communiques issued in Rabat, Fez, and Algiers, and proposals put forth by Saudi Arabia and most recently by Egypt); the European Community issued a statement in 1981; involved parties have issued two proposals (Israel and Egypt collaborated to produce the Camp David accords, and Palestinians and Jordan developed a united position in 1985); and Israel and the Palestinians have prepared proposals individually tailored to deal with problems on the West Bank and Gaza.

These plans contain a striking amount of overlap. All of them mention rights for the Palestinians; fourteen recognize the parallel rights of the Israelis. Sixteen of these proposals note the principle of a land-for-peace exchange as the basis to solve the two central problems of Israel—security and Palestinian self-determination. Most statements suggest particular efforts for negotiating party differences and point to some cooperative activities that could be undertaken, including economic unions and demilitarized zones. The peace plans are not narrowly construed but treat a multitude of problem areas.

With respect to timing, two features are notable. First, no fewer than twelve of these peace proposals were offered following or during a major period of violence. All three UN resolutions came to light in this way, and proposals issued since the start of the war in Lebanon in 1982 and the intifida in December 1987 follow the same line. Second, there is a sharp acceleration in the pace of proposal submissions in the 1980s. Eleven major plans were offered in the past decade, six of them since the start of the intifida.

Most of the plans have not been accepted by all of the relevant parties. For example, the partition plan of 1947 was accepted by the Jewish agency, but the Palestinian Arabs rejected it. Today a reverse situation applies: Israel opposes a two-state solution, but the PLO accepts it. Still, there are some interesting parallels between the early UN plan and the flurry of proposals some forty years later in the plans of George Shultz, Yitzhak Shamir, the PLO, and James Baker. All address the issues of two self-governing peoples, transition periods to achieve this end, elections, mutual recognition, economic unions, etc.

The idea of negotiating a solution seems to have arisen after the 1967 war. This theme is part of Security Council Resolutions 242 and 338, the Rogers Initiative, and the Geneva Peace Conference held in December 1973. Frequent calls for another international conference or direct negotiations between the parties appear in later proposal drafts. This is a clear sign of willingness to talk out differences and to reach agreement through discussion, not force.

Some of the proposals are long and detailed (partition resolution, Shultz plan), whereas others are short and sketchy (Saudi and Fez plans). Party propaganda appears occasionally, but not in a consistent pattern. The evolution of these proposals does show a development of focal points on which to reach accommodation. Negotiation has become more important, although the appropriate forum is still lacking agreement between the parties, the rights of Palestinians are more and more specified, and international cooperation among regional countries is gaining significance. Throughout, the status of Israel's policy objectives seems unchanged. Similarly, the territory-for-peace theme is consistent in all the proposals.

On the future of the Palestinians, the original partition resolution specified an independent state located in the West Bank and Gaza. This point does not reappear in subsequent UN resolutions but reemerges at the 1973 Geneva meetings, the joint U.S.–U.S.S.R. statement, and the Camp David accords. Plans on self-governance become increasingly specific as to voting rights and procedures. These proposals and selected points made in the eighteen plans are listed below. Table 2 cites issue positions of each peace plan.

International Plans for an Arab–Israeli Peace

1. 1947, Nov. 29 UN General Assembly Resolution 181: Partition Plan

2. 1967, Nov. 22 UN Security Council Resolution 242

3. 1970, June 19 The Rogers Initiative

4. 1973, Oct. 22 UN Security Council Resolution 338

5. 1973, Oct. 20 U.S.–U.S.S.R. Geneva Conference

6. 1974, Oct. 29 Rabat Communiqué

7. 1977, Oct. 1 U.S.–U.S.S.R. Joint Statement

8. 1978, Sep. 17 Camp David Accords: A Framework for Peace in the Middle East (Part I)

9. 1978, Sep. 17 Camp David Accords: A Framework for the Conclusion of a Peace Treaty between Egypt and Israel (Part II)

(*List continued on page 80*)

Table 2

Recommendations Proposed on Selected Issues in Arab–Israeli Peace Plans

(• denotes recommendation)

I. Plans Presented between 1947-1980

Issues	Partition Plan	UN 242 Resolution	Rogers Initiative	Geneva Conference	Rabat Communique	US-USSR Statement	Camp David Accords[a]	Europe Summit
Palestinian Goals:								
1) Jerusalem Capital City								
2) Independent State	•							
3) Elections for Self-Government	•						•	
4) Transition Period toward Self-Rule	•						•	
5) PLO Sole Representative					•			
6) Self-Determination Rights				•	•			•
7) Legitimate Rights				•	•	•		•
8) Rights to Return to Homeland								
9) Compensation for Refugees				•				
10) Settle Refugee Problem		•	•				•	
Israeli Goals:								
1) Jerusalem Capital City								
2) Freedom of Navigation		•	•				•	

74

Issues	Partition Plan	UN 242 Resolution	Rogers Initiative	Geneva Conference	Rabat Communique	US-USSR Statement	Camp David Accords*	Europe Summit
3) Secure and Recognized Boundaries		•	•	•		•	•	•
4) Political Independence of Regional States	•	•	•	•		•	•	•
5) Renounce Belligerence		•	•	•		•	•	
6) Renounce Terrorism				•				
7) Renounce Threat or Use of Force		•	•	•			•	
Land-for-Peace Goal:								
1) Peace Treaty								
2) Comprehensive Settlement				•		•	•	•
3) Territory-for-Peace Exchange								
4) Israeli Withdrawal		•	•			•	•	
5) Disband Settlements								
6) Freeze Israeli Settlements								

Table 2 (continued)

Issues	Partition Plan	UN 242 Resolution	Rogers Initiative	Geneva Conference	Rabat Communique	US-USSR Statement	Camp David Accords[a]	Europe Summit
Implementing Cooperation:								
1) Federation of Palestinians, Jordanians, Israelis								
2) Combined Self-Government Palestinians, Jordanians								
3) Economic Unit	•							
4) Demilitarized Zones		•				•	•	
5) Freedom of Access to Holy Places	•			•				•
6) International Guarantees				•		•		•
Implementing Discussion:								
1) Direct Negotiations							•	
2) UN Special Representative		•	•					
3) International Special Commission	•							
4) International Conference						•		

[a]Includes Framework for Peace in the Middle East, Framework for Peace Treaty between Israel and Egypt, and Israeli-Egyptian Peace Treaty.

II. Plans Presented between 1981-1991

Issues	Fahd Plan	Reagan Plan	Fez Plan	Pales.-Jordan Plan	Shultz Plan	Shamir Plan	PLO Plan	Egypt Plan	Baker Plan[b]
Palestinian Goals:									
1) Jerusalem Capital City									
2) Independent State	•		•				•		
3) Elections for Self-Government		•			•	•	•	•	•
4) Transition Period toward Self-Rule	•	•	•		•	•	•		•
5) PLO Sole Representative			•	•					
6) Self-Determination Rights			•	•					
7) Legitimate Rights	•				•				•
8) Rights to Return to Homeland									
9) Compensation for Refugees	•		•						
10) Settle Refugee Problem		•		•	•	•			•
Israeli Goals:									
1) Jerusalem Capital City		•							•
2) Freedom of Navigation					•	•			•
3) Secure and Recognized Boundaries		•			•	•			•
4) Political Independence of Regional States	•	•			•	•	•		

77

Table 2 (continued)

Issues	Fahd Plan	Reagan Plan	Fez Plan	Pales.-Jordan Plan	Shultz Plan	Shamir Plan	PLO Plan	Egypt Plan	Baker Plan [b]
5) Renounce Belligerence		•			•	•			•
6) Renounce Terrorism									
7) Renounce Threat or Use of Force		•			•	•			•
Land-for-Peace Goal:									
1) Peace Treaty					•	•			•
2) Comprehensive Settlement					•	•	•		•
3) Territory-for-Peace Exchange				•	•	•		•	•
4) Israeli Withdrawal	•	•	•		•	•	•		•
5) Disband Settlements	•		•						
6) Freeze Israeli Settlements		•						•	•
Implementing Cooperation:									
1) Federation of Palestinians, Jordanians, Israelis									•
2) Combined Self-Government Palestinians, Jordanians		•		•	•	•			
3) Economic Unit									
4) Demilitarized Zones		•							•
5) Freedom of Access to Holy Places	•		•						
6) International Guarantees	•		•						

78

Issues	Fahd Plan	Reagan Plan	Fez Plan	Pales.-Jordan Plan	Shultz Plan	Shamir Plan	PLO Plan	Egypt Plan	Baker Plan[b]
Implementing Discussion:									
1) Direct Negotiations		•			•	•			•
2) UN Special Representative									
3) International Special Commissions								•	
4) International Conference				•	•		•		•

[b]Includes Baker Initiative of May, and Five Point Framework of October, 1989.

(*List continued from page 73*)

10. 1979, Mar. 26 Egyptian–Israeli Peace Treaty

11. 1980, June 13 European Declaration

12. 1981, Aug. 8 Fahd Plan

13. 1982, Sep. 1 Reagan Plan

14. 1982, Sep. 9 Fez Plan

15. 1985, Feb. 11 Jordanian Palestinian Agreement

16. 1988, Mar. 4 Shultz Plan

17. 1988, June 7–9 Algiers Summit Communiqué

18. 1989, May 14 Shamir Plan

19. 1989, May 21 PLO Election Plan

20. 1989, May 22 Baker Initiative

21. 1989, Sept. 16 Egyptian Plan

22. 1989, Oct. 8 Baker Five-Point Mideast Formula

Selected Issues in Arab–Israeli Negotiations

I. Palestinian Goals

    1. Jerusalem Capital City

    2. Independent State

    3. Elections for Self-Government

    4. Transition Period toward Self-Rule

    5. PLO Sole Representative

    6. Self-Determination Rights

    7. Legitimate Rights

    8. Rights to Return to Homeland

    9. Compensation to Refugees

   10. Settle Refugee Problem

II. Israeli Goals

    1. Jerusalem Capital City

    2. Freedom of Navigation

    3. Secure and Recognized Boundaries

    4. Political Independence of Regional States

    5. Renounce Belligerence

    6. Renounce Terrorism

    7. Renounce Threat or Use of Force

III. Land-for-Peace Linkage

    1. Peace Treaty

    2. Comprehensive Settlement

    3. Territory-for-Peace Exchange

    4. Israeli Withdrawal

    5. Disband Settlements

    6. Freeze Israeli Settlements

IV. Cooperation Mechanisms

    1. Federation of Palestinians, Jordanians, Israelis

    2. Combined Self-Government—Palestinians, Jordanians

    3. Economic Unit

    4. Demilitarized Zones

    5. Freedom of Access to Holy Places

    6. International Guarantees

V. Discussion Format

    1. Direct Negotiations

    2. UN Special Representative

    3. International Special Commissions

    4. International Conference

MAJOR PEACE PLANS

1. Title: United Nations General Assembly Resolution 181: Partition Plan
Date: November 29, 1947
Background: In February 1947, Britain announced it would end its responsibilities in Palestine under the League Mandate and refer the problem to the United Nations as a result of the incompatible nationalist aspirations of Arabs and Zionists and continued violence in the region. A special investigative UN commission was formed in May 1947, consisting of eleven member countries. The commission report was ready in August, and a UN General Assembly vote was taken in November, with the following results: in favor of the resolution, 33; opposed, 13; abstain, 10. The resolution passed.

Features:

1. Partition of Palestine into two separate sovereign states—one Jewish, one Arab—by October 1948.

2. Boundaries for each state set according to population concentrations of Arabs and Jews (see map).

3. International Regime Administration of Jerusalem.

4. British military troop withdrawal by August 1948.

5. A UN commission set up to oversee the transition.

6. Provisional Council of Government for each state selected and established by the UN commission.

7. Democratic elections in each state.

8. Democratic constitutions in each state with these provisions: (a) legislative and executive bodies, (b) commitment to settle all international disputes by peaceful means, (c) commitment to restrain from threat of use of force against territorial integrity or political independence of any state, (d) civil, political, economic, religious, and human rights for everyone, and (e) no tourist or visa restrictions between the two states.

9. Rights to holy places open to everyone.

10. No expropriation of land by Jews or Arabs in each other's proposed state except for public purpose, and with full compensation.

11. Arabs and Jews become citizens of the state in which they reside. Everyone may freely choose citizenship in either state and enjoy full civil and political rights.

Reactions: Zionists, accept. Arabs, reject.

Implementation: The Zionists declared their independence and established the Jewish state of Israel on May 14, 1948. British troops withdrew on May 15. Immediate fighting between Arab states and Jews broke out, ending in January 1949. No Arab state was created.

2. *Title*:   United Nations Security Council Resolution 242

Date: November 22, 1967

Background: After the war of June 1967, when Israeli forces conquered the Sinai Peninsula, Gaza, the West Bank of Jordan, and East Jerusalem, the Israeli government initially expressed a willingness to return some of the occupied territory in exchange for negotiated peace agreements. At the Arab Summit in Khartoum, however, member states agreed on September 1 to unite in their efforts to ensure that there would be no peace with Israel, no recognition of Israel, and no negotiations with Israel so long as the Zionists had acquired the territory by force. Great Britain sponsored the resolution through the UN Security Council, which voted unanimously (fifteen member countries) to accept the proposal.

Features:

1. Emphasizes the inadmissibility of the acquisition of territory by war, which is in violation of the UN Charter.

2. Establishment of a just and lasting peace in the Middle East.

3. Withdrawal of Israeli armed forces from territories occupied in the recent conflict.

4. Termination of all claims of belligerency and respect for territorial integrity and political independence of every state.

5. The right to live in peace within secure and recognized boundaries for every state.

6. Guaranteed freedom of navigation through international waterways in the area.

7. A just settlement of the refugee problem.

8. Demilitarized zones.

9. Designation of a UN special representative to promote efforts to achieve settlement in accordance with the points in this resolution.

Reactions: Israel, accept. Palestinians, reject, then accept. Egypt and Jordan, accept. Syria, reject. (The Palestinians accepted the resolution in December 1988.)

Implementation: Gunnar Jarring was appointed as the special representative to mediate the dispute and discussed issues with the parties between 1967 and 1972, although his efforts failed. The major stumbling block was contradictory views on the scheduling of negotiations: the Arab states wanted Israel to withdraw from all territories before the discussions, whereas Israel saw withdrawal as a subject for negotiation. Each side wished to bargain from a position of strength. As time passed, this resolution came to be regarded as a workable document for solving the Arab–Israeli conflict and is cited in other peace proposals. The Camp David accords between Israel and Egypt are an example of the land-for-peace principle enunciated in this plan.

3. *Title*: The Rogers Initiative

Date: June 19, 1970

Background: By the end of 1969, Israel had crafted a policy of continued occupation over territories taken in the 1967 war, the PLO had participated directly in several battles with Israeli forces, demonstrating fighting strength and further developing Palestinian resistance groups, and Egypt had launched a War of Attrition to break Israeli resolve. U.S. Secretary of State William Rogers, appointed in the recently elected Nixon administration, noted the lack of success of the Jarring talks. Determined to make an effort at a negotiated settlement to the Arab–Israeli conflict, he presented the Rogers Plan in December 1969. The plan was designed around UN Resolution 242, and both Israel and Egypt rejected it outright. Violent attacks between the parties continued, fueled by massive, sophisticated superpower weaponry. Rogers later proposed that the disputants "stop shooting and start talking," which expressed the more limiting principles forming the initiative.

Features:

1. Cease-fire for ninety days along the Egyptian–Israeli frontier.

2. Resumption of negotiations sponsored under UN Resolution 242 directed by Gunnar Jarring.

Reactions: Israel, reject, then accept. Egypt, reject, then accept. Jordan, accept. Palestinians, reject.

Implementation: The parties finally agreed to the cease-fire, which went into effect on August 8, 1970, and was extended for another three months by the UN General Assembly on November 4. Meanwhile the regional arms race continued, with Soviet weaponry supplied to Egypt and American equipment sent to Israel. Jordan's agreement, which was contingent on controlling Palestinian guerrilla activities originating from its borders into Israel, was met with hostile and violent reactions from PLO members, who were just beginning to feel they alone could confront the Zionists better than the standing Arab armies. In September, major fighting broke out between Jordanian and Palestinian troops. President Nasser died at the end of September, and the negotiating talks resumed intermittently but without progress, in part due to the incompatibility of the parties' positions and the confusing roles of authority assumed by the United Nations and the United States, both of whom were now sponsoring the talks.

4. *Title*:   United Nations Security Council Resolution 338

Date: October 22, 1973

Background: As the War of 1973 was ending and none of the parties were achieving a decisive military victory, the United States and the Soviet Union, as major arms benefactors of Israel and Egypt respectively, sought to arrange a halt to the fighting. The UN Security Council Resolution, drafted earlier by the United States and the Soviet Union, was voted unanimously in favor: 14–0.

Features:

1. Cease-fire among all parties.

2. Implementation of UN Security Council Resolution 242.

3. Negotiations among the parties to establish a just and durable peace in the Middle East.

Reactions: Israel, reject, then accept. Palestinians, reject (they later accepted the resolution, in December 1988). Egypt, accept.

Implementation: An Israeli offensive continued for several days in spite of the cease-fire resolution. The Soviet Union threatened to send troops to the region, and as a result, U.S. forces were placed on worldwide alert to confront the Soviet threat. Later, negotiations were started in Geneva to settle the peace between Israel and Egypt, and talks led to the Sinai disengagement-of-forces agreements in 1974 and 1975, mediated by U.S. Secretary of State Henry Kissinger.

5. *Title*:   U.S.–U.S.S.R. Geneva Conference

Date: December 21–23, 1973

Background: In response to Resolution 338 in the UN Security Council, urging that negotiations be undertaken, the United States and the Soviet Union agreed to convene and cochair a peace conference. Israel, Egypt, and Jordan attended. Syria refused to participate. The Palestinians were not invited. The secretary-general of the United Nations opened the meetings. There was no substantive negotiation, but parties agreed to talk in good faith.

Features: The only overlapping positions expressed by each of the participating governments were the following:

1. Respect and recognition of the sovereignty, territorial integrity, and political independence of all states in the Middle East.
2. A realistic program for establishing negotiations between the parties on the basis of Resolutions 242 and 338 of the UN Security Council.

Reactions: Israel, agreed to participate so long as the Palestinians were not in attendance. Palestinians were not invited.

Implementation: The meetings were largely ceremonial and marked the first time Arab states had participated in a direct conference with Israel. Since no specific proposal or concluding declaration resulted from the meetings, the issue of implementation did not arise, although it was assumed that further discussions would take place in the Geneva Conference setting. This never happened.

6. *Title*: Rabat Communiqué
Date: October 29, 1974
Background: The emerging sense of Palestinian identity, since the initial creation of the Palestine Liberation Organization ten years earlier, and the growing power of this group within the Arab world led to specific steps of individual recognition to strengthen and support Palestinian nationalism at the Arab League Summit Conference held in Morocco in 1974.

Features:

1. To affirm the right of the Palestinian people to self-determination and to return to their homeland.
2. To affirm the right of the Palestinian people to establish an independent national authority under the command of the Palestine Liberation Organization, the sole legitimate representative of the Palestinian people.
3. To support the PLO in the framework of Arab commitment.
4. To defend Palestinian national unity.

Reactions: Israel, reject. Palestinians, accept.

Implementation: Since this statement was issued the PLO has increased its stature along the lines outlined here, and at the same time, Israel has refused to negotiate with the organization, arguing that the PLO is a terrorist group whose goal is Israel's demise.

7. *Title*: U.S.–U.S.S.R. Joint Statement
Date: October 1, 1977
Background: The newly elected U.S. president, Jimmy Carter, was deter-

mined to make progress toward peace in the Middle East and saw a revival of the 1973 Geneva International Peace Conference as the likely forum. In developing contacts and meeting prenegotiation conditions with various parties, the United States soon discovered incompatible positions. As a result, the Soviet Union was brought into the picture as a way to pressure the parties, and a common stand was adopted for governing a future conference.

Features:

1. A comprehensive settlement of the Arab–Israeli conflict, incorporating all parties and all issues.
2. Withdrawal of Israel from territories occupied in the 1967 conflict.
3. Resolution of the Palestinian question, including ensuring the legitimate rights of the Palestinian people.
4. Termination of the state of war and establishment of normal peaceful relations on the basis of mutual recognition of sovereignty, territorial integrity, and political independence.
5. Secure borders and demilitarized zones between Israel and the neighboring Arab states.
6. International guarantees for such borders.
7. Superpower participation in these international guarantees.
8. Negotiations within the Geneva Peace Conference framework, with participation of all parties involved in the conflict including those of the Palestinian people.

Reactions: Israel, reject. Palestinians, accept.

Implementation: As the parties worked toward procedural arrangements to govern the forthcoming Geneva Peace Conference, various differences in positions developed anew. At this point, Anwar Sadat, the Egyptian president, decided to visit Jerusalem, where he arrived on November 19, 1977, to talk to the Israelis directly. The Geneva forum and the superpower communiqué were taken over by Sadat's dramatic move and the subsequent talks at Camp David.

8. *Title*: Camp David Accords: A Framework for Peace in the Middle East (Part I)

Date: September 17, 1978

Background: Following direct contacts between officials of Israel and Egypt and increasing tension in their efforts to reach an agreement over the Sinai Peninsula and the future of the Palestinians, President Jimmy Carter invited Prime Minister Menachem Begin and President Sadat to Camp David, Maryland, for concentrated negotiation sessions. The United States offered to assist as a third-party mediator.

Features:

1. The basis for peaceful settlement of the Arab–Israeli conflict is UN Resolution 242.
2. Negotiations are necessary to carry out the provisions and principles of UN Resolutions 242 and 338.

3. Respect for the sovereignty, territorial integrity, and political independence of every state in the area and their right to live in peace within secure and recognized boundaries.

4. West Bank and Gaza: Egypt, Israel, Jordan, and the representatives of the Palestinian people should participate in negotiations on the resolution of the Palestinian problem in all its aspects.

The Transition Period:

   a. Free elections should be held to create a self-governing authority in the West Bank and Gaza.

   b. Egypt, Israel, and Jordan will agree on the modalities for establishing the elected self-governing authority.

   c. The delegations of Egypt and Jordan may include Palestinians from the West Bank and Gaza or other Palestinians as mutually agreed.

   d. The parties will negotiate an agreement to define the powers and responsibilities of the self-governing authority.

   e. Israel's military troops and civilian administration will be withdrawn once the elections are held.

   f. A transition period of up to five years will begin once elections are held.

The Final Status:

   a. Within three years of the transition period, negotiations should begin to determine the final status of the West Bank and Gaza and to conclude a peace treaty between Israel and Jordan.

   b. The solution from the negotiations must recognize the legitimate rights of the Palestinian people and their just requirements.

   c. Measures will be taken to assure the security of Israel and its neighbors during the transitional period and beyond.

   d. Negotiations will begin to establish procedures for resolving the refugee problem.

5. Egypt and Israel agree to settle their disputes through peaceful means.

6. Egypt and Israel agree to full diplomatic recognition, abolishing economic boycotts and exploring possibilities for economic cooperation.

Reactions: Israel, accept. Egypt, accept. Palestinians, reject. Jordan, reject.

Implementation: The framework for peace in the Middle East subsequently led to direct negotiations between Israel and Egypt on the future of the Palestinians, and autonomy proposals developed in this setting. The meetings began in May 1979, but Jordan and the Palestinians did not participate. Although several additional meetings were held in 1980, little progress was made. Jewish settlements in the West Bank continued to be developed. Sadat suspended Egyptian participation during that year after Israel declared Jerusalem its undivided capital. Israel requested resumption of the talks in 1981, President Sadat was assassinated in October 1981, and after two days of talks between Israel and Egypt in November, no progress was reached toward an agreement. By mid–1982, Israelis and Palestinians were involved in direct combat in Lebanon. Discussions on the framework ceased.

9. *Title*:   The Camp David Accords: A Framework for the Conclusion of a Peace Treaty between Egypt and Israel (Part II)

Features:

1. Israel forces withdraw from the Sinai.
2. Sinai returned to Egyptian sovereignty.
3. Free passage for Israeli ships through the Suez Canal.
4. Freedom of navigation for all nations through the Gulf of Aqaba.
5. Construction of a highway between the Sinai and Jordan with guaranteed free passage by Egypt and Jordan.
6. Limited military forces stationed in designated areas.

Reactions: Israel, accept. Egypt, accept. Palestinians, reject. Jordan, reject.
Implementation: Egypt and Israel produced a formal peace treaty based on this document for structuring full, mutual recognition and diplomatic relations. Sinai was returned to Egyptian control in stages, finishing by April 1982.

10. *Title*:   Egyptian–Israeli Peace Treaty
Date: March 26, 1979
Background: As a culmination of the framework developed in the Camp David Accords, talks continued between the parties and eventually resulted in a formal treaty.

Features:

1. An end to the state of belligerency between parties.
2. Israeli withdrawal from the Sinai.
3. A permanent recognized boundary between the countries and respect for territorial integrity.
4. Mutual recognition of each other's sovereignty, territorial integrity, and political independence.
5. Respect for each other's right to live in peace within secure and recognized boundaries.
6. Agree to settle all disputes through peaceful means.
7. Agree to restrict and punish threats of belligerency, hostility, or violence originating in each territory against the population, citizens, or property of the other party.
8. Establishment of normal, full diplomatic relations.
9. Freedom of passage for Israeli ships through the Suez Canal and Gulf of Aqaba.
10. Dispute resolution through negotiation.

Reactions: Israel, accept. Egypt, accept. Palestinians, reject.

Implementation: The two countries established normal relations and opened embassies in their respective capitals on January 26, 1980. Direct travel across the Egyptian–Israeli border was permitted. The Arab world pressured President Sadat against the agreement, and the day after the treaty was signed, nineteen of twenty-two Arab League member states met and agreed to impose political and economic sanctions on Egypt. As a result, Egypt was expelled from the Organization of Arab Petroleum Exporting Countries (OAPEC), the Islamic conference, and the Arab League. League headquarters moved from Cairo to Tunis. All Arab League members except Oman, Sudan, and, surprisingly, the PLO broke diplomatic relations with Egypt. Jordan was the first country to reestablish diplomatic ties in September 1984. Others followed later. Egypt rejoined the Arab League in May 1990. Although the treaty has been labeled a "cold peace," the conditions have generally held. The United States provided substantial financial assistance to each of the parties in exchange for signing the treaty.

11. *Title*:   The European Declaration

Date: June 13, 1980

Background: At various times after the 1973 war, Europeans expressed declaratory statements of positions toward resolving the Arab–Israeli dispute and continued to maintain their stand that any settlement should be pursued comprehensively, not in step-by-step fashion, and should explicitly address the legitimate rights of the Palestinians. These points departed from U.S. policy. In response to their rejection of the Camp David Accords, some PLO leaders began discussions with various European statesmen of a plan for Israeli withdrawal from the occupied territories and the establishment of a Palestinian state. The leaders held an exchange of views on all aspects of the Middle East conflict, including the Egyptian–Israeli peace treaty and the growing tensions in the area. The statement issued by the European Economic Community Summit in Venice (nine countries) resulted from these considerations and contacts.

Features:

1. UN Resolutions 242 and 338 should govern settlement of the conflict.
2. The right to existence and security for all states in the region including Israel.
3. Justice for all peoples, which implies the recognition of the legitimate rights of the Palestinians.
4. Secure, recognized, and guaranteed borders for all states.
5. Peace-settlement guarantees provided by the United Nations.
6. A just solution for the Palestinians, including their right to self-determination.
7. Negotiations to include the Palestine Liberation Organization.
8. No unilateral initiatives to change the status of Jerusalem.
9. Freedom of access to the holy places for everyone.

Reactions: Israel, reject. Palestinians, accept.

Implementation: The Camp David process, led by the United States, dominated the Great Power peace strategy at this time. In addition, various members of the European community were not of one voice on all of the issues pertaining to Arab–Israeli problems, and thus leadership for the peace process continued to reside with the United States.

12. *Title*:   The Fahd Plan
Date: August 8, 1981
Background: During 1981, Israel engaged in fighting in Lebanon involving Syrian forces, the United States announced a massive arms-sales package to Saudi Arabia including AWACS radar-defense planes, Israeli warplanes destroyed the nuclear reactor in Iraq, and by the summer, Israeli and Palestinian forces were directly involved in fighting in southern Lebanon. In July, an Israel–PLO cease-fire, mediated by Saudi Arabia and the United States, was put into effect. Shortly thereafter, Crown Prince Fahd of Saudi Arabia revealed a proposal that had been drafted jointly with the PLO.

Features:

1. Israeli evacuation of all Arab territories seized during the 1967 Middle East war, including the Arab sector of Jerusalem.
2. Dismantling the settlements set up by Israel on the occupied lands after the 1967 war.
3. Guaranteeing freedom of religious practices for all religions in the Jerusalem holy shrines.
4. Asserting the rights of the Palestinian people and compensating those Palestinians who do not wish to return to their homeland.
5. Commencing a transitional period in the West Bank of Jordan and the Gaza Strip under supervision for a duration not exceeding a few months.
6. Setting up a Palestinian state, with East Jerusalem as its capital.
7. Affirming the right of all countries of the region to live in peace.
8. Guaranteeing the implementation of these principles by the United Nations or some of its member states.

Reactions: Israel, reject. Palestinians, accept.
Implementation: The idea behind this peace plan was to consolidate a single Arab negotiating position in order to strengthen the case for the PLO objectives. However, the plan failed to win acceptance at the Arab Summit held in November 1981 due to political divisions among the Arab states. The following year, at the Arab Summit in Fez, the plan was essentially approved, with some minor amendments.

13. *Title*:   The Reagan Plan
Date: September 1, 1982
Background: On June 6, 1982, Israel invaded Lebanon with a major attack against PLO forces. The Cairo Agreement of October 1969 had designated southern Lebanon and indigenous Palestinian refugee camps as under PLO con-

trol, which gave the organization considerable independence. The goals of the Israeli invasion were both military and political—to eliminate the direct PLO threat against Israeli territory and to destroy PLO leadership. The fighting led to a cease-fire and agreement, brokered by the United States, allowing the PLO to evacuate to other countries, none bordering on Israel. The departure was completed by September 2. President Reagan, in a televised address, saw this moment as an opportunity for fresh thinking and renewed effort to continue the Camp David peace process.

Features:

1. Resolution 242 remains the cornerstone for peace.
2. Negotiations are the only way to reconcile the legitimate security interests of Israel with the legitimate rights of the Palestinians.
3. The Arab states and the Palestinians must recognize Israel.
4. Jordan and the Palestinians must participate in the peace process.
5. West Bank and Gaza:

   a. A self-governing authority should be created through free elections.

   b. Israel should adopt a settlement freeze.

   c. A five-year transition period is needed to evaluate results.

   d. The final status of the West Bank should be self-government by the Palestinians in association with Jordan.

   e. Jerusalem must remain undivided, its final status decided through negotiation.

Reactions: Israel, reject. Palestinians, nonacceptance (no outright rejection).

Implementation: Shortly after the Reagan Plan was presented, the Arab Summit was held in Fez, where a peace plan was adopted that contained considerable overlap with Reagan's points. King Hussein of Jordan tried to reach agreement with the PLO for joint participation in the plan as specified, but failed. Jordan was not drawn into the peace process, so the initiation offered by Reagan was not pursued further.

14. *Title*:   The Fez Plan
Date: September 9, 1982
Background: The Arab Summit held in Fez, Morocco, quickly convened after the PLO forces were withdrawn from Lebanon, to reaffirm their support for the Palestinian people in their struggle to recover "inalienable national rights." The Arab League members voted unanimously to accept the plan.

Features:

1. The withdrawal of Israel from all Arab territories occupied in 1967 including Jerusalem.
2. The dismantling of settlements established by Israel on the Arab territories after 1967.
3. The guarantee of freedom of worship and practice of religious rites for all religions in the holy shrines.

4. The reaffirmation of the Palestinian people's right to self-determination and the exercise of its imprescriptible and inalienable national rights under the leadership of the Palestine Liberation Organization, its sole and legitimate representative, and the indemnification of all those who do not desire to return.

5. Placing the West Bank and Gaza Strip under the control of the United Nations for a transitory period not exceeding a few months.

6. The establishment of an independent Palestinian state, with Jerusalem as its capital.

7. The UN Security Council guarantees peace among all states of the region, including the independent Palestinian state.

8. The UN Security Council guarantees the respect of these principles.

Reactions: Israel, reject. Palestinians, accept.

Implementation: There were considerable overlaps between the Fahd Plan of 1981 and the Fez proposal, both of which represent first efforts at a joint Arab peace declaration. Top Arab leaders and a senior Palestinian representative discussed contents of the plan with the five countries that are permanent members of the UN Security Council. In the end, little support was given to the plan overall, and it was abandoned.

15. *Title*:   Jordanian–Palestinian Agreement

Date: February 11, 1985

Background: Following the PLO military loss in Beirut in 1982, a split in the organization during 1983 into reactionist and mainstream forces, and a major threat to Arafat's position of power, coupled with Jordan's wish to be part of the Middle East process, King Hussein agreed to host a Palestine National Council meeting in Amman in 1984 in an effort to make amends with the Palestinian leadership.

The Palestinian–Jordanian association was important to each group, since their joint fate seemed bound together in the future status of the West Bank: the majority of Jordanian citizens were Palestinians; the West Bank, formerly under Jordanian sovereignty, was populated with Palestinians; and since 1974 the PLO had been regarded as the sole representative of the Palestinian people.

Features:

1. Land in exchange for peace as cited in the UN resolutions, including the Security Council resolution.

2. The Palestinian people's right to self-determination. The Palestinians should exercise their inalienable right to self-determination when the Jordanians and the Palestinians manage to achieve this within the framework of an Arab confederation that is intended to be established between the two states of Jordan and Palestine.

3. Solving the Palestinian refugees problem in accordance with the UN resolutions.

4. Solving all aspects of the Palestine question.

5. Based on this, peace negotiations should be held within the framework of an international conference to be attended by the five UN Security Council permanent member

states and all parties to the conflict, including the PLO, which is the Palestinian people's sole legitimate representative, within a joint delegation—a joint Jordanian-Palestinian delegation.

Reactions: Israel, reject. Palestinians, accept.

Implementation: Several months after the agreement, King Fahd, President Hosni Mubarak, and King Hussein visited the United States to solicit support for the idea of an international conference. King Hussein proposed lists of Palestinians for the joint Jordanian–Palestinian delegation, but since the PLO did not accept Resolutions 242 and 338, the United States declined to meet with the representatives. During September and October of 1985, the Palestinians were involved in several acts of violence, which damaged the diplomatic efforts behind the peace plan. In February 1986, King Hussein repudiated the plan, relations with the PLO deteriorated, and the following year Arafat and the PNC also repudiated the agreement in an effort to mend differences with PLO opposition factions.

16. *Title*: The Shultz Plan

Date: March 4, 1988

Background: With the fall of the Jordanian–Palestinian agreement, King Hussein continued to push the idea of an international peace conference for solving Middle East problems with Israel. Shimon Peres, who was serving in an unusual Israeli political coalition with Shamir, was willing to go along with the idea, but Shamir was opposed. In November 1987, an Arab Summit in Amman reaffirmed that such a conference ought to be held. By December a general uprising in the West Bank and Gaza territories shifted the focus of the conflict and negotiation strategy. U.S. Secretary of State Shultz began another diplomatic initiative aimed at resolving the current crisis. In letters to Prime Minister Shamir and King Hussein, he outlined his plan.

Features:

1. A comprehensive peace providing for the security of all states in the region and for the legitimate rights of the Palestinian people.

2. Negotiations to be based on UN Resolution 242.

3. An international conference would convene to serve as the forum for the negotiations.

4. Negotiations between Israel and a Jordanian–Palestinian delegation to address the Palestinian issue.

5. Palestinians would be represented in a Jordanian-Palestinian delegation.

6. Timetable for implementation:

Beginning: International conference would convene with Israel, Syria, Egypt, a Jordanian-Palestinian delegation, the United States, the Soviet Union, China, Britain, and France. All participants must accept UN Resolutions 242 and 338 and renounce violence and terrorism. The conference would have a continuing role but could not veto or impose a settlement.

One month later: Israel and "each of its neighbors" would begin six months of negotiations on an interim phase of self-administration for Palestinians living in the West Bank and Gaza Strip, including election of an administrative council by Palestinians.

Seven months later: Talks, to last one year, would begin between Israel and a Jordanian-Palestinian delegation on the final status of occupied territories. An interim phase of self-administration would not go into effect until these talks had begun.

One year later: Talks on the final status of occupied territories would conclude.

Two years later: Effective date for agreement on the final status of occupied territories.

Reactions: Israel, Peres accept, but Shamir reject. Palestinians, reject.

Implementation: The dynamics of the intifada led the Palestinians to reject their role in a combined Jordanian delegation, Shultz refused to meet with PLO members (because they had not accepted UN Resolution 242), Jordan in July announced its formal break with the West Bank, and a new U.S. administration came to power in January 1989, thus undermining the Shultz effort. Basic ideas of the plan were, however, picked up later.

17. *Title*:   Algiers Summit Communiqué

Date: June 7–9, 1988

Background: In response to the Palestinian intifada taking place in the West Bank and Gaza, member Arab League states convened an emergency session to investigate the ways and means for supporting the uprising and bolstering its effectiveness. As declared in the communiqué, "Out of commitment to their national and historical responsibilities, the Arab heads of state examined the present and future challenges facing the Arab nation, and the perils besetting it in this highly critical phase of its history, and reaffirmed their resolve to safeguard national security and protect Arab land."

Features:

1. Commitment to provide the Palestinian people with all forms and types of assistance needed to continue resistance and massive revolt under the leadership of the PLO until the attainment of inalienable national rights.

2. The UN Security Council should force Israel to comply with UN resolutions and provisions of international conventions to stop repressive and inhuman practices.

3. The UN Security Council should work toward securing an immediate and total withdrawal of Israel from the occupied Arab territories and should place the Palestinian territories under a provisional UN mandate to protect their citizens and guarantee the Palestinian people in the exercise of inalienable national rights.

4. The Fez Plan of 1982 should provide the basis for solving the Arab–Israeli conflict.

5. An international conference sponsored by the United Nations should be held, to include participation of the five permanent members of the Security Council and all parties to the conflict including the PLO, the sole, legitimate representative of the Palestinian people, on an equal footing and with the same rights as the other parties.

6. The Arab economic boycott of Israel should continue so long as territorial occupation exists.

Reaction: Israel, reject. Palestinians, accept.

Implementation: The following month King Hussein renounced his claims to the West Bank, and in November 1988 the Palestine National Council proclaimed the establishment of an independent Palestinian state. By December, Arafat had addressed the United Nations at a special meeting in Geneva, where he called on Israel to join in peace talks and publicly stated the PLO's acceptance of UN Resolutions 242 and 338 and its rejection of terrorism. The following day the United States opened a dialogue with the PLO, over Israeli objections. The intifada continued.

18.   *Title*:   The Shamir Plan
Date: May 14, 1989
Background: The intifada continued, and Israel, in January 1989, deported a number of Palestinians suspected of leading the resistance. The following month Prime Minister Shamir stated he would remove some of the Israeli troops from the main population centers in occupied territories when the local residents agreed to accept political autonomy as the first stage for a settlement of the general problem. U.S. Secretary of State Baker met with Israeli officials in March and pressured Israel to reduce tensions in the West Bank. The document of Palestinian autonomy and local elections was presented the next month to U.S. President George Bush, who expressed support for the plan.

Features:

1. Israel yearns for peace and the continuation of the political process by means of direct negotiations based on the principles of UN Resolutions 242 and 338 and the Camp David Accords.

2. Israel opposes the establishment of an additional Palestinian state in the Gaza district and in the area between Israel and Jordan.

3. Israel will not conduct negotiations with the PLO.

4. Israel calls for the establishment of peace relations with Arab states for the purpose of promoting a comprehensive settlement of the Arab–Israeli conflict, including recognition, direct negotiations, ending the boycott, diplomatic relations, cessation of hostile activity in international institutions or forums, and regional and bilateral cooperation.

5. Israel calls for a resolution of the refugee problem in Judea, Samaria, and Gaza to improve living conditions.

6. Israel proposes free and democratic elections among the Palestinian Arab inhabitants of Judea, Samaria, and Gaza in an atmosphere devoid of violence, threats, and terror.

a. In these elections a representation will be chosen to conduct negotiations for a transitional period of self-rule.

b. A proposal of regional elections should be adopted, with details determined in further discussions.

c. The elections shall be free, democratic, and secret.

d. Every Palestinian Arab residing in Judea, Samaria, or Gaza who is elected by the inhabitants to represent them—after submitting candidacy in accordance with the detailed document that will determine the subject of the elections—may be a legitimate participant in the conduct of negotiations with Israel.

7. During the transition period:

a. The Palestinian Arab inhabitants of Judea, Samaria, and Gaza will be accorded self-rule, by means of which they will, themselves, conduct their affairs of daily life.

b. Israel will continue to be responsible for security, foreign affairs, and all matters concerning Jewish settlers in Judea, Samaria, and Gaza.

c. Topics involving the implementation of the plan for self-rule will be considered and decided within the framework of the negotiations for an interim agreement.

d. The transition period will last for five years, and not later than the third year after the establishment of self-rule, negotiations for a permanent solution will begin.

8. Participants in the negotiation:

a. For the transition period: Israel and elected representation of the Palestinian Arab inhabitants of Judea, Samaria, and Gaza; Jordan and Egypt will be invited to participate.

b. For the permanent solution: Israel, elected representation of the Palestinian Arab inhabitants of Judea, Samaria, and Gaza, and Jordan. Egypt will be invited to participate.

9. Timetable for implementation:

a. First, dialogue and basic agreement by the Palestinian Arab inhabitants of Judea, Samaria, and Gaza, as well as Egypt and Jordan if they wish to take part, in the negotiations on the principles constituting the initiative.

b. Immediately afterward, the stage of preparations and implementations of the election process in which a representation of the Palestinian Arab inhabitants of Judea, Samaria, and Gaza will be elected.

c. During the preparations and implementations of the election process, there will be a calming of violence in Judea, Samaria, and Gaza.

d. Immediately after the elections, negotiations shall be conducted for an interim agreement for the transition period.

e. Not later than the third year after the establishment of self-rule, negotiations for a permanent solution begin. During the whole period of these negotiations until the signing of the agreement for a permanent solution, the self-rule shall continue in effect as determined in the negotiations for an interim agreement.

Reactions: Israel, accept. Palestinians, reject.

Implementation: The Palestinians rejected the Shamir Plan, viewing it as an Israeli maneuver that was without substance. The PLO, in turn, presented its own election plan shortly thereafter, and this was followed by a formal statement by Secretary Baker, an Egyptian plan, and a U.S.-sponsored Middle East formula, all of which addressed the specifics of election procedures raised in the Shamir plan.

19. *Title*: The PLO Election Plan

Date: May 21, 1989

Background: Bassam Abu Sharif, the special advisor to Arafat, prepared this program in response to the Shamir proposal.

Features:

1. The Palestinian Liberation Organization supports the holding of elections in the West Bank and Gaza to choose representatives freely and democratically. But we Palestinians are in favor of a truly democratic choice—not a sham democracy.

2. The substance of this package is the two-state solution. The state of Israel will live in peace side by side with the state of Palestine, which will be confederated with Jordan. An international guaranteed peace agreement will protect the interests of all parties, including the Palestinians and the Israelis.

3. A beginning of the withdrawal of Israeli forces and their replacement by international or multinational forces, according to an internationally assured timetable.

4. Election of representatives from the West Bank and Gaza to a legitimate body of the Palestinian people. The Israeli withdrawal need not be complete before elections are held, but Israeli soldiers and armed settlers should not be in any position to hinder or endanger voters.

5. The elections should be monitored and observed internationally to guarantee freedom of choice and protection of those elected—so that they do not suffer the same fate as did those elected in 1976.

6. A transitional period under international or multinational auspices. During this time, the Palestinian legislative assembly will elect an executive body, which will select a team to negotiate with Israel.

7. An international peace conference convened on the basis of UN Resolutions 242 and 338 that takes into consideration the deplorable conditions being endured by the Palestinians in the West Bank and Gaza. At this conference all parties in the Middle East conflict can raise any question for discussion or negotiation.

8. The PLO wants a comprehensive peace that will safeguard future generations, both Palestinian and Israeli. The PLO will continue its efforts to establish such a peace in cooperation with all parties concerned.

Reactions: Israel, reject. Palestinians, accept.

Implementation: None.

20. *Title*: The Baker Initiative

Date: May 22, 1989

Background: Secretary Baker delivered a speech to the American Israel Public Affairs Committee in Washington in which he highlighted the central features underlying the U.S. position toward resolving the Arab–Israeli conflict, particularly in light of recent developments concerning negotiations and election procedures for the West Bank.

Features:

1. A comprehensive settlement achieved through negotiations based on UN Resolutions 242 and 338.

2. Direct negotiations between the parties over territory for peace, security and recognition of Israel, and Palestinian political rights.

3. An international conference might be appropriate, but only if it does not interfere with, replace, or substitute for direct talks.

4. A settlement for self-government of Palestinians in the West Bank and Gaza in a manner acceptable to Palestinians, Israel, and Jordan.

5. Commitment to a process of negotiations clearly tied to the search for a permanent settlement of the conflict.

6. A workable free, fair election process for Arab inhabitants in the West Bank and Gaza.

7. Arabs should take concrete steps toward accommodation with Israel: end the economic boycott, end challenges to Israel's standing in international organizations, and repudiate the line that Zionism is racism.

8. Israel should give up the vision of a Greater Israel, forswear annexation of the West Bank, stop settlement activity, and allow Palestinian schools to reopen in the West Bank.

9. Palestinians should practice constructive diplomacy, amend the PLO covenant, and give up violent tactics.

10. The Soviet Union should restore diplomatic ties with Israel and help promote a serious peace process.

Reactions: Israel, reject. Palestinians, accept.

Implementation: The Israelis not only rejected Baker's approach, but in July the Likud party took further steps against the election process by formulating a policy barring the Arab residents of East Jerusalem from participation and by postponing any elections until the end of the Palestinian uprising. Jewish settlements on the West Bank continued. Later that month, Shamir and Jamil Tarifi, a prominent West Bank lawyer with ties to the PLO, admitted they had met and discussed election proposals. Shamir was criticized by right-wing Israeli leaders who regarded the talks as indirect negotiations with the PLO. During the summer, Israel announced that it would gradually reopen schools on the West Bank that had been closed as part of the campaign to stop the Palestinian intifada. Diplomatic ties at the consular level between Israel and the Soviet Union were reestablished on January 2, 1991.

21. *Title*:   The Egyptian Plan

Date: September 16, 1989

Background: As a result of ideas presented in the Shamir Plan and the Baker speech, Egypt, formally welcomed back into the Arab League in May after a ten year suspension from the organization as punishment for signing a peace treaty with Israel, agreed to become involved in the process of designing election procedures for Arab inhabitants of the West Bank and Gaza. As a first step, Egypt agreed to host negotiations between Palestinians and Israelis in order to get the two sides to sit down for a dialogue.

Features:

1. All Palestinians in the West Bank, Gaza, and East Jerusalem would be allowed to vote and run for office.

2. Candidates would be free to campaign without interference from the Israeli authorities.

3. Israel would allow international supervision of the election process.

4. Construction or expansion of Jewish settlements in the territories would be frozen during the election period.

5. The army would withdraw from the area of polling places on election day.

6. Only Israelis who live or work in the occupied territories would be permitted to enter them on election day.

7. Preparation for the election would take no longer than two months; Egypt and the United States could help form the Israeli–Palestinian committee for that effort.

8. Israel would agree to negotiate land in exchange for peace while also protecting its security.

9. The United States and Israel would publicly guarantee Israel's adherence to the points.

10. Israel would publicly agree in advance to accept the outcome of the election.

Reactions: Israel, Shamir reject, but Peres accept. Palestinians, reject.

Implementation: One of the direct results of this plan was the following formula presented by U.S. Secretary Baker several weeks later.

22. *Title*:   The Baker Five-Point Mideast Formula

Date: October 8, 1989

Background: Efforts at finding a workable Middle East peace framework were now focused on how to arrange preliminary talks between Israelis and Palestinians so that they could discuss the technicalities of organizing elections in the West Bank. This was the starting point noted in the Shamir Plan presented five months earlier. To clarify features in the Egyptian Plan and provide avenues that both sides would be able to accept, Secretary Baker put forth a specific plan reflecting the U.S. role in this process.

Features:

1. There is agreement that an Israeli delegation should conduct a dialogue with a Palestinian delegation in Cairo.
2. Egypt cannot substitute itself for the Palestinians. Egypt will consult with Palestinians on all aspects of that dialogue. Egypt will also consult with Israel and the United States.
3. Israel will attend the dialogue only after a satisfactory list of Palestinians has been worked out.
4. Israel will come to the dialogue on the basis of the Israeli government's May 14 initiative. Palestinians will come to the dialogue prepared to discuss elections and the negotiating process in accordance with Israel's initiative.
5. Palestinians would be free to raise issues that relate to their opinions on how to make elections and the negotiating process succeed.
6. To facilitate this process, the United States proposes that the foreign ministers of Israel, Egypt, and the United States meet in Washington first.

Reactions: Israel, approve then reject. Palestinians, accept.

Implementation: By March 1990, Prime Minister Shamir refused to accept the Baker plan, and the government of Israel, which had voted in favor of the plan 9–3 (by an "inner cabinet" group) in November 1989, collapsed. The leadership crisis was finally resolved on June 8, when a new government was formed, but it declared resistance to any concessions to reach peace with the Palestinians. Secretary Baker rebuked the Iraelis for stalling and rejecting his compromise formula for talks with Palestinians and complained that the new government was posing more obstacles to negotiations. "When you're serious about peace, call us," he said, and he then recited the White House telephone number. President Bush, meanwhile, broke off U.S.–PLO talks on June 20 because the organization refused to condemn an unsuccessful speedboat raid on Israel in May. During that month there was a new flare-up of violence between Israelis and Palestinians, and it appeared that PLO factions were involved.

On August 2, 1990, Iraq invaded Kuwait, Arafat and the PLO sided with Saddam Hussein, and U.S. forces were dispatched to Saudi Arabia to oppose the Iraqi moves. The worldwide coalition, led by the United States, demanded Iraqi withdrawal from the territory of Kuwait, the Arab League voted to send troops to support U.S. intervention in Saudi Arabia, and on August 12, Saddam Hussein offered to link Iraqi withdrawal from Kuwait to an Israeli withdrawal from occupied territories. The United States (and Israel) opposed such crossover connections between the Gulf crisis and the Middle East's other problems. The Bush administration wanted to free Kuwait first before returning to broader Middle East settlements.

From the outbreak of the Gulf crisis in August, the Arab alliance against Iraq wanted a wider settlement of Middle East issues, including resolution of the Israeli–Palestinian dispute. On October 8, 1990, violence erupted in Jerusalem on the Temple Mount, resulting in nineteen Palestinian deaths by Israeli police.

Later that month the UN Security Council voted to condemn Israeli security forces and asked for a UN investigation. The Israeli government rejected the terms of such an inquiry. A few weeks later, another resolution was presented that was originally intended to stress (a) UN monitoring of Palestinian protection in the West Bank and (b) Security Council endorsement for an international peace conference. The U.S. delegation sought to separate these two issues, arguing that although the United States earlier had accepted the International Conference idea in the Shultz and Baker initiative, the problem of trading concessions on the Palestinian question with Iraq's withdrawal from Kuwait now arose. U.S. policy is firmly opposed to such linkage across issue areas. To avoid a U.S. veto, the Security Council created a compromise resolution (number 681), which was passed unanimously, 15–0, on December 20, 1990. The resolution has two points: Israel's deportation of Palestinians in the West Bank is deplored, and the UN Security Council seeks to protect Palestinians in the Israeli-occupied territories and calls for UN monitoring of their safety through the offices of the Secretary-General.

It is not clear whether the monitoring can be carried out, in light of Israel's opposition to the program. The concept of the international peace conference, long supported by the Arab delegations and the PLO, specifically was included in a separate, nonbinding statement by the council president. Although the resolution is not a peace proposal, the fact that diplomatic maneuvering included extended discussions about an international conference to settle the Arab–Israeli conflict is important to the development of positional bargaining on this issue.

The Gulf War began on January 17, 1991, effectively setting aside the idea of a peaceful resolution in the Middle East. On that same day, two key PLO leaders were assassinated in Tunisia. A few weeks later, another Palestinian policymaker was shot down on the streets of occupied Kuwait. Fighting continued between Palestinian and Israeli forces in Lebanon.

The Gulf War ended in a provisional truce at the end of February, 1991. By April, a UN-sponsored permanent cease-fire was in effect. Since then, the Americans have been actively involved with all parties to the Arab–Israeli conflict, encouraging them to participate in the peace process by discussing outstanding issues in a formal negotiation environment, most likely an international peace conference.

Summary

It is evident from the content of these peace plans that positional bargaining strategy has been dominant in all negotiation efforts. Routinely, each side adopts a position and becomes fully committed to that policy stance. Because the parties are in conflict, a negotiation proposal produced by one of them tends to emphasize points that it finds agreeable but that the other side rejects. The disputants individually appear to be holding out for a fixed end that meets their exact conditions for settlement. This "digging in" strategy has stalled the resolution

process, since the only mode of compromising is through offering small concessions, piece by piece, which subsumes a great deal of time and effort.

In spite of the consistent differences on policy goals and positional bargaining
strategies used to pursue them, the parties *have* changed their substantive positions on at least one key point over the past four decades. At the time of the
UN partition resolution in 1947, the Zionists were willing to accept a two-state
solution, whereas the Arabs rejected such a plan. In the post–1967 war environment, however, the Israelis have opposed any designs for a two-state solution,
whereas the Palestinians have embraced the idea. But by merely reversing their
stands on this issue, the parties are no closer to a resolution, and the conflict
intensity remains.

The negotiation pattern practiced by the United States, as an interested Great
Power outsider, has also followed positional bargaining procedures. The U.S.
plans, including initiatives by Reagan in 1982, Shultz in 1988, and Baker in
1989, have tried to accommodate the wishes of *both* sides and incorporate features
favorable to positions adopted separately by Israel and the Palestinians. For
example, Reagan mentions a settlement freeze for Jews in the West Bank (a
pro-Palestinian position) and urges a political association between Palestinians
and Jordan (a pro-Israeli position) in his set of negotiation items; Shultz likewise
pushes for the Palestinian–Jordanian affiliation and suggests an international
conference as a vehicle to discuss such issues (a pro-Palestinian position); and
Baker goes further in trying to meet the demands of each side by suggesting
direct negotiations between the parties (a pro-Israeli position) in addition to an
international conference. This strategy has failed because the total package of
items in the negotiation set includes statements that each side refuses to accept.

The specific issue of negotiation participants is another area that demonstrates
the application of positional bargaining. Since 1974, the Palestinians and the
Arab League have accepted the premise that the PLO is the sole, legitimate
representative of the Palestinian people. The PLO not only is the natural political
partner but is the only group with the vested authority to engage in diplomatic
efforts to structure the Palestinians' future. Yet, the Israeli government has
steadfastly refused to meet with the organization, stating explicitly in the Shamir
Plan that it will not conduct negotiations with the PLO. Although there may be
elaborate and persuasive reasons for each side to stress its respective policy, the
bargaining rigidity has had a negative effect on negotiation progress in the Arab–
Israeli conflict.

The conflicting parties have made some progress in closing the bargaining
space between them through their positional bargaining negotiation strategies.
The primary result has been narrowing the set of issues for discussion. For
example, the plans generated by various groups since the intifada (Shultz Initiative, Shamir Plan, Egyptian Plan, Baker Plan) have progressively focused on
smaller and smaller areas of difference, so that the real issue now becomes the
selection of Palestinian representatives for the dialogue to take place as a first
step toward eventual elections in the West Bank. Election details have not been

developed fully, the meaning of self-rule is still in dispute, procedures for implementing stages toward independence for Palestinians are not discussed, and the land-for-peace exchange—which was to frame the negotiations overall, as outlined in Resolution 242—no longer operates as a central guideline in the bargaining. It is true that Israeli security and recognition, alongside Palestinian legitimate rights, are seen as the significant issues that must be addressed in any peace proposal. Yet, there has been no serious plan that adequately deals with the desires of both parties simultaneously. The positional bargaining strategy is not working.

Altogether, the efforts expended by all the parties—Israel, the Palestinians, the United States, the United Nations, and others—have not been successful in resolving the central problems in Middle East politics. Still, some common points have evolved on which the disputants are in agreement. The first area of agreement is the principle of a land-for-peace exchange, which emerged after the 1967 war. The second item of agreement is that negotiations should be the method for resolving party differences. The third agreement is that self-rule ought to be established through elections by Palestinians. The agreements can stand because they are general; the specific mechanics have not been worked out. Such themes, however, do suggest a basis for sustaining the peace process and evolving it into a strategy of bargaining that is governed by the principled negotiation rules advocated by Fisher and Ury.

The three points of agreement contain separate, constructive aspects that are relevant in a principled negotiation situation. They have not been primary movers in successful negotiation, however, due to the dominance of positional bargaining. First, the land-for-peace theme shows that a basic *principle as precedent* can help to guide the lines of negotiation. Second, an official stand that parties are committed to negotiation is a first step toward admitting a willingness to consider *trust* of the enemy. Third, the common but vague agreement on elections and self-rule for the Palestinians can serve as a catalyst for parties to invent *creative ideas*, a broad set of options that may be acceptable to everyone. Each of these underlying themes that can foster movement toward principled negotiation procedures will be examined below.

PRINCIPLED NEGOTIATION

To see how a principled negotiation strategy fits into the Arab–Israeli conflict resolution environment, we will examine three different types of applications. First, as an example of *principle as precedent*, the origins of UN Council Resolution 242, which was unanimously adopted in November 1967, are discussed. Because many today still feel this statement is the essence for a just solution and lasting peace, its contents and the political strategy for its adoption are very important. Second, a directly grafted illustration of the Fisher-Ury guidelines to the Middle East conflict has been specifically worked out by Harold H. Saunders. The ideas in his book *The Other Walls: The Politics of the Arab–Israeli Peace*

Process (1985), which describes ways to build *trust* and stresses the importance of overcoming human barriers to start negotiations, are presented. Third, the ultimate, substantive issues and *creative idea* generation that will have to be brought into any final settlement are examined by looking at Gidon Gottlieb's suggestions presented in his article "Israel and the Palestinians" (1989). His approach is to show how parties and outside negotiators can capitalize on existing principles of agreement through the promotion of "new thinking" to bypass frustration and to ease tension.

Principle as Precedent

Resolution 242 remains the basic framework for negotiations and peace in the Middle East. Cited continuously in peace plans offered since then, it presents ideas that most parties to the conflict find acceptable. However, there would have been no such resolution without ambiguities. Resolution 242 was unanimously adopted only because it was clearly understood beforehand that the fifteen affirmative votes would be cast with each member expressing an individual interpretation to explain the vote. The essence of the resolution is the land-for-peace exchange principle.

The U.S. interpretation has been that Resolution 242 did not call for total Israeli withdrawal, that the final secure and recognized borders were a matter of negotiation between the two sides, and that the pre–June 1967 lines were neither endorsed nor precluded as the final peace boundaries. The U.S.S.R. interpretation has continued to be that the resolution called for total Israeli withdrawal from the territories occupied during the June war. The differing interpretations are relevant in that the ambiguities of 242 allow a choice; things are not predetermined (Sisco, introduction to Caradon, Goldberg, El-Zayyat, and Eban, 1981:ix). Security Council Resolution 242 continues to be necessarily broad and ambiguous and at the same time somewhat specific to provide a basis for further negotiation progress. This allows the participants to refer to the resolution to justify their position.

Lord Caradon, the British Permanent Representative to the United Nations in 1967 and sponsor of the Resolution, has explained the substance and strategy that made possible its unanimous adoption and why it continues to serve as a basis for negotiations between the parties. He stated that during the previous summer, in the UN General Assembly, there had been long, frustrating debates, with no indication or possibility of agreement. Both Arabs and Israelis and the superpowers were arguing for opposite proposals. "It seemed," wrote Lord Caradon, "that the Middle East was doomed to continue the center of a bitter and deep-seated and irreconcilable dispute which would divide the world and lead on in the end to another conflict on a far wider scale" (Caradon et al., 1981:4).

He went on to say that personal and private discussions with various representatives from the concerned countries showed that it might be possible to escape from complete deadlock, that there might be some hope of a positive outcome. "Not agreement, that often seemed beyond the prospect of attainment—but some positive plan to prevent another conflict," as he cautiously wrote (Caradon, 1981:5). His approach, when introducing the resolution to the Council, followed the guidelines of Fisher and Ury's principled negotiation and focused on common, rather than divergent, interests. He said:

The Arab countries insist that we must direct our special attention to the recovery of the territories. The Israelis tell us that withdrawal must never be to the old precarious peace but to secure boundaries. Both are right. The aims of the two sides do not conflict. To imagine that one can be secured without the other is a delusion. They are of equal validity and equal necessity. We want not a victory in New York but a success in the Middle East. (Caradon, 1981:5)

Yet, the fate of the resolution was actually in doubt until the final vote was taken. The Soviet Union had put down a rival resolution that could have captured some positive votes, and their Deputy Foreign Minister V. V. Kuznetsov asked for a postponement on the vote. On the occasion of the actual voting, there was a good deal of uncertainty and tension. As Caradon (1981:6) described it:

I knew Kuznetsov very well. I had worked with him on other difficult issues. I greatly respected him. When he said, "I am personally asking you for two days," I knew that he could not work against me. I thought he might even be thinking of abstaining on the British Resolution. I knew I could trust him as he trusted me. I went back into the Council and said that a last-minute request had been made for a postponement of this all-important vote. I asked for a postponement until the following Wednesday evening.

So on the Wednesday the Council met again. There could be no more postponement now. This was the culmination of all our efforts. We listened to a long speech from the representative of Syria, and then unexpectedly we were called to vote, when I had imagined that this final debate would go on all night.

The President of the Council called for a vote first on the British Resolution, which had been down first. I raised my hand to vote for it. And then there was a cheer from the galleries. I looked to my right to see Kuznetsov's finger raised voting for our resolution and withdrawing his own, thus making the vote for the British Resolution 242 unanimous.

He had made good use of the two days. He had come to the conclusion that a unanimous vote and full agreement were essential. He had gone back to his Government and, I have no doubt, to Arab Governments too, and he had persuaded them.

When I was in London a few days later on other business, satisfaction was expressed about a unanimous vote in the United Nations on such a difficult and dangerous issue. I wrote to the *London Times* to say that the main credit for the unanimous Resolution must go to Deputy Foreign Minister Kuznetsov.

We have maintained our friendship. At times of subsequent crises in the Middle East he has sometimes sent me a personal message—"Our Resolution is still doing well." After the unanimous vote in the council that day I said, "The Resolution which we have prepared is not a British text: it is the result of close and prolonged consultation with both sides and with all Members of the Council. As I have respectfully said every Member of the Council has made a contribution in the search for common ground on which we can go forward.''

Resolution 242 not only set out balanced principles for a peaceful settlement based on the equal requirements of withdrawal and security. Both were essential and interdependent, according to Caradon (1981:9). It also provided for the action to put those principles into effect. The intent of the resolution was not to write a peace treaty or set out in detail what the final settlement should be, but to propose certain principles that could form the basis for a comprehensive settlement, which could be accomplished only in stages.

Some twelve years after the resolution was passed, Lord Caradon reemphasized the validity of Security Council 242 as the basis for the ultimate goal of a comprehensive settlement of the Arab–Israeli conflict. Primary in this plan is acceptance by all parties of Israel's right to exist and to live in peace in the region, and withdrawal of Israel from territories occupied in 1967. Caradon also advocated that Resolution 242 is incomplete with respect to Palestinian rights, that they are a separate people with a right to their homeland. Here, he argued, the resolution might be supplemented—not, he emphasized, ''replaced, amended or distorted, but supplemented to meet this point'' (15).

Without advocating a reversal or reduction of the Resolution 242 principles, Caradon believes additions in a new resolution are needed to bring the original one up to date and provide for its implementation. A new resolution must deal with five main issues, all of which he considers ambitious aims, to be sure; but it should not be more difficult to decide on the action to carry out the principles and purposes than it was to agree on such far-reaching ideals in the first place in 1967. The issues concern cessation of all violence and all Israeli settlements in occupied territory; the creation of a boundary commission to make recommendations for secure and recognized borders; international trusteeship over East Jerusalem, the West Bank, and Gaza during which the Palestinians could control their own affairs through elections and self-determination; provisions for international guarantees and demilitarized zones to protect all states in the area; and a peace conference with everyone, including Palestinians, participating.

Lord Caradon (17) summarized these points, again in the spirit of principled negotiation, when he wrote, ''There is, I feel sure, a mounting awareness that peace cannot come from domination and animosity but must come from equal rights and mutual respect and reconciliation.'' He believes that the final settlement can come only from an international initiative, which means returning to the first principles of Resolution 242 coupled with a new initiative to supplement, extend, and implement the original resolution. He maintains that the resolution still provides an opportunity for peace, that its purpose and fairness are perfectly plain, and that questions and doubts about the main intentions arise from wishful thinking or natural prejudice, not genuine uncertainty (10).

Trust

Harold Saunders, author of *The Other Walls: The Politics of the Arab-Israeli Peace Process*, participated, as a U.S. official, in mediating five Arab–Israeli agreements during the 1970s. He argues that diplomacy and negotiation are human and psychological processes that involve a network of interrelated steps aimed at changing the political environment to make advances toward peace possible. He believes those obstacles can be eroded by acknowledgment on each side of the other's suffering and by open acceptance of a common humanity.

In this spirit, progress toward an Arab–Israeli settlement depends first on building the human and political environment necessary for sustained negotiation and breaking down the barriers to reconciliation, which he calls "the other walls." His advice is simple and in line with the principled negotiation approach: attack the barriers; prepare the political foundations.

Saunders has developed a framework of interconnected factors relevant to the prenegotiation stage in setting the contours for a favorable political environment. The first element is that the problem needs to be defined in one voice. Second, once this occurs, it becomes possible to build a commitment by the parties to negotiate their differences. At this point, third-party assistance may be useful to bring these things into focus. A fourth factor, developing empathy and sensitivity toward the positions of both parties, becomes important in order to bring them into active bargaining. The negotiation posture advocated by Saunders closely follows the guidelines of principled negotiations.

Defining the Conflict

A first step in focusing political efforts involves defining the conflict that the peace process is designed to resolve. Areas of wide disagreement exist, but to explore the possibilities for developing a basis for negotiation, one must identify points on which agreement is emerging. Some common points, stated "in different ways from different premises and with different objectives in mind," exist in the following areas (Saunders, 1985:17): (1) the objective of Middle East diplomacy should be to achieve a just peace in the Middle East; (2) a just peace requires international guarantees for peace among *all* states of the region; (3) peace among all states of the region will require Israeli withdrawal from territories occupied in 1967; (4) if Israel is to withdraw from territories occupied in 1967, there must be a transition period under an interim authority during which the political life and the security of the area from which Israel has withdrawn can be organized; and (5) freedom of worship and religious rights for all faiths concerned with the holy shrines of Jerusalem and the West Bank must be guaranteed.

Saunders argues that this gives common ground for negotiation, even though no common view of the prenature of the settlement yet exists. Each party must understand how the other side defines the problem and simultaneously acknowledges the existence of the other side, treating each other as individual human beings. Israelis and Arabs still define the problem in sharply different ways, and Saunders (24) recommends that a first task in trying to break down the barriers to negotiation is to understand what might change a party's picture of the problem.

Building Commitment to Negotiation

The most critical period in the peace process comes when leaders are deciding whether to commit themselves to a negotiated settlement (Saunders 1985:24). They have to judge whether a negotiated solution would be better than the present situation, whether a fair settlement could be fashioned that would be politically manageable, and whether the balance of forces would permit agreement on such a settlement. Before a new direction can be taken in this early period, the political environment must be rearranged. In preparing for negotiation, Saunders advises (27) both Israelis and Palestinians to envision a settlement that reflects the craving of both peoples for separate political expression of their identities and reflects how the land must be shared and to determine how the two parties would coexist there, specifically the nature of the relationship that would exist between the two peoples under a peace settlement. But here Sanders (28) finds a paradox. "The shape of a settlement, it seems, can become clear only in the middle of coexistence as defined through dialogue or negotiation, yet the dialogue does not begin partly because neither side can see the shape of a settlement it could live with."

One side may be ready to negotiate but may refuse to do so because it does not want the humiliation of offering to negotiate and finding that the adversary will not negotiate seriously. The judgments involved would require some understanding of what the other side really needs and wants, of leaders' strategy for achieving their aim, and of leaders' ability to develop political support for such a settlement. Each side must be able to believe that any concessions it makes can be reciprocated.

Progress toward negotiation requires an understanding and willingness to work with the politics of decision making. Serious negotiations will be possible only when leaders on each side begin to be concerned with presenting their positions so that the other side can see how its needs will be met (Saunders, 1985:30). A party may believe that the balance of power so favors the adversary that the adversary will not negotiate seriously. The Palestinians consider Israel so powerful militarily and in control of the West Bank and Gaza as to feel no pressure to negotiate. The Palestinians will not commit themselves to negotiation that would lay them open to criticism for beginning something and coming away with nothing. In Israel, de facto control over the territories is seen as preferable to any conceivable outcome from negotiation. The Israelis engage in superficial negotiation without really wanting an agreement.

Role of Third Parties

On the global stage, the Middle East states have consistently seen relationships with the big powers as a normal part of the regional political scene. Parties to the conflict look to third parties as facilitators, mediators, catalysts, or full partners to provide legitimacy or pressure for their efforts to negotiate peace.

In the Arab–Israeli conflict, the world community has faced a dilemma: it cannot impose a solution, but the parties to the conflict have not been able to find a solution for themselves. It is accepted that parties to the conflict must be parties to the peace, yet the parties to the conflict have been unable or unready to make peace and have consistently drawn outsiders into the efforts to achieve a settlement. Saunders's view is that the nature of third-party involvement should be determined by the extent to which the party is able and willing to contribute to the negotiation. The United States and the Soviet Union have legitimate interests in the Middle East. The issue in the Arab–Israeli peace process is thus how much political capital either nation is willing to spend in encouraging the Arab and Israeli parties toward serious negotiation and compromise (Saunders, 1985:110).

Developing Empathy and Sensitivity

To bring the parties to active negotiation, it is essential to identify the substantive and psychological issues facing political leaders who want to negotiate. This involves continuous "political reshaping" of the environment. Each side has political groups whose picture of the problem does not acknowledge the other side as having a share in the problem. Palestinians and Israelis have claims and histories in the same land, but many on each side act as if the other people and their claims do not exist. Each side's picture includes a judgment that the other side cannot accept it as part of a solution to the problem in ways consistent with its identity and dignity. In the exploratory period, the aim is to identify these aspects as human problems (Saunders, 1985:119). Saunders has suggested the following points to encourage the parties to negotiate in good faith.

To encourage Israelis (51–53):

1. Recognize the unique suffering of the Jewish people, particularly in the Nazi Holocaust.

2. Accept Israel as a state in the Middle East with the right to engage in the pursuits and relationships that are normal to states at peace.

3. Assure Israel's security in those relations.

4. Prepare to negotiate peace with Israel on a reciprocal basis.

5. Make such a clear and compelling offer to negotiate peace that Israelis will have no choice but to respond.

6. Take into account the psychological factors of a historic sense of belonging in the biblical lands, the suffering caused by centuries of persecution, a special sense of victimization, and the deep-rooted need for security and acceptance.

To encourage Palestinians (67–69):

1. Recognize the identity of Palestinians with the right of self-determination.
2. Recognize that Palestinians have suffered an injustice. They have been asked by history or by the world community to forfeit land and homes in order to create a national home for Jews, who have suffered by the actions of other peoples and civilizations.
3. Accept their humanity, their peoplehood, and their feelings of dignity.
4. Allow them to participate directly in any peace process.
5. Be sensitive to their view that other groups make efforts to divide them into moderates/extremists, PLO/non-PLO.
6. Allow them the greatest possible legitimacy in negotiating, which will include some blessing from the PLO.
7. Make gains from negotiating realistic and attractive enough to generate pressures that will reduce opportunities for dissidents to block the peace process.

From his analysis, approach, and assessments, Saunders (120) offers some propositions that he believes would help each side begin thinking of the other side as human, which would help advance the peace process. First, the more the two peoples have opportunities to meet as individuals with normal human, professional, and business concerns, rather than as occupier and occupied, the more difficult it will be for each side to treat the other as no more than a faceless mass. Second, the more each side is able to recognize the injustice that the other has suffered, the more each side recognizes the humanity of the other. Third, the more each side is willing to use an exploratory period to learn which gestures would be important in changing its picture of the other side, the more the other side will begin to change its own picture. Finally, the dialogue must explore how to develop a balance of forces that would allow a fair deal if parties negotiate. Leaders must convince leaders and people on the other side that they are prepared to make some of the concessions that would be necessary to produce an agreement with which both sides can live.

Saunders's analysis derives from his philosophy that mutual acknowledgment by Israelis and Palestinians of each other's humanity and pain, combined with acceptance of each other in relation to one's own integrity, would provide common ground for meeting. The Israelis' picture of their problem has been shaped over the decades by Arab leaders' threatening rhetoric. The Arabs' picture of the peace process after Camp David was shaped by Begin's rhetoric. The political question is not just *whether* the other side can accept but *what* one side can do to make it easier for the other side to accept. The essence of the peace process is to reshape the political environment along mutually agreeable lines that are also realistic politically.

Creative Ideas

Gottlieb (1989) promotes contours of a conceivable solution to the Arab–Israeli dispute based on fresh thinking about unfamiliar notions concerning communal conflict. He points out the gap between rhetoric and acceptable policy alternatives for all sides and suggests that focusing on areas of agreement will help alleviate fears and encourage the parties to pursue real negotiations further and in more creative ways. Whereas Saunders emphasized larger issues of sensitivity to human psychological dimensions and the importance of establishing a positive political climate for parties to consider serious negotiation, Gottlieb offers a list of items usually seen as points of contention, and shows the extent of agreement already in place.

Gottlieb sets the stage by asserting that Israelis and Palestinians alternate between a hard and a soft rhetoric. The hard speech of rejection gets the most attention, but underneath are the outlines of a conceivable formula acceptable to both sides. "The softer subtext suggests that Israel will be ready to offer maximal self-rule and political rights for the Palestinians in the West Bank and Gaza, the formula called 'self-rule plus' and that the Palestinians will be prepared to accept a 'demilitarized state' linked to Jordan" (Gottlieb, 1989:110). The principles involved in a possible solution are not those conventionally associated with mainline demands of either side but must be sought through the subtexts of broad themes. It is at this level that Palestinians and Israelis coincide, to a significant extent, in their positions.

Gottlieb's first advice is to avoid heavily laden code words that serve as symbols for hard-line policy demands. He includes here the concepts of "state," "withdrawal," "sovereignty," "self-determination," and "land for peace." These words are obstacles to open discourse on settlement options. They should be either abandoned in policy discussion or disaggregated into their individual components (112). Listed below are the specific areas where Gottlieb sees agreement between the parties or otherwise offers ways to circumvent the symbolic hard-line views.

The End of Israeli Rule over Palestinian Arabs

This issue is the key to any progress and, contrary to common opinion, is not a point of contention. "All sides agree that Israel should no longer rule over the more than 1.5 million inhabitants of the West Bank and Gaza. This principle is the foundation of the Camp David accords and is equally central to the Shamir initiative" (112).

Palestinian–Jordanian and Israeli Links

It is plain to see that both Israel and the PLO wish Jordan to play a key role in the permanent solution for the territories. The notion of a confederal link between Jordan and the Palestinians is generally accepted, although the PLO insists that independent statehood is sought. There are different images of "state" in international politics, and Israeli and Palestinian leaders speak of institutions common to the two peoples, encompassing economic, political, and functional concerns (113, 115).

Distinctions must be made between a confederation of a territorial nature, a confederation between states, and one between peoples. Likud may not be opposed to a confederation between the Palestinian people and Jordan, provided the issue of sovereignty can be sidestepped. Likud has long sought to solve the question of the rights and status of the Palestinian Arabs before the status of the land. A separation of the two issues—the political rights of a people and their territorial claims—is fundamental to any approach that the nationalist center is prepared to entertain. Flexible and innovative formulas can be found in the framework of the confederal idea. Complex political and juridical notions such as "state" and "republic" with all their ideological significance, will have to be adjusted to the specific, real, and symbolic needs of Israel and the Palestinians (115).

Foreign and Trade Relations

The Israeli concept of self-rule for the Palestinians excludes the conduct of foreign relations, but the Palestinians' aspiration for a state will turn foreign relations into a central issue when a permanent solution is negotiated. Yet, in a benign relationship, a confederation could be guided by principles of neutrality and demilitarization. It could be given international standing apart from Jordan and could acquire full membership in the community of nations. Such functional arrangements already exist, for example, in the BENELUX countries (116).

Ideology, State, and Homeland

There is a distinction between "state" and "land." They are separate concepts. The boundaries of the land of Israel are biblical and broadly synonymous with the old British Mandate area. They include all of Palestine west of the Jordan River. Before 1967, the state of Israel was demarcated by the 1949 armistice lines. From a Palestinian nationalist perspective, the refugees of the 1948 war dream of their return to homes in areas west of the armistice lines in those parts of Palestine that Arafat would not concede to the Jewish state. The PLO's decision to consent to a two-state solution is an indication that state and homeland can be separate concepts for Palestinians too. Here the opposing positions of Israel and the PLO are now symmetrical (117).

States rather than homelands have rights and duties under international law. The notion of homeland was no juridical standing. However, it is entirely possible by treaty to give legal expression and legal status to the concept of homeland as distinct and separate from the concept of the state. Such a juridical construct can be designed to overlap with or arise side by side with the concept of state while remaining distinct from it. A people may thus perceive that it has rights in a homeland that stretches across state boundaries (118).

Sovereignty

This is a redundant notion, serving no function in the solution to this conflict. It should be possible to avoid altogether the debate over sovereignty by distributing its various attributes among the parties in a way that satisfies their essential demands in the confederational scheme (119).

Self-Determination

The Evian Agreements of 1962 to resolve French rule over Algeria can serve as a valuable precedent in negotiations over a Palestinian settlement. Those agreements provided that the Algerians would vote in a self-determination consultation whether to accept or reject the accords that had been negotiated. The accords established that the right of self-determination can be exercised by a people when it votes in a plebescite on a negotiated agreement (120).

Boundaries and Other Functional Lines

Israelis and Palestinians alike appear to accept the notion that a multiplicity of lines serving different functional purposes will separate the parties. Security boundaries, political limits, and economic lines need not be identical. In turn, they deal with a physical barrier and cooperative approaches to practical problems (water sharing, access to holy places). Association through separation is possible (120–121).

Security Arrangements

It is a fact that each side presents a threat of unleashed violence to the other. Without security arrangements that satisfy Israel, there will be no agreement. Various lines demarcated for different military purposes (patrols along the Jordan River, early-warning stations, areas for redeployment, demilitarized zones) can be considered if one takes Arafat at his word that "a peace settlement will contain every conceivable condition necessary to guarantee Israel's security" (123).

Refugees, Right of Return, and Citizenship

A dual system of passports for Palestinian "nationals" and for "citizens" of the confederation could deal with the refugee issue. The international community will be called upon to help with the problem of compensation and the right of return. Compensation for those choosing to return to the West Bank and Gaza can be dealt with. The principle of compensation for all Palestinians who choose not to return is not contested by anyone (123–124).

Jerusalem

At this stage, it may be wise not to explore the future of this city, due to the deep emotional attachments by the parties (124).

Gottlieb does not underestimate the formidable task of closing and finalizing agreement on these points and believes it depends on the individual leadership among Israelis and Palestinians. But he feels strongly that this softer and gentler approach—following Fisher and Ury's principled negotiation strategy—shows the way for possible coexistence between the parties.

CONCLUSION

There is a thick layer of negotiation history in this Middle East conflict. The buildup is substantial and appears to be on an accelerated pace. More and more plans are presented and discussed as time goes by, and each proposal seems to be zooming in on the precise, narrowly defined issues at hand. The elaborate efforts to form negotiation positions and present them in public arenas have brought some success too. Encouraging signs point to common agreement among the parties and, more important, to their mutual recognition of shared interests.

The positional bargaining strategy remains far more central and completely dominates the negotiation environment. Yet, for all the energy in planning and proposal-generation, there have been few achievements of joint agreement by parties. By contrast, principled negotiation techniques continue in the background and are treated as peripheral formulas that may be useful if all else fails. This recommended strategy has yet to receive true testing in the Arab–Israeli dispute; it simply has not been applied as a full-scale effort. Thus, the bulk of negotiation buildup is derived from positional bargaining, affecting the parties who are by now hardened and worn by the roles and rules captured by this traditional approach to conflict resolution.

Principled negotiation entered late into this picture and requires, in any case, a significant shift in negotiation orientation; the standard mindset for thinking about discussing issues with an adversary is derived from positional negotiation perspectives. The principled approach, in short, has experienced but a tiny start. However, basic ideas in principled negotiation—(a) the notion of mutual trust; (b) creative-idea generation to invent options of mutual gain to the disputants; and (c) the development of principles as precedents—have deeper roots in understanding and analyzing the Arab–Israeli conflict and resolution approaches. In the next chapter these themes are developed further to illustrate how negotiation is sustained in broad, principled bargaining categories yet is pursued, usually, in positional bargaining games.

6

Sustaining Negotiation

INTRODUCTION

Negotiation is a process of two or more parties combining their conflicting points of view into a single decision. It is designed to be a positive-sum exercise, on the assumption that both parties will prefer the agreed outcome to the status quo, and implies that everyone will be better off with an agreement than without one. Although the parties are fixed, the values are flexible, and a decision is made by changing the evaluation that parties give to those values in order to combine them into a single form through a bargaining process. I. William Zartman (1977) has identified several approaches to negotiation.

First is the Psychological Approach, which looks at the parties themselves more than at the bargaining process and seeks to explain negotiated results in terms of behavioral and attitudinal characteristics of the negotiating personnel. This corresponds to building the *trust* factor in principled negotiation.

Next is the Convergence-Concession Approach, in which the parties react to each other's concession behavior. This approach views negotiation as a type of learning process, capturing intuitively and experimentally the flow of bargaining activity. This corresponds to *creative-idea generation* in principled negotiation.

Last is the Formula/Detail Approach, where attention focuses on negotiating the list of items to be included in the agenda and grouping them under commonly agreed principles. Here, decisions are first needed on the "negotiability" and "terms of reference" of the issues, where a formula is tied to an overall purpose behind the negotiations (Zartman, 1977:631). This corresponds to *principles as precedent* in principled negotiation.

Zartman states that major negotiations of recent times were conducted through a search for a single formula satisfactory to all sides, followed by a further search for the implementation of this formula, through specification of the details necessary to affect the agreement (632). Negotiation is not a determinant process, is not merely a reaction to past moves from the other side but is also the initiation of forward-oriented moves to guide the other party toward the preferred alternative. It involves subject assessments to find an acceptable formula that includes selected values from both parties' proposals.

Theories of negotiation frequently start from the assumption of individual rationality: each side is trying to maximize its own payoff. As a result, an agreement is seen as an equilibrium point at which the opposing interests are balanced. However, negotiations can proceed smoothly only as long as they are guided by the collectivist desire for fairness; problems arise whenever the individualistic motivations take over. A successful negotiation begins when the conflict is ripe for settlement, when parties are able to formulate mutually acceptable first bids.

Various propositions have emerged, and lessons have been drawn from the conflict regulation process as it has been applied to the Arab–Israeli dispute. These have been grouped to correspond with Zartman's three approaches to negotiation to illustrate the features of trust, creative-idea generation, and precedent principles, which affect the possibilities for successful negotiations based on a principled, not positional, basis. In each case, major studies are examined and dissected in a search for principles of negotiation that succeeded or failed.

THE PSYCHOLOGICAL APPROACH: TRUST

The Arab–Israeli Conflict: Psychological Obstacles to Peace, by Daniel Heradstveit (1981), is one of the major studies that focus on attitudes and perceptions of adversarial national elites to explain why the disputants have failed to negotiate terms for peace. Extensive interviews with more than two-hundred leaders from Egypt, Jordan, Lebanon, Syria, and Israel, as well as some Palestinians, were conducted periodically in the 1970s to measure belief systems. Individuals who were active in shaping the policies of the conflict, who represented the mainstream of thought, were asked to describe and evaluate characteristics of their own self-image and the image of their enemy, in the context of understanding why this conflict persists. The basic premise of the study is that by identifying the stumbling blocks in the way to peace and by showing how competing interpretations within and across elites inhibit moves toward settlement, participants might ameliorate the relations between the conflicting parties. Heradstveit places the ultimate source of party differences with the psychological mindset, relying on negative images and preconceptions about the enemy and rigid conditions for peaceful change. He introduces the idea of "cognitive invariant"—the stable and basic orientations of actions that operate in novel, highly uncertain situations.

From a decision-making perspective, these cognitive sources influence how events are interpreted and shape both the objectives and the alternative courses of action that come into play in negotiating and bargaining settings. What are the beliefs that define an actor's interpretation, diagnosis, and prescription of the Arab–Israeli dispute? How do these operational codes relate to settlement conditions and possibilities for negotiation? What characterizes the perceptions and thinking of those who are favorable to conciliatory moves and those who are not (Heradstveit, 1981:10)?

Responses to six questions formed the data used to identify and analyze these issues. The first question was, *What do you think are the basic good and bad aspects of your side in the conflict?* Not surprisingly, both Arabs and Israelis see themselves as just, peaceful, and moderate (the positive elements) but claimed that their own points of view were not always explained well enough or that a lack of unity prevented a clear articulation of policy (the negative aspects). In general, bad policies were seen to derive from the opponent's bad behavior (50–51). In short clear, self-righteous perspectives emerge in the minds of these national elites.

When asked to explain *the good and bad aspects of the opponent*, Israelis and Arabs gave answers that tended to be more specific, diverse, and asymmetric. Arab respondents referred to Israel's technical advances, economic strength, successful propaganda, and unity in goals and strategies and expressed admiration for the dedication of the Jewish people to fight for their existence. But these views were coupled with several strong, negative impressions of Israelis as militaristic, revengeful, and racist. The Israeli elites, in specifying positive images of their enemy, tended to refer to personal traits of Arab people, including their sense of pride, self-confidence, and hospitality. However, they also described Arabs as fanatic, irrational, lacking in imagination, and hateful. Each side holds a mirror image of the other in terms of perceiving negative attributes of its enemy, whereas the positive features show a zero-sum mentality: each side admires traits of the enemy that it lacks (52).

A third question asked was, *Do you think the other side is threatening you?* The answers reveal that fear in the conflict is caused primarily by evaluating the opponent's intentions rather than the opponent's actual behavior. "Concrete changes in the situation, concrete events, and the opponent's actions in the past do not seem to be included in causal analysis of why there is a threat. The strong focus on the intentions of the opponent is striking and is common to both Arab and Israeli respondents," wrote Heradstveit (58). These findings are entirely consistent with the negative portrayals each side sees in the other, that is, if an adversary is characterized as revengeful and hateful, long-term objectives that are detrimental to one's own policies would follow.

In the counterquestion *Do you think the other side believes you are threatening them?*, both sides claimed that generating fear was used as a device to promote policies and that threat accusation was effective for self-advancement. Each party, in addition, expressed an opinion built on power analysis: The Arabs claimed that Israelis feel threatened because of Arab strength; the Israelis stressed that Arabs should not feel threatened because of Israeli military superiority.

There is a double message here. The disputants seem to be saying that fear is created in the mind of the beholder, yet the power quotient provides the basis of threat and is used to justify the status quo of perceptions (59).

Turning to specific reasons underlying the conflict, participants in the study were asked, *If you could point out one single factor as the main cause of the conflict in the Middle East, what is it?* Remarkable parallels emerged in the responses, indicating that the parties can focus together on a small set of causal agents. Principally, these views settled along two points: first, whether the state of Israel has a right to exist, and second, whether each party can rationally consider policies that would facilitate a peaceful settlement (65).

The final question, perhaps the most important one to the study, was, *Given what you would like to see happen in the Middle East in the near future, what do you think are the most effective ways to achieve these aims?* Arabs and Israelis alike naturally emphasized that peace and justice were the primary goals, albeit from their own, opposite perspectives. The responses tended to be very general and abstract; little articulation of actual resolution possibilities showed up. As Heradstveit (67) stated, "What the elites typically seemed to discuss, even when asked about the near future, were abstract preferences like total peace or total absence of conflict." There was hardly any articulate thinking about what would initiate processes toward conflict resolution.

For some participants in the survey, resolution of the conflict was a question of more moderation on one or both sides. Once an attitude change in this direction came about, a solution would follow; conflict resolution is a process of changing attitudes, not of changing situational influences and constraints (67). Change could occur when all countries in the area respected each other's rights, and this could happen if outside assistance was brought in to mediate the conflict, said the respondents. This set of beliefs is somewhat surprising, since the history of negotiation by mediators has not been successful. Yet, such a perspective may merely confirm the mutual agreement between the parties that alone they are incapable of reaching a peaceful solution to the dispute due to the psychological barriers.

This study analyzed the processes of causal attributes in the Middle East conflict by asking the elites how they accounted for their own behavior and the actions of their opponent. The responses show sources of imperfection and erroneous tendencies in information processing. The author argues that these deviations arise from four sources: private stimuli, past experience, protection of self-esteem and defense against threat, and saliency of features of the conflict situation to each adversary (72). The general explanation rests on the idea of attribution theory, which hypothesizes that when conflicting parties observe their opponent, the adversary's behavior is understood to derive from internal properties—abilities, traits, and motives. At the same time, one's own behavior is explained as a response to the situation, specifically environmental pressures and constraints.

The causes of the Arab–Israeli dispute are thus a combination of dispositional and situational forces where each side ascribes negative traits to the other and simultaneously justifies its own actions as governed by external operating factors. It is another way of saying that although I cannot control my own actions, in a modified setting they might be different. My enemy's actions, however, are unchangeable, due to the cognitive invariants that define my opponent. This study underscores the rigid symmetry of self-views and mirror images of the enemy party.

Three positions for evaluating conflict-resolution possibilities were identified through an analysis of the interview material of the study: (1) a negotiated settlement based on UN Resolution 242, (2) the creation of a Palestinian state, and (3) the status quo.

Participants were asked to evaluate each option. From their replies, Heradstveit constructed profiles of conciliatory and nonconciliatory perspectives that are connected to possible negotiation encounters between the two sides. He labeled the two positions according to whether individuals see realistic possibilities for reaching a compromise with the enemy. There is a pluralism of goals on both sides in the conflict, and the assumption is that moderate forces will be important and will lead the way to conflict resolution when issues can be viewed in an integrative way with common solutions presented.

Heradstveit cites several examples of the conciliatory position for each side, represented by people whom he calls Innovators, and shows elements of moderation and agreement between the enemy parties. First, the parties view the conflict in non-zero-sum terms. Second, the parties advocate that territorial division and reclamation be decided through negotiation. Third, the parties believe that a Palestinian state should be created alongside the state of Israel.

By contrast, the uncompromising position is characterized by a zero-sum understanding of the conflict, which extends to control over lands as well as the existence of an Israeli or Palestinian national entity (102–3). He labels this group of people Traditionalists.

The author concluded that elites who hold pluralistic views of the enemy—Innovators—are much more likely to favor compromise policies than those who hold a unitary perspective. "Those with dogmatic images of their opponent (Traditionalists) consistently stick to hawkish policy positions with little flexibility," wrote Heradstveit (115).

The study identified constraints on cognitive functioning, constraints that may result in policies that are not optimal in relation to how the contending parties want relations between themselves to develop. Errors and biases of elites may have repercussions on conflict resolution in several ways:

1. The rigidity of established paradigms in information processing about the opponent in the conflict inhibits compromise postures. If the enemy behaves in an expected way, images are reinforced; if the enemy behaves in a manner not expected, this is attributed to environmental forces and constraints. Thus, it is not necessary to change beliefs about the enemy (124).

2. An observed moderate change in the opponent's behavior will be seen as temporary. Unexpected moves are interpreted not as signs of possible moderation but as reactive: the enemy is nice to us now because he is forced to do this (125).

3. There is a systematic bias involved in perceived freedom of choice, where each side sees the opponent as having numerous alternative policy options while one's own situation has a narrow, deterministic latitude (126).

4. An overemphasis on the psychological aspects of the problem limits the need for concessions on concrete interests. Discussion about the opponent is heavily focused on intentions—dreams and not the operational program (127).

How can the biases in enemy images be countered? Awareness is not sufficient. The psychological processes reflect, in part, a conflict of interest that may be much more difficult and complicated than differences arising from the psychological mechanisms. The maintenance of enemy images is not independent from the realities that the attributions represent. Still, in the end, variations in policy recommendations of elites involved in the conflict can be traced to fundamental differences about the meaning ascribed to the conflict itself, where beliefs about the opponent are critical.

The specific views of Innovators and Traditionalists among the inhabitants of the West Bank are examined in Walter Reich's book *A Stranger in My House: Jews and Arabs in the West Bank* (1984). Reich asked local leaders to describe the ideology backing their perspectives. He arranged open-ended, free-spirited interviews with prominent individuals, including activists in the Jewish settlement movement and former Palestinian mayors of Nablus and Hebron, to understand the depth of their vision and commitment and to document the intensity and variety of feelings held by each side. The result is a rich portrayal of positions, ranging from rigid, uncompromising stands to more conciliatory expressions, and reveals a more complete picture of the operating psychological mindset and cognitive invariants identified by Heradstveit.

The range of political opinion expressing solutions to the Arab–Israeli conflict derived from Reich's interviews forms a continuum, from those who are willing to engage in negotiations leading to change and compromise to the hard-liners characterized by their rigid adherence to nonnegotiable terms. The opinions of eight people interviewed can be divided into finer distinctions along the Innovator-Traditionalist scale. A sampling of their opinions follows. They are grouped into four categories: (1) Innovators, who are willing to compromise; (2) Semi-Innovators, who want to compromise but see major obstacles, (3) Semi-Traditionalists, who do not want to compromise in spite of the opportunities, and (4) Traditionalists, who do not envision any compromising.

Israeli Innovator

Yoram Ben-Porath, a professor at the Hebrew University and a member of Peace Now, is dedicated to persuading Israelis to risk giving up the occupied territories for peace. He feels that since the 1967 war his country has been in a position to define a Jewish state more precisely and negotiate with Arabs. Although he does not agree with the Arabs' stand entirely or see Israelis the way Arabs do, he does not want to deny Arabs "the kinds of rights and aspirations that I also consider to be my own" (Reich, 1984:86). The problem, he says, is that Jews and Palestinians come together with long histories of victimization, which encourage both to exaggerate the power and cruelty of the other while simultaneously justifying their own actions. What would the Arabs have done if they had won? They would have destroyed Israel, which gives the basis to Israeli fears. Arabs, he argues, cannot understand how their image has been clouded by Palestinian acts of terrorism, which inhibits negotiation potential. At the same time, he realizes that Palestinians struggle to present a unified front in the face of significant disagreements among themselves on how to proceed to deal with Israel, the enemy. He advocates the creation of an independent Palestinian state, one that would exist alongside Israel under tremendous asymmetry of power. With Israel as the stronger party, this would minimize the possibility of Arab violence, soften the threat to Israel's national security, and allow for reversibility of its actions of surrendering the West Bank to the Palestinians. He believes that if Israel continues to hold on to the territories, it gives in to religious settlers who want a utopia, which is unacceptable both from political and military viewpoints, and that ultimately the country will be affected internally—it will take on a less democratic character and will be less acceptable by its own people and by the outside world (85–95).

Palestinian Innovator

Mustafa Natshe, the former acting mayor of Hebron, believes the most important issue is whether the Israeli government recognizes the Arabs' right to self-determination. There is room for two states in the area, one Arab and one Israeli, which, according to him, should be created along the lines of the 1947 UN partition plan. He admits, though, that it is difficult to argue about borders, short of legitimate recognition, but believes the Israelis want more and more land, citing acquisitions in 1947 and gains in 1967. It is power that enables them to pursue this policy. He believes the Israelis do not want a peace drawn on an equal-power basis with the Arabs but would rather rule by virtue of strength alone. At some point, he says, the Arabs will have power and then things may change. As for the West Bank Jewish settlements, he feels they are illegal, since there is no solution to the Palestinian problem, and can be uprooted easily because there is not a tradition of long-term residency. However, once a solution has been established, he thinks it would be all right for Jews to move to the area and for Arabs to return to points in Israel that they left in 1948 (39–50).

Israeli Semi-Innovator

Yisrael Medad, a Jewish settler, is an aide to Geula Cohen, MP, who represents the Renaissance Party (Tehiya), a right-of-center political group. He argues that the West Bank problem is a unique situation because it involves a return to a land by people who were expelled from it but who kept its memory and reality alive every day for two-thousand years. Thus, normal solutions that might apply elsewhere do not fit this case. He makes a distinction between arguing for rights—the Palestinian problem—and arguing for existence—the Jewish problem. The latter is far more serious. The solution proposed by Tehiya advocates annexation of the West Bank by Israel under a special arrangement where the Arabs would be offered full political rights including voting in national elections for the Knesset, provided they first accepted the principle that the state would be Jewish. In this plan, all the Arabs would be lacking would be the right to sovereignty, which he believes is not entitled to everyone under all conditions. Since he strongly feels that the Arabs will never be satisfied until they regain all of the land, this is a way to yield some rights and protect existence for the Jewish state (33–37).

Palestinian Semi-Innovator

"Karim" is an unidentified West Bank Palestinian. (Reich here states that those who have strayed from the PLO line, undercut its agenda, or embarrassed its program have sometimes been punished, so he chooses to preserve this man's identity in return for candid opinions.) "Karim" believes it was a mistake not to accept the UN partition plan of 1947, for then the Palestinians would have been much better off. With the development of the PLO, its positions toward acquiring a state have changed over the years, from advocating a secular democratic state in all of Palestine open to Jews, Muslims, and Christians to proposing a West Bank ministate alongside of, but without the recognition of, Israel. Could the Arabs ever really accept Israel in any form? he asks. The area is Arab; the people have been there for centuries. Israel's presence is strange. The Arabs who were expelled from their land want to return to their country—including all of western Palestine. He believes that the recognition of Israel can never be anything but a tactic used by those who have no power but that in the long run things will change in the power balance, which will enable the Palestinians to retreat from this temporary proposition. Why? Because each side wants all of what the other side has: if there were only two people, one Arab and one Jew, it would be the same. There would be war, and it will always be that way (68–71).

Israeli Semi-Traditionalist

Elyakim Haetzni, another settler, an attorney and a secular Jew, believes the Arab–Israeli problem can be resolved through partition. According to his calculations, the Arabs already have more than three-fourths of Palestine but prefer to call it Jordan in order to be able to demand the rest in the name of Palestine. He would like to see a strong, free Palestinian state on the east bank of the Jordan River, possibly in alliance with Israel, and autonomy in local affairs for Palestinians who continue to reside in the West Bank. Israel has the right to keep the land by reason of conquest. This is a perfectly legitimate method of acquiring territory in international relations, and from this perspective, there is no reason to abandon the settlements (20–32).

Palestinian Semi-Traditionalist

Sam'an Khoury is the managing editor of *Al-Far Al-Arabi* (*The Arab Dawn*), a Palestinian newspaper that closely follows the PLO line. He believes that the Palestinian people must be free and that until then, unity in political positions is very important. The PLO is all the Palestinians can rely on: the Israelis are against us, and the Arabs are not helpful. For all to live in peace and freely, there should be two states in Palestine. The West Bank should be turned into an independent state for the Arabs. He passionately feels that living under occupation inhibits his own freedom of expression and affects all other Palestinians in the same way, which does not allow for openness and honesty about what the Palestinians really think of Israel, its legitimacy, or the long-range future (59–67).

Israeli Traditionalist

Rabbi Moshe Levinger, a Jewish settlement leader, argues that the West Bank is religiously significant to Jews, who have lived almost continuously on the land since biblical times. It is the place where David was proclaimed King of Judah (and later of Israel); it has been a seat of Jewish learning despite persecution of Jews by various groups. The land was given to the Jews by God, and it is their responsibility to live on the land, to honor God's teachings, and thereby to enlighten the world. This is the religious mission of Zionism—to return to the land described in the Bible. He strongly believes that the land automatically belongs to the Jews, who are obliged to live there as a worthy, God-fearing people. Because of this birthright, the land cannot be divided nor negotiated. Important things that belong to someone cannot be compromised; this would be abnormal. Besides, the land represents more than mere property; it is a holy place where the Jews have an obligation pact with God to live a holy life (13–19).

Palestinian Traditionalist

Bassim Shaka'a is a former mayor of Nablus on the West Bank and actively supports the PLO. He has organized townspeople to resist and obstruct the Israeli occupation and sees little hope of an accommodation with Israel. The Jew is the stranger on this land, he argues. It is the Arab whose home has been invaded. The Jew had possession of the territory for only several hundred years, two-thousand years ago. This is my house, he states, and I cannot compromise on possession of it. Moreover, negotiations with an occupier are impossible. How could any Arab negotiate with an Israel bent on ruthless expansion? he asks. The 1948 borders are simply the beginning, and the Israelis aim to expand their state. They must withdraw from the West Bank. Eventually, he thinks, Israel will be forced to accept a Palestinian state in the region, and toward that end there can be no compromise (53–58).

The passion on both sides, the appeals to justice and history, and the distrust reflect mirror images that Arabs and Jews hold of each other, consistent with the intensification of nationalist ideology and the growing rivalry. The paradox is that although the moderate perspectives of Innovators may be necessary at the negotiating table, the rigid views of the Traditionalists are also essential to understanding a bargain that might be acceptable. This is where the role of those in the center of this continuum become important. The issue becomes one of finding a peaceful solution between parties, a solution that builds trust between two peoples who inherently cannot accept one another when they rely on ideological conviction for support.

THE CONVERGENCE-CONCESSION APPROACH: CREATIVE IDEAS

The Peace Brokers: Mediators in the Arab–Israeli Conflict, 1948–1979, by Saadia Touval (1982), contains the stories of success and an analysis of failure in resolution attempts of nine designated negotiation teams. As Touval wrote in his introduction: "It is not for lack of attempts to resolve it that the Arab–Israeli conflict has gone on for so long. For over sixty years, repeated efforts have been made to reconcile the incompatible claims to Palestine made by Arab and Jewish national movements, but to no avail" (Touval, 1982:xi).

Touval's task was to describe and evaluate the work accomplished by selected mediators who represent major attempts to promote a settlement or to significantly reduce the intensity and scope of the conflict. He readily admits that numerous other negotiations by governments, international organizations, and private individuals have become part of the total picture in Middle East conflict-resolution activities—groups who sought to promote peace, reduce border strife, or resolve specific issues related to water development projects, navigation rights, exchange and treatment of prisoners, and property matters. The mediation efforts he selected for analysis range from Count Bernadotte's work in 1948 through the Camp David accords in 1978–79. The author structures and appraises each group of negotiation opportunities around a specific set of questions (xiii):

What interests prompted the mediators to undertake the role? What did they expect to gain from their intervention, besides the obvious satisfaction of helping the Arabs and Israelis to resolve their conflict peacefully? What effects did their interventions have for Arab–Israeli power relations? For regional and global power struggles? Should the conclusion of agreements and the reduction of tensions really be credited to the mediators, or would the agreements have been concluded irrespective of the mediators? How can one explain the success of some and the failure of others? What qualities and techniques on the part of mediators were conducive to success?

In the assessments, Touval provides information about negotiator style and personal qualities in light of the international conditions in the immediate geographic region, as well as in the more general setting of superpower relations. In looking for reasons why some objectives toward peace have been achieved while others have ended in confusion, stalemate, or rejection, he weighs individual party stakes, the variety of substantive issues involved, and elements of timing, overall strategy, and tactics. He displays the goals of each party—both immediate and long-term—and shifts in goal priorities and shows how the internal changes in the countries involved may reorder national priorities and how the international environment is linked up with local assessments and desires. Overall, Touval believes that mediators are well-intentioned individuals, good people who are genuinely interested in resolving this protracted conflict, who want to improve conditions for all parties concerned, who are eager to find compromises acceptable to all adversaries, and who are dedicated to the task.

What he found is that a very complex set of factors comes into play in any negotiation efforts dealing with the Arab–Israeli conflict, factors that are almost impossible to isolate from each other. Why do some negotiations succeed and others fail? The answer is neither simple nor straightforward, and unfortunately, from this analysis we do not learn precisely how important the personality of the mediator is to the final outcome, or whether it is outside pressures and threats of sanctions that intimidate the parties to cooperate, or if adversaries' evaluations of their own situations and their own needs to make concessions (without any threatening gestures) play a lead role. All these elements contribute to the final result and help set the stage for the next round.

Perhaps a formula for failure does exist, one that contains so many variants that most negotiation activity can be incorporated under it. Touval may have unveiled some of the more obvious patterns that lead to stalled, sluggish lack of progress toward peaceful resolution. Alternatively, this conflict might be especially marked by adversary reluctance to consider compromise or by dogged persistence to change the status quo.

This study is neither cynical nor overly critical in evaluating mediation efforts. Fault-finding points in a variety of directions to show that no consistent obstacle appears to hinder the process of making peace. It is useful, however, to display this rich information into a more compressed picture for the purpose of noting correlational patterns across some of the significant factors identified by Touval. The tables below were constructed out of the descriptions presented by Touval and are intended to incorporate relevant data across the mediation efforts to show cross-case comparisons. They represent extractions from his analysis.

Table 3 shows the relationship of the situational level of conflict between the parties at the time of the mediator and the mandate of issues placed into the negotiation setting. What is readily apparent is that successful negotiation outcomes usually occurred in military issues. Both cease-fire and disengagement agreements were achieved several times, whereas larger political matters consistently went unresolved. The settlement has never been resolved regardless of

Table 3
Mediation Attempts in the Arab–Israeli Dispute:
Immediate Situation and Negotiation Objectives
(Adapted from Saadia Touval, *The Peace Brokers*)

Mediator	Time	Situation	Objectives	Outcome
Bernadotte	May 1948 to Sept. 1948	War	1. Cease-fire	success
			Intermediate Steps: 2. Common services for population	failure
			Intermediate Steps: 3. Protect holy places	failure
			Settlement: 4. Promote peaceful adjustment	failure
Bunche	Sept. 1948 to Jan. 1949	War	**Cease-fire:** 1. Continue truce	success
			Intermediate Steps: 2. Common services for population	failure
			Intermediate Steps: 3. Protect holy places	failure
			Settlement: 4. Promote peaceful adjustment	failure
UN Conciliation Commission	Dec. 1948 to Nov. 1951	Postwar and Stalemate	**Intermediate Steps:** 1. Common services for population	failure
			Intermediate Steps: 2. Protect holy places	failure
			Settlement: 3. Promote peaceful adjustment	failure
			Intermediate Steps: 4. International regime for Jerusalem	failure

Table 3 (continued)

Mediator	Time	Situation	Objectives	Outcome
			Intermediate Steps: 5. Reparations for refugees	failure
Anderson	Dec. 1955 to March 1966	Stalemate	**General:** 1. Counter USSR influence	failure
			General: 2. Show US fair to Arabs	failure
			Settlement: 3. Promote peaceful adjustment	failure
Jarring	Nov. 1967 to 1972	Postwar and Stalemate	**General:** 1. Reach international consensus on principles to moderate conflict and guide toward settlement	failure
			Settlement: 2. Promote UN Resolution 242	failure
Rogers	June 1970 to April 1972	War, Postwar and Stalemate	1. Cease-fire	success
			General: 2. Resume Jarring talks	success
			General: 3. Expel USSR military presence	failure
			General: 4. Promote US as "honest broker"	failure
			Intermediate Steps: 5. Disengagement along Suez Canal	failure

Table 3 (continued)

Mediator	Time	Situation	Objectives	Outcome
African Premiers	June 1971 to Nov. 1972	Stalemate	**General:** 1. Resume Jarring talks	failure
			Intermediate Steps: 2. Withdraw Israeli military to June 5, 1967, lines	failure
Kissinger	Oct. 1973 to March 1975	War, Postwar and Stalemate	1. Cease-fire	success
			General: 2. Counter USSR influence	?
			Intermediate Steps: 3. Disengagement between Egypt and Israeli troops	success
			Intermediate Steps: 4. Disengagement between Syria and Israel	success
			General: 5. Arrange international peace conference	success
Carter	Dec. 1977 to March 1979	Stalemate	**Settlement:** 1. Pursue comprehensive settlement	failure
			Settlement: 2. Reconvene international peace conference	failure
			Intermediate Steps: 3. Withdraw Israeli military to June 5, 1967, lines	success
			Intermediate Steps: 4. Normalize Israeli-Egyptian relations	success

the immediate situation or the coupling with other issues into the negotiation effort. Compromise agreements are more likely to result from wartime situations than from periods of stalemate, which reinforces the conclusion that military issues are more easily settled than political matters, which lack the intensity of a crisis environment. These generalizations are true regardless of the era of negotiation—whether the 1940s or the 1970s—are not tied to individual negotiators. However, after the 1973 war, when the United States took on an enhanced role as solution-finder in the Arab–Israeli dispute, the level of success in negotiated outcomes increases and extends to previously stalemated arenas. The efforts of Kissinger and Carter are very important.

Table 4 displays attributes of negotiator style and authority base alongside the mediation outcome. Here the chief predictors of success show that individuals have a better record in resolution issues than do groups, that American backing is more important than the role of any international organization, and that knowledgeable negotiators who structure a friendly, relaxed environment promote successful outcomes.

The history of mediation in the Arab–Israeli conflict provides ample evidence of the conditions leading to failure in dispute resolution, whereas the factors accounting for successful outcomes are more limited. Parties to the conflict are likely to be more receptive to solution ideas if they can be assured of compensation in light of revising their policies on key issues. In addition, the flexibility of parties seems to be most evident at two stages in conflict development: the early and later stages. States are least likely to agree to negotiation terms during times of conflict escalation.

In a more detailed appraisal of the causes of success and failure of each mediation attempt, Touval demonstrates that at least four sets of factors come into play: (1) personal factors pertaining to the negotiator(s), (2) support factors that determine the level of authority and backing from the international community, (3) process factors, including style of discussion, and (4) issue factors.

The first element, personal factors, refers to a host of mediator traits such as level of knowledge, bargaining skills, motivation to resolve the conflict, and warmth and charm and flexibility of the individual negotiators. The second item refers to outside support and possible compensation to the parties. Touval basically divides this factor into international organization backing and Great Power backing (usually it is the United States in the negotiation example). The latter yields a far greater likelihood of success. A major element in the negotiation process is the decision-making structure, where individual authority is preferred over that of a group, where the objectives and priorities in the mission are clear, where proposals are thoroughly considered in advance and discussed fully with all parties (surprises should be avoided), and where the media has limited exposure to the evolution of discussion of the issues. The final item, issue factors, reaffirms the notion that core issues should be avoided and that resolution works best with fractionated issues and a step-by-step approach to compromises. Touval concludes that an overall approach to resolution of issues ought to be confined

Table 4
Mediation Attempts in Arab–Israeli Dispute:
Negotiating Style and Resource Base
(Adapted from Saadia Touval, *The Peace Brokers*)

Mediator	Time	Negotiating Style	Resources	Outcome
Bernadotte	May 1948 to Sept. 1948	Formal, distant Not knowledgeable Comprehensive approach	Individual mediator International organization (UN)	success and failure
Bunche	Sept. 1948 to Jan. 1949	Relaxed and friendly Knowledgeable	Individual mediator International organization	success and failure
UN Conciliation Commission	Dec. 1948 to Nov. 1951	Cumbersome Not knowledgeable	Group mediation International organization (UN) Big Power (US)	failure
Anderson	Dec. 1955 to March 1966		Individual mediator Big Power (US)	failure
Jarring	Nov. 1967 to 1972	Formal, distant Knowledgeable	Individual mediator International organization	failure
Rogers	June 1970 to April 1972	Not trustworthy Knowledgeable	Individual mediator Big Power (US)	success and failure
African Premiers	June 1971 to Nov. 1972	Cumbersome Partisan	Group mediation International organization (OAU)	failure
Kissinger	Oct. 1973 to March 1975	Relaxed and friendly Knowledgeable Step-by-Step approach	Individual mediator Big Power (US)	success
Carter	Dec. 1977 to March 1979	Relaxed and friendly Knowledgeable	Individual mediator Big Power (US)	success and failure

to finding stability in the conflict situation rather than seeking to discover a solution to the problem. Touval (1982:330–31) contends that mediation was not successful in modifying basic Arab or Israeli attitudes, nor has it *resolved* the Arab–Israeli conflict. By helping to conclude limited agreements that *reduce* the conflict, mediators can, however, contribute to an evolution toward peace.

THE FORMULA/DETAIL APPROACH:
PRINCIPLE AS PRECEDENT

Under what conditions can negotiations between the Arabs and the Israelis succeed? The treaty resulting from the Camp David Framework for Peace, signed by Egyptian President Anwar Sadat and Israeli Prime Minister Menachem Begin on September 17, 1978, was a significant turning point in recent Middle East history. Although some have argued that these agreements forged the foundations for peace in the region by terminating the state of belligerency between two major antagonists, others have criticized the accords for failing to achieve a comprehensive settlement that would have resolved the Palestinian issue. Nonetheless, the lengthy negotiations carried out over many months through the good offices and mediation of the United States, which in the end produced a set of documents signed by the parties, were an indication that some aspects of conflict resolution could be achieved. Agreeable compromises were formulated, and all three parties gained something.

William B. Quandt's book *Camp David: Peacemaking and Politics* (1986) provides an excellent description and analysis of the unfolding events leading to the agreements. In spite of the lack of success of attempts by the parties to resolve their differences in the past, this negotiation effort worked. Why it worked, and why it almost failed, are the key questions that Quandt examines. His search for answers includes a lot of detail and is reported from the perspective of the role played by the United States. The successful outcome depended, he argues, on the unusual commitment and continuous involvement of the top superpower's highest foreign-policy decision makers. The lesson appears to be that enormous amounts of both effort and power-backing are necessary to diffuse any of the enmity characterizing the Arab–Israeli dispute. Establishing a viable movement away from the status quo and toward peace demands an abundance of energy, persistence, patience, and creative plans. Is it worth it? Could the task be repeated, leading again to positive outcomes?

There are several reasons to account for the negotiation success, argues Quandt, including the political climate at the time, the role played by the United States as mediator, the personalities of the leaders, and the nature of the issues resolved. However, this effort at conflict resolution came close to failure many times, and precisely the same factors could be singled out to blame the process if it had ended this way, heading in a counterproductive direction.

Political Climate

By the mid–1970s, the final big war between Israel and the combined force of the Arab neighbors was over, having ended with a successful show of military might by each side. The Arabs had recovered a sense of pride, which had been severely damaged with the humiliating defeat in the 1967 war. Israel and Egypt had reached two interim agreements over the territory of the Sinai Peninsula during 1974 and 1975, showing a history of prior negotiation success. There was a new U.S. president, who placed a high priority on resolving the Arab–Israeli dispute and who dedicated substantial time and effort to the problem. A new government assumed power in Israel. Menachem Begin, the new prime minister, represented a more conservative strand in foreign policy, yet this offered the opportunity for a fresh approach in discussing the possibilities for dispute resolution. Together, these factors provided a positive atmosphere for the parties to show political courage.

U.S. Role

The power and global position of the United States, presidential involvement, and the person of Jimmy Carter—his hopes, his dreams, his style, and his commitment—strongly influenced both the process and the outcome of the negotiations. Quandt's view is that the U.S. role was absolutely essential to the project's success, by providing power, promises, and sidepayments to the antagonists.

Leaders' Personalities

Carter was a believer in the maxim that hard work could produce results, and he hated to admit defeat. With little flair for making deals, he possessed a strong sense of doing what was right. He was impatient with fine diplomatic distinctions and the taboos surrounding certain buzzwords. He was an idealist. Begin and Sadat were bold and demanding. Begin was an ideologue, rigidly committed to protecting the cause of Zionism. Sadat was theatrical and believed in dramatic gestures; he wanted his place in history as an Arab leader. In short, these men were favorably disposed to the challenge of political courage demanded by the negotiation possibilities.

Issues Resolved

Non-core issues were most successfully treated, whereas the central, fundamental problem, specifically the future of the Palestinians, received relatively little attention. Although it was the largest territory to be negotiated in exchange for peace, the Sinai has not been viewed as major land for Israeli security purposes, as compared with the West Bank, Gaza, or the Golan Heights. Few people live in the area, there is not an abundance of resources (other than a small oil field and a tourist attraction afforded by the coastal region adjacent to the Red Sea), and neither Israel nor Egypt saw the territory as a major plot of land to be developed and protected at all costs. However, Sinai is significant strategically, serving as a buffer between the Suez Canal and the Straits of Tiran. Since both Egyptians and Israelis rely heavily on communication by sea, control over the Sinai is important. However, Sinai is only remotely connected to the festering issue of the rights for the Palestinian people.

In summary, the four factors contributing to a positive negotiating outcome suggest that a favorable political environment, combined with strong commitment by the United States and particular personalities of strong leadership, may result in solutions to non-core problems in the Arab–Israeli conflict. The absence of any single element may substantially reduce the likelihood of a peaceful resolution; and this formula provides little clue for negotiating core issues in a conflict. How often will these favorable winds be present? What modifications and additional elements will give guidelines for resolving core problems?

Because these parties were enemies, mutual trust was lacking, and hostile perceptions of each other's motives and intentions to a large extent dominated the negotiating environment. Carter, however, genuinely believed that part of the problem between the Egyptian and the Israeli leaders came from this distrust and lack of confidence, which could be overcome by helping each to understand the other better. This view was not borne out by the events at the Camp David summit, however; Begin and Sadat were barely on speaking terms (Quandt, 1986:224). Rather than following the pathway of minimal agreement on which to build, Israel and Egypt identified a series of demands that were obstacles to a conflict resolution. The issues ranged from Israeli relinquishment of airfields in Sinai to the source of authority for the interim administration of the West Bank and Gaza, from security arrangements in Sinai to the question of providing the Palestinians with a voice in determining their own future (221).

Each leader, toward the end of the Camp David summit, threatened to walk out of the negotiations or bring them to an end on unsatisfactory terms (237). At the last, the treaty drafters decided to leave some issues vague and unsettled, postponing problems until a later time (251). As Quandt stated: "Left to themselves, Sadat and Begin would probably not have overcome their suspicions and would have broken off the talks over any number of issues. For both leaders it was easier to accept suggestions from Carter than from each other. Direct negotiations may sound fine in theory, but they had little part in achieving the Camp David Accords" (257).

From the inauguration of Jimmy Carter as president on January 10, 1977, until the peace treaty was signed some two years later, the peace process moved through four clear stages. Throughout, the divisive issues and party policies remained relatively unchanged. Whereas both Egypt and Israel believed in the guiding principle of exchanging territory for peace, each held tenaciously to specific national-interest goals. Table 5 summarizes the gap between their objectives across selected, broad problem areas. It is readily apparent that they shared little common ground.

During the entire negotiating process, these positions changed very little. In

Table 5
Israeli–Egyptian Goals over Territory for Peace

Issues

State	Territory for Peace	Normal Diplomatic Relations	Sinai[a]	Golan Heights[b]	West Bank and Gaza[c]	Freedom for Palestinians
Israel	agree	yes	retain	retain	retain	prevent
Egypt	agree	yes	return	return	return	encourage

[a]Sinai is 23,442 square miles, population in 1986 was 200,500.

[b]Golan Heights is 1,176 square miles, population in 1988 was 24,300.

[c]The West Bank is 2,270 square miles, population in 1988 was 895,000; Gaza is 140 square miles, the population in 1988 was 589,000.

Source: Figures derived from *The Europa World Year Book 1991*, vol. 1 (London: Europa Publ. Ltd., 1991), pp. 950, 1441.

the four identified stages, the specific modifications and accommodations, adopted primarily by the United States in its central role as mediator, and Israeli and Egyptian reactions can be seen in Table 6. This material has been prepared as a condensation of the text descriptions offered by Quandt.

It is fairly clear that some of the initial objectives in this negotiating exercise had to be abandoned in order to make significant progress in any area. For example, the solution strategy moved from a comprehensive approach dealing with all issues in the Arab–Israeli conflict to a limited framework for peace between Egypt and Israel. Personal contact between antagonists seemed not to provide the breakthrough for cooperation and mutual understanding that President Carter had imagined. And the scope of involvement by the Arab side was reduced to a single player. Syria, Jordan, and, most significantly, the Palestinians did not participate in the effort to find a peaceful resolution of the dispute. As a result, the main issue in the conflict, namely, the future of the Palestinian people, was not considered in detail.

Summing up the balance between success and failure scores from the Camp David road to peace in the Middle East, Quandt stresses a number of points on each side of the scale. On the side of success, he credits Carter's commitment to finding a peaceful resolution to the problem and his talent for mastering details necessary to forging such an agreement. U.S. Secretary of State Cyrus Vance brought valuable skills as an international lawyer, and Egypt and Israel were willing to accept U.S. mediation to make peace and normalize relations. On the side of failure, Quandt faults Carter for lacking an understanding of the Palestinian issue, for overestimating the role of Egypt to set the groundwork for negotiations on this problem, and for underestimating Begin's attachment to the West Bank and Gaza. Thus, in working on the Egyptian–Israeli negotiation, the Camp David peace process lost sight of broader Middle East conflict settlement, the original goal of American policy.

Is the Camp David approach a model for or an obstacle to future negotiations? Although the Accords do not provide a model to be easily copied in future negotiations, the legacy resulting from this long and difficult process is significant. Camp David may have prevented the possibility of war, at least between Egypt and Israel, who now live under conditions known as a "cold peace," yet wars relating to the Arab–Israeli conflict were not abated (the Israeli invasion of Lebanon began in 1982). The concept of territory for peace can work, but since the treaty Israel has formally annexed East Jerusalem and has extended Israeli law to the Golan Heights, and violence has become a way of life in the West Bank.

Among the lessons learned from this extraordinary effort, Quandt identifies commitment, tenacity, and sincerity as significant elements in any successful negotiation, in combination with a skillful blend of inducements and pressures by the central, strong mediator to encourage reluctant parties to negotiate (Quandt, 1986:337). He admits, in conclusion, that power is at the core of

Table 6
Stages in Camp David Peacemaking
(Derived from Quandt)

Phase 1   From Carter's Inauguration to Sadat's Jerusalem Visit
                    January 20, 1977 - November 19, 1977

The American Role

Negotiating Style:

1) Policy made at the highest level because issues are controversial, stakes are high, public interest is great.
2) Believes the status quo is unstable.
3) Prepare to pay heavily in promises of aid and arms to get an agreement.
4) Actively committed to finding a solution to the conflict; item has high priority.
5) Dedicated to trying a fresh approach toward resolving the issue.
6) Prefers a comprehensive solution over the step-by-step strategy adopted by Kissinger.
7) Will pursue solution formulae with a sense of justice, not amoral deals.
8) Prefers to concentrate on agenda of broad principles with implementation in stages.
9) Wants to lead process to resolve the conflict.
10) Intends to build strong personal relations with party leaders.
11) Believes the parties need to negotiate directly.

Issues:

1) A comprehensive peace settlement.
2) Reaffirmation of UN Resolution 242.
3) Normal relations and an end to belligerence.
4) Israeli withdrawal from territories, mutually recognized borders.
5) Security arrangements and guarantees.
6) Provision for a Palestinian entity and a means sought to permit self-determination in deciding their future status.
7) Exchange of territory for peace between parties.

Process:

1) Seek advanced agreement before participating in Geneva Conference.
2) Develop "negotiating drafts" directly from party views.
3) Bilateral meetings with Israel, Egypt, Jordan, Syria.
4) Pressure on Israel to change position toward Palestinians.
5) US-USSR Joint Statement issued.
6) US-Israeli Joint Statement issued.
7) Request Egypt to take a "bold step" for peace.

Table 6 (continued)

Israeli Policy and Reactions	Egyptian Policy and Reactions
Style:	Style:
1) Emphasize rigid ideology.	1) Promise flexibility.
2) Prefer inactive US role.	2) Prefer active US role.
3) Prefer bilateral negotiations.	3) Prefer bilateral negotiations.
4) Oppose Geneva Conference.	4) Prefer secret agreements.
Issues:	Issues:
1) Peaceful relations before territory exchange.	1) Territory exchange before peaceful relations.
2) Piecemeal settlement.	2) Comprehensive settlement.
3) Ignore Palestinian issue.	3) Incorporate Palestinian issue.
Process:	Process:
1) US-Israeli Joint Statement, October 5, 1977.	1) Sadat announces he will visit Jerusalem November 9, 1977.
Status:	Status:
Israel feels US pressure yet gets a joint statement to define common goals.	Egypt satisfied by strong US role yet frustrated by joint US-Israel and US-USSR statements.

Phase 2   From Sadat's *Jerusalem* visit to Camp David Summit
November 20, 1977 - September 5, 1978

The American Role

Negotiating Style:

1) Central role as conflict mediator continues.
2) Joins "Political Committee" in direct Egypt-Israel negotiations.
3) Demands nonpolemical agenda and discussion.
4) Considers way to apply pressure and influence.
5) Modify Arab role from multilateral representation and focus solely on Egypt as key to the Arab position.

Issues:

1) Exchange of territory for peace between parties, now Israel and Egypt only.
2) Link Israel-Egypt peace to Palestinian issue.

137

Table 6 (continued)

Process:

      1) Establish Secret Planning Group to formulate specific proposals for President Carter.
      2) Pressure Israel to accept rights for Palestinians.
      3) Invite Israel and Egypt to Camp David Summit.

Israeli Policies and Reactions	Egyptian Policies and Reactions
Style:	Style:
1) Begin is intransigent.	1) Sadat is impulsive.
2) Begin is immersed in detail.	2) Sadat seeks broad strategy.
3) Begin wants declaration of principles.	3) Sadat wants specific promises.
Issues:	Issues:
1) Territory-for-peace exchange with no Palestinian linkage.	1) Territory-for-peace exchange with Palestinian linkage.
Process:	Process:
1) Begin visits Egypt.	1) Agree to begin direct negotiations with Israel.
2) Agree to begin direct negotiations with Egypt.	2) Establish two joint committees: Political and Military.
3) Establish two joint committees: Political and Military.	
Status:	Status:
Frustrated by US pressure yet accept invitation to Camp David Summit.	Frustrated by lack of results, accept invitation to Camp David Summit.

Phase 3   Camp David Summit, September 5 - September 17, 1978

The American Role

Negotiating Style:

      1) Optimistic about Carter's persuasive powers to win trust of Begin and Sadat.
      2) Belief that party conflict and hostility can be overcome and replaced with common interest and commitment to peace.
      3) Try to get Begin and Sadat to establish a good personal relationship.
      4) Limit expectations to joint statement for guidelines for future negotiations rather than a detailed agreement.
      5) Tell Sadat that agreement on general principles serves little purpose.

Table 6 (continued)

6) Tell Begin that Israeli position on the West Bank, Gaza, and Palestinians is a serious obstacle to peace.
7) Media blackout, no press briefings during summit.

Issues:

1) An Egypt-Israel peace treaty framework with or without linkage to the Palestinian issue.
2) The principle of withdrawal on all fronts, in condition of peace and security.
3) Withdrawal is a multidimensional concept to be handled in stages.
4) Security and withdrawal are intimately related. A long-term Israeli security presence in the West Bank and Gaza is a legitimate objective.
5) Sovereignty and borders are issues that cannot be resolved without Jordanian and Palestinian participation.
6) A recognition of the Palestinian problem in all its aspects, including legitimate rights of the people to enable the Palestinians to participate in the determination of their own future.
7) Israeli moratorium on settlements.

Process:

1) Day 1-2:
Meetings with Sadat and Begin reveal "common interest" and personal contact. Means to resolve dispute fail. These men do not communicate, do not get along personally.
2) Day 3-10:
Numerous negotiation document drafts developed, discussed separately with Egyptians and Israelis; little progress. Tranquil atmosphere promoting claustrophobia, not peace. No meetings between Sadat and Begin.
3) Day 11-13:
Inform parties three days remain to form some agreement and plead for concessions form both sides.
Twenty-third negotiation draft accepted by Israel and Egypt as Camp David Accords:
    a) A framework for peace in the Middle East (general principles for solving the Palestinian issue)
    b) A framework for the conclusion of a peace treaty between Israel and Egypt (detailed formula for returning Sinai to Egyptian sovereignty)

Israeli Policies and Reactions	Egyptian Policies and Reactions
Style:	Style:
1) Begin can walk out at any time.	1) Sadat cannot afford failure; has great expectations.
2) Begin concentrates on procedure.	2) Sadat concentrates on substance.
3) Begin is detailed and technical.	3) Sadat is imprecise with words.
4) Begin is not interested in Sinai agreement, only West Bank and Gaza.	4) Sadat is not interested in West Bank/Gaza agreement, only Sinai.

Table 6 (continued)

<u>Israeli Policies and Reactions</u>

Issues:

    1) Desire separate peace with Egypt not linked to Palestinian issue (separate peace avoids full Arab power or US pressure).

Process:

    1) Refuse Sinai concessions until link with West Bank is dropped.
    2) Threaten to walk out of negotiations.
    3) Pressure Carter to adopt Israeli position.
    4) Sign Camp David Accords with semi-link between Sinai and Palestinian issue.

Status:

    Israel is promised a bilateral peace treaty with Egypt and avoids specific agreement on Palestinian issue. Three months to negotiate a treaty.

<u>Egyptian Policies and Reactions</u>

Issues:

    1) Desire no separate peace but a comprehensive settlement linked to Palestinian issue (separate peace gives Israel no further incentive to negotiate).

Process:

    1) Insist on West Bank link to Sinai.
    2) Threaten to walk out of negotiations.
    3) Pressure Carter to adopt Egyptian position.
    4) Sign Camp David Accords with semi-link between Sinai and Palestinian issues.

Status:

    Egypt is promised the return of Sinai and gets broad link to Palestinian issue in framework statement. Three months to negotiate a treaty.

Phase 4   From Camp David Summit to Peace Treaty, September 17, 1978 - March 26, 1979

<u>The American Role</u>

Negotiating Style:

    1) Continue to develop negotiation drafts for consideration by each party.
    2) Carter's personal involvement continues.
    3) Issues separated into technical (handled at subministerial level) and political (presidential involvement).
    4) Pressure parties for agreement.

Issues:

    1) Concern over Arab opposition to Camp David documents.
    2) Concern over Israeli domestic criticism to Camp David documents.

Process:

    1) Bilateral meetings with Israel and Egypt.
    2) Final treaty document drafted and signed by the parties.
    3) Promise $3 billion military aid to Israel; $1.5 billion military aid to Egypt.

Table 6 (continued)

<u>Israeli Policies and Reactions</u>

Style:

　　1) No hurry for an agreement.

Issues:

　　1) Timing of the withdrawal: establish
　　diplomatic relations before returning
　　territory.
　　2) Priority of obligations: the treaty with
　　Egypt should supersede other Egyptian
　　commitments.
　　3) Commitment to solve Palestinian
　　issue: prefer vague language

Process:

　　1) Jewish settlements on West Bank
　　continue.
　　2) Sign treaty.
　　3) Accept US aid.

Status:

　　Israel gets the separate peace treaty
　　with Egypt and $3 billion military aid.

<u>Egyptian Policies and Reactions</u>

Style:

　　1) Hurry to get an agreement.

Issues:

　　1) Timing of the withdrawal: elections
　　for Palestinians before establishing
　　diplomatic relations.
　　2) Priority of obligations: the treaty with
　　Israel counts the same as other
　　Egyptian commitments.
　　3) Commitment to solve Palestinian
　　issue: prefer specific, detailed
　　language.

Process:

　　1) Arabs pressure Egypt to withdraw
　　from negotiation process.
　　2) Sign treaty.
　　3) Accept US aid.

Status:

　　Egypt gets Sinai back and $1.5 billion
　　military aid.

negotiations and that some issues cannot be resolved through reason and compromise.

CONCLUSION

Several factors have emerged for sustaining an environment conducive to negotiation in the Arab–Israeli dispute. It is most obvious, perhaps, that the issue of mutual trust between the parties—stressed as a significant part of principled negotiation—is absolutely essential. Currently, however, images of enemy perceptions tend to be continuously reinforced through the counteraction of nationalist ideology, which weakens the socialization and development of this particular component. As to the expansion of creative ideas to resolve aspects of the dispute, a positive sign is that problem fractionalization—turning issues into smaller, manageable parts—is a more successful method for reaching resolution. On establishing principles as precedents, the Camp David accords remain as a model for implementing the land-for-peace exchange in a manner providing benefits to both parties. The role of a third party—mediators representing the United Nations or a single Great Power, usually the United States—has a long and intense history in trying to sustain a favorable environment for negotiation on Middle East problems.

All of these elements are related in the following way. Usually, a conflict becomes easier to resolve as the threat factor is increasingly balanced with trust (Wehr, 1979). Whatever third-party intervenors can do to reduce the level of threat and raise the level of trust increases the chances for a favorable negotiation setting. Facilitating communication between parties, in an effort to modify an initially hostile political atmosphere, makes the setting more conducive to mediation and peace. This is because third-party mediators can listen to the perceptions and rationale offered by the disputants, help identify conditions that may permit partial solutions, propose small steps away from intense confrontation, and generally provide a medium of exchange between antagonists. One outcome of the numerous negotiation attempts and extensive discussions about the issues in the Arab–Israeli dispute is that parties have come closer to understanding the basis for each other's position, even though they may not be in sympathy with it. Factors such as miscommunication, misperception, stereotyping, and mirror images are important considerations that have to be dealt with before bargaining can really work.

It is argued that conflict can be more readily resolved once cognitive and perceptive aspects have been eliminated (Wehr, 1979). Differences may be rooted in the various orientations of policymakers who use different analysis models that lead to different conclusions when faced with the same information. The causes of disagreement are more likely to be isolated when parties are in contact, either directly or through a mediator who provides interpretations that represent all points of view and opinions. Understanding the positions of antagonists without subscribing to either position, helping parties vent frustrations and judging when and how a conflict-resolution proposal might work, and imagining ways to combine alternative solutions and ensure good communication are all negotiation skills that have been part of several of the efforts over the Arab–Israeli conflict.

The message in sustaining negotiations is that notions of winning have to be modified from zero-sum to non-zero-sum perceptions. In spite of the history of numerous failures, this factor has bred some success in the negotiation picture in the Arab–Israeli conflict. Winning is the goal of all parties engaged in a dispute, yet there are also intangible goals that may offset the concrete reward of victory, such as responses to humiliation, to a perception of injustice, or to a sense of lack of consideration and respect. The balance of all of these forces suggests that in a workable strategy for solving the issues between Palestinians and Israelis, small settlements are preferred over total resolution plans. Resolution might meet the felt needs and interests of all parties, but is possible only with extensive negotiation encounters, ample political courage on the part of all relevant policymakers, and a full set of resources and promises for each side to back feelings of doubt and to overcome the mistrust factor. These are the lessons for sustaining a momentum of negotiation.

7

From Conflict to Negotiation: Predictions

What are the steps involved in moving from a conflict environment to a favorable negotiation setting? The purpose of this chapter is to analyze the linkage between elements in the conflict frame and components in the negotiation process. At various points in the following discussion, a series of propositions are listed that focus on particular conditional arrangements that may enhance the possibilities for serious and comprehensive negotiations to begin to resolve the Israeli–Palestinian conflict. In essence, the basic argument is that both sides will be willing to engage in direct talks and consider settlement once they have developed sufficient communication links to alter their mutual negative images, developed a commitment to negotiate their differences, and agreed to focus on certain realities of the situation, namely their common interests, the perceived or actual changing power balance between them, and the costs of stalemate. From this scheme, a final word on negotiation prospects in this long-standing conflict is offered at the conclusion. But first, a short analysis, from a theoretical perspective, of the effects of territorial partitioning.

PARTITION CONSEQUENCES

The first officially sanctioned and partially implemented solution to the growing disturbance between the Arabs and the Jews was the UN partition plan of November 1947. This plan in effect laid the groundwork for further, more intense conflict and nearly a half century later is still relevant, since any negotiation must take this fact into account. What were the implications of this solution attempt?

Divisions have profound political ramifications, and dividing territory to solve national rivalry problems almost always leads to hostility, not peaceful coexistence. G. Henderson, R. Lebow, and J. Stoessinger (1974), in their analysis of partition, drew some conclusions about the patterns of interstate relations that emerged in the postdivision period and suggested likely future outcomes. The consequences of partition may lead to three possible solutions: unification into a single state; mutual acceptance of the status quo, normalizing relations; or limited confederation, combining autonomous and joint organization across governmental responsibility (Henderson et al., 1974:437–38).

Unification of the disputed territory of the British mandate, imposed through military conquest of one side by another, seems quite unlikely in the near future. Unification reached through political victory is an alternative possibility. According to this scenario, the internal political and economic weakness of one of the divided units leads to the collapse of its regime, thereby allowing unification to proceed without significant military resistance. It is most likely to happen in cases where the disparity in size, population, and economic resources is sufficiently great to give one side a decisive advantage. Essentially this characterization fits the descriptive differences between Israelis and Palestinians. However, the absence of religious, ethnic, or linguistic cleavages or widespread popular sentiment favoring unification (though the PLO has expressed the idea of a unified, secular state where Jews, Muslims, and Christians would live together) and the outside opposition to such a plan suggest it would be an unrealistic outcome.

Peaceful coexistence, Henderson et al. discovered, is possible following a stalemate of unsuccessful bids at military conquest by parties when each of the partitioned units has a resurgent economy and political stability and receives continual support from its respective superpower ally. In this environment, rapprochement is possible. In no way do these conditions describe the divisional conflict between Arabs and Jews. The basis for perceiving strong internal incentives for reducing hostilities is growing yet is still weak.

The third solution arrangement, a limited federation of interests, has no application among partitioned states and remains a hypothetical possibility. It has been suggested by Abba Eban and others as one way to negotiate a settlement in the Arab–Israeli dispute, however, and was encouraged in the UN partition resolution.

Relations between divided states do change, Henderson and colleagues concluded, as a function of the degree of stability and legitimacy of each unit in the partition, relations between each unit and its respective superpower, and relations between the superpowers themselves. For example, Henderson et al. hypothesize that as divided units develop internal strength and as hostility between their respective superpower backers decreases, the units are likely to possess greater freedom of action and seek improved relations with each other. All divided units begin with intense mutual hostility and, through the course of their existence, may not necessarily achieve an advanced stage of declining hostility. This plateau is reached only as the result of peculiar and fortuitous combinations of circumstances (Henderson et al., 1974:438–39).

The defining characteristics of initial division usually result in intense hostility marked by mutual nonrecognition, ideological conflict, attempts to fortify and close the border, attempts to subvert the opponent's regime through propaganda, and possible militarization of the conflict. Middle-term division, by contrast, means declining hostility between units. Defining characteristics may include tacit or formal acceptance of coexistence, dilution of claims to sole-successor status, a decline in ideological confrontation, the salience of the border to permit exchange of persons and ideas, a decline in subversion, and a mutual recognition that military confrontation is less likely. Symbolic acts often associated with this stage included an exchange of visits between leaders, public statements renouncing military solutions, agreements on border questions, and public recognition of the partition line as an inviolable boundary (439–40).

Partition, intended to resolve conflict by separating hostile ethnic communities and allowing each to satisfy its demands for separate political units, has not proved very successful. Why? Hostility between the minority group and the dominant community helps promote interstate conflict. In addition, conflicting groups have rarely agreed on where the boundary between them ought to be drawn; this has led to bitter territorial disputes. Henderson et al. found that in every country that was ultimately partitioned, the conflicting ethnic groups were to some extent geographically intermingled. In the Middle East, the existence of a substantial Arab minority in Israel and, since 1967, even greater numbers of Arabs in Jerusalem, the West Bank, and Gaza has forced Israel to implement security measures that contribute to Arab–Israeli hostility. The inhumane treatment of Jewish minorities in Arab states has angered Israelis, and public opinion polls reveal that Jewish immigrants from Arab states have the most uncompromising attitudes toward Israel's neighbors.

No partitioned country was able to agree on a mutually acceptable border (444). In every instance, fighting broke out, and the de facto border became the cease-fire line between the conflicting groups. Inevitably, one or both sides were dissatisfied with this line and laid claim to additional territory on the basis of historical association and/or ethnic consanguinity. In the case of Palestine, the Arab side has denied the right of Israel to exist as a nation and lays claim to the total territory of mandated Palestine. The Israelis, for their part, have seized territory originally set aside for the Palestinians in the 1947 UN plan and, since 1967, have held substantial portions of additional land. The Arabs are pledged to liberate the territories conquered by Israel while Israel seeks security frontiers of sufficient depth to protect the nation from attack. The border issue is unresolved, each side laying incompatible claims to disputed borders and territory.

Henderson and colleagues conclude that there is little hope of resolving outstanding issues between partitioned countries because territorial disputes diffuse slowly and because the damaging aspects of such conflicts frequently mean that expressions of hostility and plans for war become self-fulfilling. In the Middle East this has led to a series of military confrontations. Defeat in war and ensuing political and economic discontent on both sides have reinforced the intensity of the original conflict, where political activity serves as a basic instrument in the creation of emotions that kindle the psychology of division. Division is a catalyst for political mobilization, and when confrontational activity intensifies on either side, the division will run deeper (448).

Many factors affect the psychological and political orientations that maintain divisions. Among them are ethnic, linguistic, and religious elements; stability and legitimacy of government; distribution of natural resources; length of historical experience; influence of neighboring states; and the role of the Great Powers—although the relative importance of each of these components is hard to estimate. Henderson et al. suggest that partition creates internal needs for ideological identification as a result of confrontation, crisis, and strife between groups. The ideology component breeds propaganda, and propaganda breeds hostility. Because partitioned states are swiftly mobilized, problems that are communal suddenly become national. This situation does little to encourage the forces of compromise and rationality needed to reduce the tensions created, let alone provide solutions for resolving the conflict. The only possibility for escaping the conflict syndrome is direct bargaining and mutual compromise, in short, negotiation. Henderson et al. offer three propositions:

1. Once organizations created out of hostility begin to speak to each other, propaganda will recede, ideology will soften slightly, and the organizations that fostered separateness will change.
2. If communication can develop into an expanding number of joint functions and tasks for organizations on both sides of the division, group reinforcement processes will begin to support unity over disunity.
3. If this stage can be succeeded by attempts at reduction in armed forces, emotional tensions will ebb, and prospects for rapprochement or unity will brighten (454).

Today, Middle East diplomacy is still concerned with debate over the application of land for peace to the remaining disputed territories, even though the details of compromise and concession hold many complications. In the peace process, settlement is no longer viewed as all-or-nothing by the warring parties, and the attainment of a final, lasting peace is not the principal objective of the policymakers. Rather, because final settlement looms so far in the distance, peacemakers have focused their energy on finding a suitable mechanism to reengage a search for such a peace sometime in the future. Steps in this process have come to substitute substantive progress toward peace. The equation of "process, therefore peace," argues Robert Satloff (1986–87:25), reached its height when various principal actors, namely Jordan, Israel, and Egypt, proposed imaginative processes to advance the cause of peace, proposals ranging from a U.S.–PLO dialogue to an international peace conference with direct Israeli–PLO talks.

"Land for peace" remains a problem because Israel's minimum requirements exceed the Arabs' maximum concessions and because the Palestinians' minimum requirements exceed the Israelis' maximum concessions. This reflects the difficulty of achieving a peace plan when it is impossible to conceive of either side abandoning its basic strategy. Yet, no one has given up entirely, and this has to be seen as a sign of encouragement.

The prognosis for a healthy negotiation climate in the Arab–Israeli dispute is not good. Nor is it hopeless. Seemingly intractable problems have been resolved before; not all international crises lead to further war. In light of intransigence, the protracted nature of the conflict, historical practices of attempts to resolve Middle East disputes, problems created by the partition solution, and the battle marks from all of the Arab–Israeli wars, how is it possible to develop a climate that fosters movement of either side toward a negotiated settlement? In understanding this process of moving from conflict to compromise to peace, we are helped by the insights of negotiation theorists. Much of the negotiation literature, however, deals only with the methods, procedures, and mechanics of the bargaining process where formalized negotiation is already under way.

How to negotiate successfully is the thrust, rather than whether to negotiate at all. Although some of these features are important before the parties come to the table—notably flexibility, alternative hard and soft strategies, and salient focal points—they operate in a more subtle way. For internationalized disputes, the parties continue to operate in a milieu of domestic political environments during the prenegotiation stage without benefit of constant, direct interaction, and response from the other side. This means a momentum of cooperation and accommodation is far more difficult to establish.

Three typologies of negotiation, developed by Frederich C. Iklé (1967), Glenn Snyder and Paul Diesing (1976), and I. William Zartman (1985), address the problem directly by putting forth propositions to explain the onset of negotiation. Iklé's pioneering study, *How Nations Negotiate*, focuses on common interests between parties as one very important predictor for starting negotiations. Snyder and Diesing, analyzing sixteen cases of crisis with significant bargaining content, postulate how the conditions that parties bring to a negotiating environment relate to given outcomes in a cost-benefit framework. Zartman's intent is to discover a climate of changing power balance between parties, which in his words makes a conflict "ripe for resolution." He focuses on postcolonial Africa. Each approach contains a logical base for structuring negotiation potential generally, and from the variety of propositions presented, we are able to draw some inferences that fit the Arab–Israeli dispute.

COMMON INTERESTS

Negotiation occurs when the perceived common interests of disputing parties supersede the significance of conflict issues that divide them. Negotiation is a process in which explicit proposals are put forward ostensibly for the purpose of reaching agreement on an exchange or on the realization of a common interest where conflicting interests are present. There must be both common interests and issues of conflict. Without common interest, there is nothing to negotiate for, and without conflict, there is nothing to negotiate about (Iklé, 1967:2–3).

According to Iklé, folk wisdom about negotiation postulates that it is the best way to resolve conflict and avoid the use of force. It requires a willingness to compromise, and it demands concessions from both sides. It implies that no side can expect to win everything but that fair solutions can be discovered. And if a conflict exists over many issues, the less controversial ones should be solved first, since initial agreement will lead to further agreement. These beliefs and expectations are, however, riddled with ambiguity. How are fair solutions fashioned and judged? Will postponed issues become harder or easier to solve? Why is compromise the preferred norm? Iklé (1) argues that negotiation is an instrument of diplomacy that may be used either to settle conflicts short of war or to exacerbate hostilities and erode foundations for peace. Thus the main focus for understanding negotiation is to determine how the process of discussion and agreement is related to the outcome.

He classifies five types of negotiation, of which two—normalization agreements and redistribution agreements—are relevant here. Negotiation for the purpose of a normalization agreement is meant to terminate the abnormal or to formalize arrangements tacitly arrived at, such as to stop fighting through a cease-fire or truce, to reestablish diplomatic relations, or to end a temporary occupation in exchange for a military alliance and to regularize other postwar uncertainties through a peace treaty.

Negotiations for normalization are strongly influenced by the instability of the abnormal situation they are supposed to settle. If fighting continues while negotiations are prolonged, each side may gain through force what it failed to gain through bargaining. After a temporary suspension of fighting, however, the threat of a resumption of hostilities tends to become less effective for bargaining purposes, unless supported by existing military capabilities or preparations that make a new offensive both likely and dangerous to the opponent. In the event that no agreement is reached, continued fighting will change the fortunes of war and may erupt again into fighting. Conversely, hostilities may gradually subside despite the failure of negotiations, so that a tacit truce will in fact be established (29–30).

Negotiations for the purpose of a redistribution agreement are characterized by a demand of an offensive side for a change in its favor, consisting of a new distribution of territory, political influence, institutional powers and rights, economic and military assets, or the like. Essentially, what the offensive side gains, the defensive loses; hence the offensive side has to couple its demand with the threat of worse consequences if the demand is refused. In the most acute form, the offensive side presents its central demand in the form of an ultimatum and makes specific threats. If the offensive side is successful, agreement in this type of negotiation will lead to a change in the status quo, as the defensive side complies with all or part of the demand. If the offensive side is unsuccessful, an agreement may still result whereby the defensive side consents to exchange some face-saving formula for a formal withdrawal of the demand. If either side is stubborn, redistribution negotiations may end without any agreement. In this case, either the status quo is preserved tacitly or the offensive side carries out part or all of its threat (31).

In redistribution, the conflicting interest is the principal topic of negotiation, whereas the common interest remains tacit or is shunted into peripheral bargaining. The conflicting interest stems from the demand by the offensive side. The common interest lies in the mutual desire to avoid violence, that is, the offensive side would rather keep its gains more modest than carry out its threat, and the defensive side would rather relinquish something than challenge the threat. Occasionally a complementary interest in an exchange is added to this basic common interest, such as the formal withdrawal of a threat in exchange for a face-saving formula or the preservation of long-term friendship in exchange for a modest concession.

There is an interesting difference in the reaction of public opinion to negotiation for normalization and for redistribution. A cease-fire, an armistice, or a peace treaty—the ostensible goal of negotiation for normalization—is usually supported by public opinion on both sides. In negotiation for redistribution, the offensive side usually appears as the disturber of peace, unless the redistribution is aimed at the liberation of occupied areas or colonies (32–33).

Why does a defensive side negotiate? In certain cases they may decide it is better to yield, since not doing so may provoke the offensive side to carry out its threat, leading to even greater losses. However, in many redistribution negotiations, the defensive party decides against yielding, either because the costs would be too great or because it seems unlikely that the threat would be carried out. The defensive side runs several risks by negotiating on a redistribution demand, according to Iklé (33). First, the negotiators of the defensive side might feel they ought to demonstrate flexibility and offer concessions toward satisfying the offensive demand. Second, they may come to regard a situation that has been the subject of prolonged negotiations as abnormal and may deem it appropriate to change the status quo in order to normalize it. Despite these risks, the government of the defensive side may have countervailing reasons for meeting with its opponents even though it concludes that it need not yield. The defense side may be in favor of negotiation because it thinks negotiation has certain advantageous side effects. In addition, when faced with certain offensive demands, some may favor negotiation in order to find out what the opponent really wants. They feel the opponent's true goal must be more reasonable or more realistic, and then a solution satisfactory to both sides could be found.

Proposals play a key role in the process through which the parties come to terms. Indeed, the confrontations, revisions, and final acceptance of proposals at the conference table are sometimes all that is meant by negotiation. Proposals are surface markers that indicate more substantial developments underneath. Governments prepare them to spread propaganda, to maintain contact, to stave off violent actions, or for similar reasons that do not concern agreement. Ostensibly, proposals always represent an offer in that they give a description of the terms that are alllegedly being made available to the opponent. Yet, in contrast to business negotiations, governments can always withdraw their offers after they have been accepted. In short, proposals are meant to influence an opponent to change expectations about one's anticipated minimum demands and to alter anticipations concerning the opponent's minimum terms (194).

The manner of negotiating and the conditions under which a party accepts or rejects an agreement affect its bargaining strength in the future (76). Thus, parties want to protect or improve their position for potential subsequent negotiating sessions over new or unresolved issues. This means the outcome of negotiation ranges from total disagreement to complete agreement, with varying mixtures and specificity in the eventual settlement (59).

Iklé outlines a broad framework of considerations that enter into any negotiation environment and, on this basis, explains why agreement may or may not be achieved. His predictions emphasize elements of motive, intention, and reasoning rather than the demonstrable behavior of the participants. The other two theories build from his analysis and develop specific propositions that are empirically testable.

CHANGING POWER BALANCE

Negotiation occurs when a conflict is ripe for resolution, that is, there is a threat of conflict escalation, alternative policy tracks exist, and a changing power balance between parties is occurring. When successful, conflict resolution through negotiation depends on the identification of the ripe moment in different patterns of crisis and conflict escalation. Zartman develops several related propositions to describe the point at which parties are willing to negotiate (Zartman, 1985:232–36):

1. Conflict is ripe for resolution when both sides are unable to achieve their aims, resolve the problem, or win the conflict alone and feel uncomfortable in the costly status quo.

2. Conflict is ripe for resolution when both sides realize that matters will swiftly get worse if they have not improved in ways that negotiation seems to define. Here a catastrophe threatens the mutual checks the parties impose on each other.

3. Conflict is ripe for resolution when a crisis has just occurred with losses on both sides and the basic conflict remains unresolved.

4. Conflict is ripe for resolution when the parties perceive a sense of urgency, for without a deadline for agreement, opponents become accustomed to living with an abnormal situation.

5. Conflict resolution depends on rendering the conflict option unattractive and on conveying an attractive option of accommodation and negotiation. Repeated inability to achieve aims contributes to a search for alternatives, although the ineffectiveness of the original country goals has to be demonstrated rather than argued, for predictions of failure are not convincing.

6. In cases of asymmetry between the parties, conflict is ripe for resolution when the stronger side starts slipping and the weaker side begins to rise.

In sum, the success of negotiation is tied to the perception and creation of a ripe moment when the parties are locked in a mutual, destructive stalemate marked by a recent or impending catastrophe, when unilateral solutions are blocked and joint solutions have become conceivable, or when the relative strength of parties begins to shift. Opponents in conflict can come to perceive these moments themselves, but they frequently need the help of outside mediators. Once the moment has come, parties and mediators can turn to the creative trial-and-error attempt to find an acceptable way out of the conflict.

How is such a moment identified? Zartman states that the moment of conflict-resolution ripeness stands out conceptually even though it is buried in the maze of individual events. A clear definition of this opportunity may allow recognition of a ripe moment only after it has passed. In other words, there is a retrospective assessment built into Zartman's basic propositions, when prospective sensing of the approaching moment is the real clue to testing whether this framework of negotiation is accurate and useful. The perception of a negotiation scenario is described vaguely by Zartman in the following words: "Once the approach is sensed, there is the difficult task of bringing the parties to recognize that the time has come" (1985:237).

Once parties have been convinced that they need a way out, a proposal for solving the conflict is prepared. It must appear relatively just and satisfactory to both parties, and therefore it needs to cover major issues of the conflict and include important demands from both sides to ensure compliance with a potential agreement. Parties cannot be expected to give up their claims without receiving compensation. In some cases it will be possible to work directly toward a solution; in others, it may be possible to agree only on a first step that points the conflict in a more manageable direction (241).

These conditions can be met, providing there is an effective communication link between the parties. Processes are required to alter perceptions, promote the points of view of the parties, and test whether an accurate, agreed-on information base can be achieved. Initiatives by one party are inhibited by fear that they will be perceived as a confession of weakness or of defeat. Furthermore, a willingness to negotiate might imply a willingness to compromise, and leaders of parties to a dispute are rarely in a position to demonstrate such a willingness. Conflict resolution is best carried out in concert. If conciliators are available to the parties to bring trust, reliability, good faith, and credibility to negotiating environments, the chances for success are improved (238–39).

Altogether, Zartman argues that a successful negotiation process can begin when parties perceive an urgency to discuss or resolve the issues of conflict, when shifts in power balance between the conflict parties are apparent, and when strong internal leadership exists on each side. Although it is not clear whether these elements are necessary or sufficient conditions, they do suggest where to look to determine prospects of a negotiation climate in the Middle East crisis.

STALEMATE COSTS

Negotiation occurs when the costs of stalemate exceed the value of compromised settlement. The bargaining process gives parties the opportunity to attempt to influence each other's decision in the context of identified conflicting and common interests. The relative strength of the two sets of interest is critical, according to Snyder and Diesing (1976). They hypothesize that conflict is ripe for resolution when the value to be gained in settling outweighs the sacrifice both parties would have to make to reach agreement (Snyder and Diesing, 1976:476).

A settlement must benefit both parties by improving their general relations and removing obstacles to their alignment and must compensate for losses each party would accrue in accepting the other's minimum demands. Bargaining occurs only if the perceived common interest in reaching agreement is strong enough and/or the conflicting interests are weak enough to create a range of potential settlements that both parties would prefer over the absence of agreement (475). Moreover, Snyder and Diesing suggest a chain-linked set of relations that define successive stages of the bargaining process. The entire process originates at the ill-defined or unbounded prenegotiation period. The logic and realistic basis for eventual, potential negotiated settlement develops along the following lines:

- In a prenegotiation period, each party holds a general belief system comprising a set of initial expectations about the other party's likely behavior during the conflict, as well as images of the self and of the opponent. One party thinks of its own behavior as defensive or legitimate and the other's as aggressive or illegitimate; the other party holds the reverse view.

- An initial bargaining strategy is chosen on this basis.

- Expectations and strategy are resistent to change, and hence incoming information is interpreted to conform to them.

- If information continually contradicts expectations and cannot be assimilated, expectations are adjusted, though as little as possible. A small adjustment of expectations leads to a change of tactics, for example, conciliatory gestures.

- A change of strategy from firm resistance to accommodation occurs only when new information (created cumulatively or through a sudden, dramatic input) clearly indicates that a key expectation on which the whole strategy is based is wrong.

- Parties develop their initial estimates and expectations of relative resolve and bargaining power by comparing each other's interests and military forces. They change these estimates during the bargaining process by further comparisons of the intensity of interests and by direct observation of each other's behavior (494).

On the basis of their argument and analysis of different twentieth-century international crises, Snyder and Diesing concluded that the outcomes of crises were governed by varying conditions:

1. Conflicts resolved through negotiations reached by even compromises from each party occurred under conditions of equal bargaining power, coupled with mutual perceptions that each side was resolved to go to war or begin an escalation process leading toward war rather than accept the other's initial demand but that each was willing to accept less than its original demand. This realization led to internal assessments of goals and a process of mutual concessions.

2. Conflicts resolved through negotiations reached by unequal compromises or one-sided capitulation resulted from a mutual recognition of inequality where (a) one party's interests in the issue were much greater than the other had expected; (b) one party received more support from its allies than its opponent had expected; or (c) one party took a firm position initially and later realized it did not have sufficient military strength to risk war. Typically the imbalance was so great that the less-resolved party had no alternative but to back down completely.

3. Conflicts not resolved through negotiation but ending in war contained strong and mirror-opposite legitimacy beliefs held with equal intensity by each side.

Snyder and Diesing suggest that perceptions of legitimacy are potent in determining bargaining power and outcomes. The party that believes it is in the right, and that communicates this belief to an opponent who has some doubts about the legitimacy of its own position, nearly always wins. What creates and structures legitimacy? It often derives from defense of a long-term status quo against the attempt to change by threat of force, say Snyder and Diesing. In such cases, the defender wins except when both sides share the belief that some change in the status quo is more legitimate than its perpetuation. Mutual perceptions of legitimacy or justice of claims severely restrict possibilities for negotiated settlement.

The relative bargaining power of each party will be a function of the asymmetry of interdependence across issues and interests. Parties are interdependent on two levels: the issue in conflict, where each is dependent on the other's concession for the satisfaction of its interests; and common interest, where each is dependent on the other's cooperation for gaining or preserving shared values. Each side attempts to exploit the opponent's dependence on common-interest factors to achieve gains or avoid losses at the conflictual level. (499)

Between adversaries, whether a party decides to stand firm depends on its estimate of whether the other will be firm considering the other's valuation of whatever is in conflict and the parties' comparative military capabilities. In addition, bargaining involves attempts to influence by communication the other party's expectations and decisions. Thus it activates and perhaps modifies the political power that is already latent in existing relations and focuses the interplay of power on a particular issue. Bargaining may also change estimates and values of outcomes, specifically to lower the cost of yielding for both parties. Values may force a reappraisal of what is at stake, and the relative bargaining power then stands revealed. Following such a bargaining process in a prenegotiation period makes the conflict ripe for resolution, argue Snyder and Diesing (488). From this point, the parties negotiate a compromise, or stand firm, or fight (477).

By Snyder and Diesing's analysis, conflicts resolved by negotiated agreement followed a definite pattern of coercive and accommodative strategies applied by the opponents. An initial adoption of a coercive strategy clarified the opponents' comparative resolve, exposed the bargaining-power balances, and revealed the likelihood of breakdown or war if both continued to stand firm. Snyder and Diesing (489) assert that this period of mutual firmness is essential before parties can be in a position to estimate whether and how much they must reduce their demands. Bargainers wish to build up their own resolve image gradually and test the adversary's resolve thoroughly before they feel safe in committing themselves firmly.

Although coercive tactics predominate in the confrontation phase of a crisis and accommodative tactics in the resolution phase, each is leavened with some mixture of the other. For example, Snyder and Diesing suggest that conciliatory gestures accompanying coercive moves reduce the risk that coercion will provoke more intransigence in the opponent. Both sides try to communicate a willingness to accommodate on some issue, with a determination to stand firm on others. Unfortunately, the problem with such mixed strategies is that the message is a complex one to be transmitted accurately to one's opponent (491).

Snyder and Diesing predict that bargaining efforts to achieve formal negotiations will fail, and a crisis will become war, when correction of misperception reveals a conflict of interests so deep that it cannot be resolved either by unilateral retreat or by mutual compromise. As long as two parties mistakenly believe there is a possibility of a settlement, negotiation drags on and the outbreak of war is delayed. When misperceptions are finally corrected and both sides realize there is no chance that either will make a concession acceptable to the other, war occurs. In sum, the outcome of a crisis and the possibilities for negotiated agreement reflect the inherent bargaining power of the parties, combined with their relative posture for war or risk of war (502).

The propositions they offer can be formed into categorical syllogisms to show the logic of connection from one element to the next. The flow of argument is as follows:

1. The legitimacy of claims conveyed by each side determines the asymmetry of their issues and interests.
2. The asymmetry of party issues and interests determines the image of self and opponent, and expectations of negotiation.
3. The images of self and opponent, and expectations of negotiation, determine the relative power balance between the parties.
4. The relative power balance between the parties determines the coercive and accommodative strategies used by each side in the negotiation.

5. The coercive and accommodative strategies used by each side in the negotiation determine the negotiation outcome.

6. The negotiation outcome determines the intentions and expectations each side holds regarding the other's future behavior.

For practical comparisons with the Arab–Israeli dispute, the main concepts are claims of legitimacy, power balances, and threat and compromise strategies. All of them are determinants of bargaining outcomes.

NEGOTIATION PROSPECTS

The ideas of Iklé, Zartman, and Snyder and Diesing contain points of similarity as well as divergence. First, all portray the potential for negotiation as a bilateral, dyadic process, implying that parties reach tacit, mutually reinforcing positions and share the value of settlement before the onset of actual negotiating procedures. The entire approach followed here to identifying obstacles to peace and to marking a climate with negotiation potential has focused on the relational aspects characterizing the parties. The structural connection, rather than separate policies pursued by any party alone, has been used to make predictions. As an alternatives perspective, though, it could be imagined that the realistic possibilities for negotiation rest with a single party to the conflict, specifically the stronger unit, Israel. Does the state of Israel dictate entirely the course of events— promoting war, calling for negotiation, or remaining silent in treating the issues of the Arab–Israeli conflict? Is the country so powerful that the other players do not figure into the calculations for influencing a peaceful or conflictual direction? Iklé gives some attention to this matter in suggesting the conditions under which a defensive side would be willing (or unwilling) to consider changes in the status quo. Although his key propositions do not focus on the single party as pivotal to a negotiation settlement, he recognizes the importance that a single actor to a dispute may assume.

A second shared feature among these theorists on negotiation is that all of them posit a linkage between commonality and conflict intensity between enemies. For example, Iklé argues that as the relationship between perceived common interests and issues of conflict changes in a direction favoring emphasis on the common interests, negotiation is likely to happen. Snyder and Diesing connect the costs and the benefits of stalemate continuance versus negotiated settlement. In each case, the broad, intended hypothesis is the same: as areas of potential agreement widen and attitudes toward compromise and settlement seem more inviting, maintaining the conflict environment becomes unproductive, costly, and unwise. Thus negotiation begins. This connection becomes a tautology that, standing true in the abstract, by definition provides little in the way of guidance for making prospective assessments. In other words, if parties negotiated, they must have altered their views. But how might we discover beforehand whether the dominant perceptions and values placed on settlement and compromise have modified? Are there other predisposing factors identified to enable prediction?

A third common element to all propositions about negotiation relates directly to the question above. In general, causal variables are identified by the separate theorists as a means to understand and appraise negotiation potential. For example, threats of further conflict escalation, strong domestic leadership, and high costs associated with military defense show up in the propositions of Zartman and Snyder and Diesing. However, theorists who have tried to account for conflict resolution have sometimes identified the same group of independent variables for predicting the outbreak of violence, not negotiation. Is it possible that the predictors of war are also the determinants of negotiated settlement? If so, then if movements and trends among these factors were identified, how would accurate predictions be constructed? Zartman states that a threat of conflict escalation may lead to negotiation (in order to avoid another costly stalemated conflict), whereas mainstream arms-race theorists generally suggest that conflict escalation continues in a single, unstoppable path leading to the opposite effect. Snyder and Diesing's chief proposition isolates the costs of stalemate as the central independent variable to promote a healthy environment for negotiated settlement. Yet this can be challenged by the Prisoner's Dilemma model, in which the prediction of rational behavior holds that parties will continue without settlement (so long as they are enemies, have issues of conflict between them, and lack mutual trust) and will bear additional costs, since it is ultimately a safer strategy for protecting one's interests and avoiding a double-cross.

The problems with these negotiation propositions are largely matters of logic and argument: the tautology, inconsistent predictions, and bilateral versus single party approach could be examined with data on Arab–Israeli negotiation attempts, crises, and wars to determine how the hypotheses worked. At this stage, though, a separate issue becomes salient. During the entire range of the dispute, there have been but two serious negotiations, each brokered by an outside power, the United States. These include the Sinai Agreements of 1974 and 1975, and the Camp David peace process, which culminated in the 1979 treaty between Israel and Egypt. In many ways these negotiations have been viewed as unique to the conflict: the factors and features defining the parties' interests and the particular role played by the United States may never be repeated. The events may not represent true negotiating possibilities for the outstanding core issues, and even the flow of activities is limiting. Drawing detailed comparisons between the political environment in the Middle East during the 1970s and the possible developments of the 1980s and 1990s may reveal only the mass of differences without showing whether negotiations may begin anew on separate issues and between another set of players. At the same time, these dramatic events do indicate that intractable problems are at least partially resolvable; negotiations do occur between bitter enemies.

The negotiations between Israel and Egypt in the 1970s do offer some support for the propositions mentioned here. They began after (not before) the October

1973 war, consistent with Zartman's prediction that negotiation follows war. Each side was represented by strong leaders—Sadat and Begin. If strength includes a willingness to pursue a new policy toward hostile neighbors (a policy without precedent) and to tolerate internal dissension, this supports another Zartman hypothesis. The contentious issue, whether the land of Sinai should be held by Israel for security reasons or should be returned to Egypt for reasons of sovereignty, was not subject to extensive claims of legitimacy by both sides. The area, though significant for what it represented, was not viewed as critical to the future existence of either country. The absence of intensive and nearly identical arguments about rights and legitimacy concerning Sinai facilitated a favorable environment for negotiating, as predicted by Snyder and Diesing. Finally, due to the efforts and generosity of the United States in promoting and securing a negotiated agreement, achieved in part by considerable foreign assistance in money and weaponry to each side, one of the propositions of Iklé is confirmed. It will be recalled that he argues that a defensive side becomes willing to negotiate if it is convinced that certain advantageous side-effects will follow.

By 1990, two more major conflicts had occurred, involving the Israelis and the Palestinians directly, the war in Lebanon and the intifada. Serious negotiating toward settlement has not yet severed the threat of future violence. The outstanding land issue now concerns the West Bank and Gaza, much smaller territories than Sinai and areas densely populated with Palestinians, unlike the barren desert of Sinai. The disputing parties here are far more asymmetric. On the one side is Israel, a sovereign state with numerous military victories and years of foreign support from the United States, which is undisputably the strongest contender. On the other side are the Palestinians, who lack statehood, have no history of military success, and have more symbolic than real foreign support. Moreover, Palestinian leadership is not unified, even though Arafat is a long-term, solid representative of the PLO. But any person for either side who aspires to maintain the central leadership role must follow a careful path between conservative and progressive policies. Attempts to forge new policy lines—to deal with the enemy—are discouraged. For example, for the first time in the history of Israel, Jews were tried by the government for holding peace talks with members of the PLO. (The meeting, held in Rumania in November 1986, was tacitly sanctioned by Arafat, but more extremist Palestinian elements tried to prevent it from taking place and threatened to kill those involved. During the Rumanian meeting, both Israel and the PLO delegates called for an end to violence and expressed their desires to see negotiations and an active search for peace. Neither side, however, committed itself explicitly to any final map for a peace settlement.)

Reactions by Israelis and Palestinians alike to the Rumanian meeting, which was intended to foster peaceful relations and to create a favorable environment for negotiation, produced resentment and conflict. Each side bolstered its claim of legitimacy on the land in question and expressed fundamental needs to argue its own line of justice at the expense of the grievances of the other side. This shows, among other things, a sign of despair. No theorist on negotiation addresses the problem of predicting the course of events once despair sets in. Snyder and Diesing do predict, however, that if contentious issues are argued on grounds of legitimacy, expressed in equal amounts by both sides, conflicts are more likely to be resolved through force than by peaceful negotiation.

Against this movement toward antagonism and away from negotiation is a countervailing dynamic that may be connected more positively to a peaceful resolution of the dispute. All the theorists discussed here note the significance of proposal presentation as an indicator of a healthy climate for arranging negotiation. Iklé wrote about the functions of proposals, Zartman identifies them as "alternative policy tracks," and Snyder and Diesing refer to the "value of compromise settlement." When proposals are offered, negotiation is more likely to happen than without them, even though a proposal may bear little relationship to a final outcome. Proposals suggest points of discussion or may reveal a modified stand by a party in the conflict. They signal a change, a flexibility, and perhaps a chance to achieve a compromise settlement to the dispute. Thus the presentation of proposals and the basic ideas contained in them can be charted as an indicator of encouraging negotiations.

Although different in content and position, most of the proposals generated during the past one and a half decades address six issues related to dispute resolution: (1) Israeli withdrawal from territories taken in the 1967 war, (2) a recognition of the Palestinian people's rights, (3) respect for the sovereignty of Israel, (4) an emphasis on negotiating these issues, (5) the importance of achieving peace in the area, and (6) the establishment of designated Palestinian territory and jurisdiction. All proposals issued since the intifada focus on self-governance and elections for the Palestinians in the West Bank and Gaza.

What is notable in the evolution of these proposals is a gradual but marked movement toward convergence of ideas offered by various parties to reach a resolution of the conflict. All proposals consistently discuss some form of change in Israeli control over the occupied territories, although they diverge in outlining the extent, timing, and conditions to govern the action. Most plans in fact speak of Israeli withdrawal. The Israelis themselves have produced plans for a limited removal of their presence over disputed territories, although the Shamir Plan rules out withdrawal. This item is an unchanging one. Second, most proposals mention the legitimacy and justice and rights of Palestinians. In the 1967 Security Council Resolution 242 (reaffirmed in 1973 by UN Resolution 338), the reference is restricted to "refugees." After that time, however, the rights of the Palestinian people is stated explicitly. Third, the emphasis on a negotiated settlement and the creation of a lasting peace in the region come mainly from outside powers, which is hardly surprising. As items in resolution proposals, neither is mentioned by the Arab side until the Jordanian-Palestinian statement in 1985. Fourth, the respect for sovereignty and territorial integrity for all states in the region, including Israel, is a continuing theme for Israel itself and also is contained in the proposals generated by outside parties. It becomes part of the Arab proposals presented in the 1980s. Altogether, there is movement toward agreement on

Palestinian rights, Israeli sovereignty, peace, and negotiated settlement. The proposals of the 1980s note these points.

Across these four areas there is definite evidence of convergence, even though the points of agreement lack specificity. It is usually far easier to reach unanimity on general, abstract goals, such as the desire for peace and the need for a negotiated settlement, than it is to risk conflict escalation. But a comparison with earlier periods in this dispute shows that such agreement may be cautiously considered as a sign of progress toward some limited solution.

Looking at the dynamics of change in positions, we see it is the Arab side that has shown the greatest modification in its demands, in effect bringing its vision more in line with plans presented by outside parties. One of the elements in all Arab plans, though, is the demand for the creation of an independent Palestinian state. Since the UN partition solution of 1947, the idea lay dormant until the 1974 Rabat Summit. This idea is soundly rejected by Israel and the United States; it has not been directly addressed by the external powers proposals included in this analysis. Thus, although centrifugal movement toward settlement appears on some issues, intensified opposition becomes focused on self-determination for Palestinians. The Israeli government has held with its autonomy plan—where people, not land, would be independent—since 1979, which both Arabs and outside parties reject. Nonetheless, even though the gap is still very wide with respect to resolving this specific issue, the marks of agreement are significant. There is evidence of growing common interests, in support of the negotiation theorists.

Which direction is likely in light of these current conditions? According to the negotiation theorists, parties will develop a commitment to negotiate if under the following scenarios:

1. *The offensive side increases its power to tip the balance in its favor* (Iklé, Zartman). Thus substantial expansion of military power by the Palestinians and guaranteed, real military support from Arabs, in order to supersede the Israeli military might, would enhance the possibilities for serious negotiation to begin. Unlikely.

2. *The defensive side is promised significant side payments in agreeing to negotiate land for peace* (Iklé). Thus real expansion of aid to Israel from its major benefactor (the United States) would encourage the parties to negotiate. Unlikely.

3. *The parties are given a deadline for agreement to underscore the sense of urgency in reaching resolution* (Zartman). Thus proposals and active negotiation participation by the United States, the Soviet Union, and perhaps Europeans to impose restrictions to force the parties to come to agreement would achieve this end. The mechanism of an international conference as written into the 1985 Jordanian–Palestinian Agreement and discussed in the Shultz and Baker plans and included with the documentary materials of UN Security Council Resolution 681 of December, 1990, might help to achieve this end. Possible.

4. *The parties are asymmetric with respect to the legitimacy of claims conveyed by each side* (Snyder and Diesing). Thus if Israel tones down its claims for ''Judea and Samaria'' while the Palestinians continue to carry on the intifada as part of a wider

public campaign to intensify attention on rights in the West Bank, negotiation may occur. Possible.

5. *Both parties share the belief that some change in the status quo is better than its perpetuation* (Snyder and Diesing). Thus a significant increase in dissatisfaction among both Israelis and Palestinians over the current occupation and administration of the West Bank territory is articulated and publicized to the other side. Possible.

The first three suggestions depend on action by outside parties; the last two derive from internal positions. The final point is particularly interesting, for it speaks to the issue of despair noted earlier. Rather than serving as a hindrance and hardening positions, despair may offer a pathway to remedy the situation. But on this point, only time will tell. The first three propositions are relevant to this Arab–Israeli conflict, for as L. C. Brown (1984) argued, consistent with Middle Eastern politics, dispute resolution will continue to rely on external powers. But in light of the current environment, only propositions three and five are realistic for the near future.

What are the effects of the asymmetry of power and the belief that some change is better than a continuation of the status quo? The late Simha Flapan, addressing a group of peace-minded Arabs and Israelis in 1986, stated:

I am perfectly aware of the difficulties involved in dialogue. First, there is the asymmetry involved in the objective situation. The Jewish people have realized their right to self-determination. They have a modern, dynamic state, one of the best armies, equipped with sophisticated weaponry and, according to persistent rumors, a formidable nuclear capacity. . . . Palestinian reality is defined by a lack of sovereignty, dispossession, exile, and occupation. To them suffering is not a memory, not a trauma of the past as it is for the Jewish people, but a daily experience. Is a dialogue possible between the conquered, oppressed, and occupied—and the occupier? I think it is possible because there are forces in Israel which struggle to put an end to the occupation, oppression and rule over another people. The objective asymmetry places on us, the Israelis, a major responsibility but it does not liberate the PLO from adopting a strategy which will make the Israeli peace camp strong enough to change its government and policy. (*New Outlook*, November–December 1986)

What, then, would be the bargaining power of the Palestinians in any future negotiations? What could they hope to achieve? There is one source of strength deriving from the general realization that a lasting settlement in the Middle East will have to include the Palestinians. This bestows on them considerable political power in the Arab world as well as internationally. One of their demands is the right to self-determination and the exercise of national sovereignty, hence the crucial significance of the idea of a Palestinian national authority in the West Bank and Gaza. In this conception, complex questions dealing with demilitarization, inspection, international guarantees, etc., would have to be settled, but without compromising the principle of Palestinian sovereignty over Palestinian territory or the principle of Israeli security. The idea of a Palestinian state confederated with Jordan seems unacceptable to the majority of Palestinians. Equally unlikely would be the establishment of a Palestinian state divorced from the PLO and the power and authority it wields among Palestinians.

But matters may take a different course. The failure of peace diplomacy as a result of inflexible attitudes on both sides or the outright breakdown of talks could lead to the resumption of hostilities between Israel and the Arab countries. A situation could come about as the result of neither a comprehensive solution nor a total deadlock but of only a partial solution in which each party obtained something and felt that to accept it would not constitute a defeat. The narrow focus of any such agreements, however, contains obvious dangers.

Conflict theory makes it clear that disputes over pragmatic and instrumental values are more easily resolved than disputes over fundamentals. The disengagement of forces on the Egyptian and Syrian fronts represents the resolution of a dispute that concerned peripheral rather than central issues of the Arab–Israeli conflict. The core of the Israeli–Palestinian conflict, namely nationalist rivalry and attendant ideology, has been left untouched in the course of negotiations thus far. Whether settlement of nonfundamental issues can lead to settlement of fundamental issues remains an open question. But it seems obvious that the more vague the definition of the territorial withdrawal demanded of Israel and of the meaning of Palestinian rights, which are at the center of the conflict, the more difficult the resolution of these issues becomes.

A year into the intifada, Israeli society was becoming increasingly polarized over the Palestinian question. The two major parties, Labor and Likud, were deadlocked. Labor supported a dialogue with the PLO and the exchange of land for peace, although it opposed the creation of a Palestinian state. Labor's peace formula rested in the return of the West Bank to Jordanian control, even though Jordan has renounced all claims to the West Bank. The Labor party proposed elections for the territories, and members of the Labor party had actually met with Palestinians in an effort to move things forward. Likud, however, stated its position: not talking with the PLO, no exchange of land for peace, and no Palestinian state. The Likud formula called for Israel to retain the occupied territories and for the Palestinians to be granted limited autonomy. Likud felt that the intifada could be ended by force, whereas Labor and even the army felt it was a political problem that could be solved only by a political solution. The two parties had opted to form a coalition government, leaving neither one free to pursue its political agenda. At various points Labor threatened to pursue a unilateral peace initiative in the hope that it would cause a breakup of the coalition and force new elections in which the Labor party hoped to gain the advantage.

In the international arena, Israel has come under strong criticism by Western nations for its brutal handling of the intifada. Even the United States was beginning to view Israel as an obstacle to peace. Prime Minister Shamir came to Washington in April 1989 to put forth his own election proposal. Essentially, the plan called for elections in the West Bank and Gaza to select Palestinian representatives who would negotiate a five-year transitional period of self-rule.

Palestinians would have jurisdiction over their own daily affairs while Israel would retain control over foreign affairs, security, and issues pertaining to the Israeli settlers. A later round of negotiations would determine the final status of the territories.

Palestinians viewed the plan with suspicion, as a tactic to buy time to put down the intifada and to undermine the PLO's public relations success in the world. The Shamir Plan set the condition that there would be no change in the status of the territories, that Israel would surrender not one section of the land. The PLO saw Shamir's plan as having little to offer; the plan violated their primary goal of achieving statehood.

Those who advocate armed struggle insist that the Palestinians, like all people, have an internationally recognized right to resist occupation and to fight for liberation. Conversely, others, mainly residents of the occupied territories, argue that Israel has killed many Palestinians during the intifada. If the Palestinians were to take up weapons, it would be an invitation for the slaughter of thousands and perhaps for a mass expulsion of the Palestinians from the territories. The inclination to escalate the conflict with the use of arms comes from a deeply held belief that Israel will seek a settlement only when the occupation becomes too costly. A decision to reinvoke armed struggle as part of a resistance campaign would be guided by the admission that all other avenues to a solution have been blocked and there is nothing left to lose.

This academic debate was cut short when the Gulf crisis erupted into open combat between the American-led coalition and Iraq. The clear implication was that the forces of moderation and mediation were outpaced by the thunder of militarism and military strategy. Both Palestinians and Israelis sought solace in the conflict environment. Because war is about power, specifically the dispute over power distribution and hence political control, the Israelis viewed triumph over Saddam Hussein and his well-armed Arab forces as vindication for their long-held, unwavering stand that a negotiated compromise over territory would be unwise because, fundamentally, Arab recognition and acceptance of the Jewish state is still in doubt. The Palestinians, openly expressing jubilation on learning that Scud missiles had hit citizens in Tel Aviv, saw the military might of Iraqi forces as a real and substantial counterthreat to Israeli military strength in the region. For them, the structural positioning of two forces of raw power, more balanced than ever, opened an opportunity for change in the political landscape, possibly tipping the balance in their favor.

The Gulf conflict, in spite of the sidelined role ostensibly assumed by Israelis and Palestinians alike, brought forth the intense, hostile undercurrent that has defined the basic relations between the two parties and their mirrored enemy images for years. The triumph of war over negotiated settlement in this chapter of Middle East affairs indicates the extremely delicate line separating militants and moderates and the ease of moving into armed-struggle solutions rather than working toward negotiated peace. From the Palestinian and the Israeli perspectives, it seems more and more clear that separation is the only way, the only real option for the future. Any slowdown in this process tends to play into the hands of militants on both sides and only polarizes the situation. The opportunity for peace may be fragile, but working toward negotiation will likely strengthen the role of the moderates.

But what exactly is meant by this elaborate ritual of prenegotiation positioning and bargaining? John Cross (1977) has identified the nature and function of bargaining processes from two different views. First, bargaining is a charade. The parties have a common (but unstated) understanding of what the final agreement will be, and the elaborate sequence of bids and counterbids, threats, and other uses of force has as its sole purpose the gratification or appeasement of third parties. Second, bargaining is a mechanism for dividing the fruits of co-operation among two or more participants. The emphasis is on division rather than cooperation. No matter how complicated the original situation may be, and no matter how many dimensions may be required to define an agreement, it is usually simplified to a single dimension. There is the selection of a settlement point along the boundary of possibilities on the assumption that each party gains satisfaction only from self-payoff and is essentially indifferent to the payoffs received by others.

These interpretations of the bargaining process presume that the set of possible agreements is known to both parties. But this is not necessarily so. Much of what is happening centers on a search for mutually beneficial agreements. Negotiation may actually consist of a series of component bargains in which the parties discover that two issues afford possible exchanges, and an agreement may be struck before the next pair of tradeable issues has even been discovered (Cross, 1977:587). Unfortunately, the literature on negotiation is almost silent on this search-and-settling-in aspect of the process. Most models of bargaining stress the full-information, one-dimensional problem and rely on a paradigm in which the two parties concern themselves with the division of the payoff.

Prenegotiations may take more time than either party initially expected. The use of force or coercion, which increases the costs of delays in agreement, will reduce the duration of the negotiation. Also if a party's learning rate is high, the duration of the negotiation will be reduced.

If negotiation is defined as a process of value and behavior modification in which peaceful means are used to alter divergent positions toward a common convergence of values, then the use of persuasive techniques and their success in modifying negotiators' values toward an initially desired end should encourage states to help achieve acceptable outcomes. Mutual power and influence relationships, if employed effectively and credibly, should result in eventual concessions and a convergence of formerly conflicting interests. Learning and flexibility in position-taking may be impeded if a negotiator's perceptual framework is closed to new conceptions of the opponent. The closed-mindedness and intense suspicion have been a major stumbling block in activating negotiations between the Arabs and the Israelis.

In the negotiation process, the mutual use of power to maximize one's own interests while achieving a common convergence of interests creates a complex, mixed-motive ambience of trust and suspicion. The objective and the subjective environments also have a direct impact on the negotiator. A negotiator's subjective interpretation and expectations of the opponent's position and behavior provide the basis for strategic planning, whether the image is true or biased.

Bargaining outcomes are conceived as the culmination of power plays between participants. They are normally not the result of a single effort. Convergence of interests is a gradual process because persuasion is a gradual process. Mutual attempts to use power to influence the other side's positions and goals are not only a means of self-interest maximization but also a fundamental search process to identify likely areas for accommodation, sensitive issues best to be delayed, limits of acceptability, strengths of commitments, and optimal timing for agreement.

Bargaining is a rhetorical contest characterized by discussion, posturing, and persuasive appeals that depend on expectations of the opponent's concession-making pattern. The process entails threats, commitments, reactions, initiatives, accommodations, and promises. Negotiators—or parties who anticipate negotiating—operate within two limits: they act to increase common interests and expand cooperation; they also act to maximize their own interests and to prevail in terms of ensuring that an agreement is valuable for themselves. Ultimately, psychological attributes of decision makers and their general orientation toward accommodation and conciliation structure the negotiating environment. Parties that display suspicion, authoritarianism, and anxiousness *or* high self-esteem are more likely to be hard and difficult bargainers. Those representatives who possess a cognitive complexity of the problems to be settled and who are compassionate toward one another are more concerned with finding an accepted resolution to outstanding issues. Therefore, before serious discussion on any settlement starts, the psychological barriers have to be lowered, the polarity gap reduced. Paradoxically, since the history of the Arab–Israeli dispute is a cycle of violence followed by peace plans followed by violence again, perceptions of the enemy tend to polarize and become more rigid with time. Yet it seems as if the periods of conflict in international war and the localized intifada may be a part of the forward thrust toward a settlement.

The symbolism of victimization and suffering, of basic acceptance for a national homeland, continues to define a central element of the Arab–Israeli conflict. Both sides have grievances, both are frustrated, each seeks legitimacy for its cause. Regional political rules emphasize power and coercion, which operate as temporary devices for dispute resolution. Psychological reorientation and fresh avenues of negotiation strategy have rarely been tried, yet the possibility remains that this type of bargaining could produce settlement outcomes that are at least as satisfactory as, and no more costly than, choices reached by military power.

Will the pattern persist? One can hope for a workable political negotiation strategy to satisfy all parties at this stage, even though the bargaining will be hard fought.

Bibliography

Adan, Avraham. *On the Banks of the Suez*. San Raphael, Calif.: Universe, 1980.

Ajami, Fouad. "The Arab Predicament." In *The Arab–Israeli Conflict: Perspectives*, edited by Alvin Z. Rubinstein. New York: Praeger, 1984.

———. "The End of Pan Arabism." *Foreign Affairs* 57 (Winter 1978–79): 355–73.

Alexander, Yonah. "The Jewish Struggle for Self-Determination: The Birth of Israel." In *Self Determination: National, Regional, and Global Dimensions*, edited by Yonah Alexander and Robert Friedlander. Boulder, Colo.: Westview, 1980.

Allon, Yigal. *The Making of Israel's Army*. New York: Universe, 1970.

Almog, Shmuel, ed. *Zionism and the Arabs*. Jerusalem: Historical Society of Israel, 1983.

American Friends Service Committee. *A Compassionate Peace: A Future for the Middle East*. New York: Hill and Wang, 1982.

Aviner, Shlomo. *The Making of Modern Zionism: The Intellectual Origins of the Jewish State*. New York: Basic Books, 1981.

Axelrod, Robert. "Argumentation in Foreign Policy Settings: Britain in 1918." *Journal of Conflict Resolution* 21, no. 4 (December 1977): 727–44.

Azar, Edward E. "Peace Admist Development: A Conceptual Agenda for Conflict and Peace Research" *International Interactions* 6, no. 2 (1979): 123–43.

Azar, Edward E. and Stephen Cohen "Peace as Crisis and War as Status Quo: The Arab–Israeli Conflict Environment" *International Interactions* 6, no. 2 (1979): 159–84.

Azar, Edward E. "The Theory of Protracted Social Conflict and the Challenge of Transforming Conflict Situations." In *Conflict Processes of the Breakdown of International Systems*, edited by Dina Zinnes. Boulder, Colo.: Monograph Series in World Affairs, vol. 20, no. 2. 1983.

Azar, Edward, and John W. Burton, eds. *International Conflict Resolution: Theory and Practice*. Boulder, Colo.: Lynne Rienner, 1986.

Azar, Edward, P. Jureidini, and R. McLaurin. "Protracted Social Conflict: Theory and Practice in the Middle East." *Journal of Palestine Studies* 8, no. 1 (1978): 41–60.

Barringer, R. E. *War: Patterns of Conflict*. Cambridge, Mass.: MIT Press, 1972.

Bar-Siman-Tov, Yaacov. *Linkage Politics in the Middle East: Syrian between Domestic and External Conflict, 1961–1970*. Boulder, Colo.: Westview, 1983.

Bartos, Otomar J. "Simple Model of Negotiation: A Sociological Point of View." *Journal of Conflict Resolution* 21, no. 4 (December 1977): 565–79.

Bartunek, Jean M., Alan A. Benton, and Christopher B. Keys. "Third Party Intervention and the Bargaining Behavior of Group Representatives." *Journal of Conflict Resolution* 19, no. 3 (September 1975): 532–57.

Baum, Phil, and Raphael Danzinger. "A Regenerated PLO: The Palestine National Council's 1988 Resolutions and Their Repercussions." *Middle East Review* 23, no. 1 (Fall 1989): 17–25.

Begin, Menachem. *The Revolt*. New York: Nash, 1977.

———. *White Nights: The Story of a Prisoner in Russia*. New York: Harper and Row, 1977.

Beliny, Willard A. *Middle East Peace Plans*. New York: St. Martin's, 1986.

Ben-dor, Gabriel. "The Institutionalization of Palestinian Nationalism, 1967–1973." In *From June to October: The Middle East between 1967 and 1973*, edited by Haim Shaked and Itamar Rabinovich. New Brunswick: Transaction Books, 1978.

———. "Nationalism without Sovereignty and Nationalism with Multiple Sovereignties: The Palestinians and Inter-Arab Relations." In *The Palestinians and the Middle East Conflict*, edited by G. Ben-dor. Ramat Gan, Israel: Turtledove Publishers, 1978.

Ben-Gurion, David. *Israel: Years of Challenge*. New York: Holt, Rinehart and Winston, 1976.

Benvenisti, Meron. *Conflicts and Contradictions*. New York: Villard, 1986.

———. *1986 Report: Demographic, Economic, Legal, Social, and Political Developments in the West Bank*. Jerusalem: West Bank Data Base Project, 1986.

———. *The West Bank Data Project: A Survey of Israel's Policies*. Washington, D.C.: American Enterprise Institute, 1984.

Bethel, Nicholas. *The Palestine Triangle: The Struggle for the Holy Land, 1935–1948*. New York: Putnam, 1979.

Birkland, Carol S. *Unified in Hope: Arabs and Jews Talk about Peace*. New York: Friendship Press, 1987.

Blalock, Hubert M. *Power and Conflict: Toward a General Theory*. Newbury Park, Calif.: Sage, 1989.

Blitzer, Wolf. *Between Washington and Jerusalem: A Reporter's Notebook*. New York: Oxford University Press, 1985.

Brown, L. Carl. *International Politics and the Middle East: Old Rules, Dangerous Game*. Princeton: Princeton University Press, 1984.

Brzezinski, Zbigniew. *Power and Principle: Memoirs of the National Security Advisor, 1977–1981*. New York: Farrar, Straus and Giroux, 1983.

Burton, John W. *Conflict and Communication: The Use of Controlled Communication in International Relations*. New York: Free Press, 1969.

Butterworth, Robert Lyle. "Do Conflict Managers Matter? An Empirical Assessment of Interstate Security Disputes and Resolution Efforts, 1945–1974." *International Studies Quarterly* 22, no. 2 (June 1978): 195–214.

Caradon, Lord, Arthur J. Goldberg, Mohamed H. El-Zayyat, and Abba Eban. *U.N.*

Security Council Resolution 242: A Case Study in Diplomatic Ambiguity. Washington, D.C.: Institute for the Study of Diplomacy, Georgetown University, 1981.

Carter, Jimmy. *The Blood of Abraham: Insights into the Middle East*. Boston: Houghton Mifflin, 1985.

———. *Keeping Faith: Memoirs of a President*. New York: Bantam, 1982.

Chapman, Colin. *Whose Promised Land?* Tring, England: Lion Publishing, 1983.

Cohen, Geula. *Women of Violence: Memoirs of a Young Terrorist, 1943–1948*. Translated from the Hebrew by Hillel Halkin. New York: Holt, Rinehart and Winston, 1966.

Cohen, Raymond. "Problems of Intercultural Communications in Egyptian-American Diplomatic Relations." *International Journal of Intercultural Relations* 11 (1987): 29–47.

Cordesman, Anthony H. "Peace in the Middle East: The Value of Small Victories." *Middle East Journal* 38, no. 3 (Summer 1984): 515–20.

Cross, John G. "Negotiation As a Learning Process." *Journal of Conflict Resolution* 21, no. 4 (December 1977): 581–606.

Curtis, Michael. "The Uprising's Impact on the Options for Peace." *Middle East Review* 21, no. 2 (Winter 1988–89): 3–12.

Dayan, Moshe. *Breakthrough: A Personal Account of the Israel-Egypt Peace Negotiations*. New York: Knopf, 1981.

———. *Moshe Dayan: Story of My Life*. New York: Morrow, 1976.

Deutsch, Morton. *The Resolution of Conflict: Constructive and Destructive Processes*. New Haven: Yale University Press, 1973.

Dinstein, Yoram. "Self-Determination and the Middle East Conflict." In *Self-Determination: National, Regional, and Global Dimensions*, edited by Yonah Alexander and Robert A. Friedlander. Boulder, Colo.: Westview, 1980.

Divine, Donna R. "The Dialectics of Palestinian Politics." In *Palestinian Society and Politics*, edited by Joel Migdal. Princeton: Princeton University Press, 1980.

Druckman, Daniel. "Boundary Role Conflict: Negotiation As Dual Responsiveness." *Journal of Conflict Resolution* 21, no. 4 (December 1977): 639–62.

———, ed. *Negotiations: Social Psychological Perspectives*. Beverly Hills, Calif.: Sage, 1977.

Eban, Abba. *An Autobiography*. New York: Random House, 1977.

———. *My People: The Story of the Jews*. New York: Behrman House, 1968.

Elan, Amos. *Herzl*. New York: Holt, Rinehart and Winston, 1975.

———. *The Israelis Founders and Sons*. New York: Holt, Rinehart and Winston, 1971.

Eliav, Arie Lova. *Land of the Hart: Israelis, Arabs, the Territories, and a Vision of the Future*. Philadelphia: Jewish Publication Society of America, 1974.

Elizur, Yuval, and Eliahu Salpetter. *Who Rules Israel?* New York: Harper and Row, 1973.

Feste, Karen A. *The Arab–Israeli Conflict: A Decision-Making Game*. Washington, D.C.: American Political Science Association, 1977.

———. *Conflict in the Middle East: A Public Policy Simulation*. Washington, D.C.: American Political Science Association, 1975.

———. "Exploring Negotiation Possibilities in the Arab-Israeli Conflict." *Crossroads*, no. 29 (1989): 50–80.

Fisher, Roger, and William Ury. *Getting to Yes: Negotiating Arguments without Giving In*. New York: Houghton Mifflin, 1981. Reprint, Harmondsworth, England: Penguin Books, 1983.

Flapan, Simha. *The Birth of Israel: Myths and Realities.* New York: Pantheon, 1987.
———. *Zionism and the Palestinians.* London: Croom Helm, 1979.
Gabriel, Richard A. *Operation Peace for Galilee: The Israeli–PLO War in Lebanon.* New York: Hill and Wang, 1984.
Garfinkle, Adam M. " 'Common Sense' about Middle East Diplomacy: Implications for U.S. Policy in the Near Term." *Middle East Review* 17, no. 2 (Winter 1984–85): 24–32.
Glassman, Jon D. *Arms for the Arabs: The Soviet Union and War in the Middle East.* Baltimore: Johns Hopkins University Press, 1978.
Goitein, S. D. *Jews and Arabs: Their Contacts through the Ages.* New York: Schrocken, 1964.
Goldman, Nahum. *The Jewish Paradox.* New York: Grosset and Dunlap, 1978.
Gottlieb, Gidon. "Israel and the Palestinians." *Foreign Affairs* 68, no. 4 (Fall 1989): 104–26.
Graber, Doris A. "Conflict Images: An Assessment of the Middle East Debates in the United Nations." *Journal of Politics* 32, no. 2 (1970): 339–78.
———. "Perceptions of Middle East Conflict in the U.N., 1953–1965." *Journal of Conflict Resolution* 13, no. 4 (December 1969): 454–484.
Greilslammer, Ilan, and Joseph Weiler. *Europe's Middle East Dilemma.* Boulder, Colo.: Westview, 1987.
Gresh, Alain. *The PLO: The Struggle Within: Towards an Independent Palestinian State.* London: Zed, 1983.
Grose, Peter. *A Changing Israel.* New York: Vintage, 1985.
Haber, Eitan. *Menachem Begin: The Legend and the Man.* New York: Delacorte, 1978.
Haig, Alexander M., Jr. *Caveat: Realism, Reagan, and Foreign Policy.* New York: Macmillan, 1984.
Hallaj, Muhammed. "Zionist Violence against Palestinians." *The Link* 21, no. 3 (September 1988): 2–6.
Hareven, Alouph, ed. *Can the Palestinian Problem Be Solved?* Jerusalem: Van Leer Foundation, 1983.
Harkabi, Yehoshafat. *Arab Attitudes toward Israel.* Jerusalem: Ketter, 1972.
———. *The Bar Kokhba Syndrome: Risk and Realism in International Politics.* Chappaqua, N.Y.: Rossel, 1983.
———. *The Palestinian Covenant and Its Meaning.* London: Valentine, Mitchell, 1979.
Hazo, Robert G. "Conditions for Peace." *American-Arab Affairs*, no. 1 (Summer 1982): 120–26.
Heller, Mark A. *A Palestinian State: The Implications for Israel.* Cambridge, Mass.: Harvard University Press, 1983.
———. "Politics and Social Change in the West Bank Since 1967." In *Palestinian Society and Politics*, edited by Joel Migdal. Princeton: Princeton University Press, 1980.
Henderson, G., R. Lebow, and J. Stoessinger. *Divided Nations in a Divided World.* New York: David McKay, 1974.
Heradstveit, Daniel. *The Arab–Israeli Conflict: Psychological Obstacles to Peace.* Oslo, Norway: Universitetsforlaget, 1981.
Hersh, Seymour M. *The Price of Power: Kissinger in the White House.* New York: Summit, 1983.
Hertzberg, Arthur. *The Zionist Idea.* New York: Antheneum. 1981.

Herzl, Theodor. *The Jewish State*. 1896.
————. *Old New Land*. New York: Markus Wiener Publishing and the Herzl Press, 1987.
Herzog, Chaim. *The Arab–Israeli Wars: War and Peace in the Middle East*. New York: Random House, 1982.
————. *The War of Atonement: October 1973*. Boston: Little, Brown, 1975.
Hoffman, John E., and Benjamin Beit-Hallahmi. "The Palestinian Identity and Israel's Arabs." In *The Palestinians and the Middle East Conflict*, edited by G. Ben-dor. Ramat Gan, Israel: Turtledove Publishers, 1978.
Holsti, K. J. *International Politics: A Framework for Analysis*. 3d ed. Englewood Cliffs, N.J.: Prentice Hall, 1977.
Hopmann, P. Terrence, and Theresa C. Smith. "An Application of a Richardson Process Model: Soviet-American Interactions in the Test Ban Negotiations, 1962–1963." *Journal of Conflict Resolution* 21, no. 4 (December 1977): 701–26.
Huntington, Samuel, and Jorge Dominguez. "Political Development." In *Handbook of Political Science: Macropolitical Theory*, edited by Fred Greenstein and Nelson Polsby, vol. 3. Reading, Mass.: Addison-Wesley, 1975.
Iklé, Frederich C. *How Nations Negotiate*. New York: Praeger, 1967.
Jewish Agency for Palestine. *Memorandum to the Palestine Royal Commission*. Jerusalem 1936.
Johnson, Lyndon B. *The Vantage Point: Perspectives of the Presidency*. New York: Holt, Rinehart and Winston, 1971.
Kahane, Meir. *They Must Go*. New York: Grosset and Dunlap, 1981.
————. *Time to Go Home*. Los Angeles: Nash, 1972.
Kalb, Marvin, and Bernard Kalb. *Kissinger*. Boston: Little, Brown, 1979.
Kazziha, Walid. *Palestine in the Arab Dilemma*. London: Croom Helm, 1979.
Kelman, Herbert C. "The Political Psychology of the Israeli Palestinian Conflict: How Can We Overcome the Barriers to a Negotiated Solution?" *Political Psychology* 8, no. 3 (1987): 347–63.
————. "The Palestinianization of the Arab–Israeli Conflict." *Jerusalem Quarterly*, no. 46 (Spring 1988): 3–15.
Kenen, I. L. *Israel's Defense Line: Her Friends and Foes in Washington*. Buffalo, N.Y.: Prometheus, 1981.
Khouri, Fred J. "Major Obstacles to Peace: Ignorance, Myths, and Misconceptions." *American-Arab Affairs*, no. 16 (Spring 1986): 37–62.
Kissinger, Henry. *White House Years*. Boston: Little, Brown, 1979.
————. *Years of Upheaval*. Boston: Little, Brown, 1982.
Kollek, Teddy, with Amos Kollek. *For Jerusalem: A Life by Teddy Kollek*. New York: Random House, 1978.
Kurzman, Dan. *Ben-Gurion: Prophet of Fire*. New York: Simon and Schuster, 1983.
————. *Genesis 1948: The First Arab–Israeli War*. New York: New American Library, 1970.
Lall, Arthur. *The UN and the Middle East Crisis, 1967*. New York: Columbia University Press, 1968.
Landau, Chaim (ed.) *Israel and the Arabs*. Jerusalem: Central Press. 1971.
Lanir, Zvi. *Israel's Involvement in Lebanon: A Precedent for an "Open" Game with Syria?* Tel Aviv, Israel: Center for Strategic Studies.

Lapidoth, Ruth. "The Autonomy Negotiations: A Stocktaking." *Middle East Review* 15, 3/4 (Spring/Summer 1983): 35–44.

Laqueur, Walter. *A History of Zionism*. New York: Schocken, 1978.

———, ed. *The Israel-Arab Reader: A Documentary History of the Middle East Conflict*. New York: Bantam, 1970.

Laqueur, Walter, and Barry Rubin. *The Israel-Arab Reader: A Documentary History of the Middle East Conflict*. New York: Penguin, 1984.

Latour, S. "Some Determinants of Preference for Modes of Conflict Resolution." *Journal of Conflict Resolution 20*, no. 2 (June 1976): 319–56.

Lenczowski, George. *The Middle East in World Affairs*. 4th ed. Ithaca: Cornell University Press, 1980.

Leonard, James. "The Autonomy Talks: Muddling Through." In *Israel, the Middle East, and U.S. Interests*, edited by Harry S. Allen and Ivan Volgyes. New York: Praeger, 1983.

Lesch, Ann Mosley, and Mark Tesler. *Israel, Egypt, and the Palestinians: From Camp David to Intifada*. Bloomington, Ind.: Indiana University Press, 1989.

Levy, A. M., and A. Benjamin, "Focus and Flexibility in a Model of Conflict Resolution." *Journal of Conflict Resolution 21*, no. 3 (September 1977): 405–25.

Lewis, Bernard. *The Jews of Islam*. Princeton: Princeton University Press, 1984.

Lewis, Flora. "Middle East Back Sliding." *New York Times*, March 12, 1989.

Luttwak, Edward, and Dan Horowitz. *The Israeli Army*. London: Allen Lane, 1975.

Machiavelli, Niccolò. *The Prince and the Discourses*. Modern Library Series. New York: Random House, 1940.

McDowall, David. *Palestine and Israel: The Uprising and Beyond*. Berkeley: University of California Press, 1989.

McLand, Charles B. *Soviet–Middle East Relations*. London: Central Asian Research Center, 1973.

Mandel, Robert. *Perceptions, Decision-Making, and Conflict*. Washington, D.C.: University Press of America, 1979.

Meir, Golda. *My Life*. New York: Putnam, 1977.

Mendelsohn, Everett, *A Compassionate Peace: A Future for Israel, Palestine, and the Middle East*. A Report Prepared for the American Friends Service Committee. Revised edition. New York: Noonday Press. 1989.

Meyer, Lawrence. *Israel Now: Portrait of a Troubled Land*. New York: Delacorte, 1982.

The Middle East and North Africa. Thirty-seventh Edition. London: Europa Publications, Ltd., 1990.

Milstein, Jeffrey. "American and Soviet Influence, Balance of Power, and Arab–Israeli Violence." In *Peace, War, Numbers*, edited by Bruce Russett. Beverly Hills, Calif.: Sage, 1972.

Moore, John Norton, ed. *The Arab–Israeli Conflict: Volume III: Documents*. Princeton: Princeton University Press, 1974.

———. *The Arab-Israeli Conflict: Volume I: Readings*. Princeton: Princeton University Press, 1974.

Naess, A. "A Systemization of Ghandian Ethics of Conflict Resolution." *Journal of Conflict Resolution 2*, no. 1 (June 1958): 140–55.

Neff, Donald. *Warriors at Suez*. New York: Simon and Schuster, 1981.

———. *Warriors for Jerusalem: The Six Days That Changed the Middle East*. New York: Simon and Schuster, 1984.

Neumann, Robert G. "The Middle East in the Next Decade." *American-Arab Affairs*, no. 126 (Summer 1988): 1–15.

Nixon, Richard. *The Memoirs of Richard Nixon*. New York: Grosset and Dunlap, 1978.

Norton, Augustus R., and Martin H. Greenberg, eds. *The International Relations of the Palestine Liberation Organization*. Washington, D.C.: Sidney Kramer Books, Southern Illinois University Press, 1989.

O'Ballance, Edgar. *No Victor, No Vanquished: The Yom Kippur War*. San Raphael, Calif.: Presidio Press, 1978.

Ott, M. C. "Mediation As a Method of Conflict Resolution: Two Cases." *International Organization* 26, no. 4 (1972): 595–618.

Oz, Amos. *The Hill of Evil Counsel*. London: Fontana/Collins, 1980.

———. *In the Land of Israel*. New York: Harcourt Brace Jovanovich, 1983.

———. *Touch the Water, Touch the Wind*. New York: Bantam, 1979.

Peri, Yoram. *Between Battles and Ballots: Israeli Military in Politics*. Cambridge: Cambridge University Press, 1983.

Perla, Shlomo. "Israel-Jordan Armistice Talks in 1949—A Case Study of Israel's Predilection for Direct Negotiation with the Arabs." *Middle East Review* 23, no. 1 (Fall 1989): 26–34.

Perlmutter, Amos. "Crisis Management: Kissinger's Middle East Negotiations, October 1973–June 1974." *International Studies Quarterly* 19, no. 3 (September 1975): 316–43.

———. *Israel: The Partitioned State*. New York: Scribner, 1985.

Peters, Joan. *From Time Immemorial: The Origins of the Arab-Jewish Conflict over Palestine*. New York: Harper and Row, 1984.

Pirages, Dennis. "Political Stability of Conflict Management." In *Handbook of Political Conflict: Theory and Practice*, edited by Ted Robert Gurr. New York: Free Press, 1980.

Pratt, Cranford, et al. *Peace, Justice, and Reconciliation in the Arab–Israeli Conflict: A Christian Perspective*. New York: Friendship Press, 1979.

Quandt, William B. *Camp David: Peacemaking and Politics*. Washington, D.C.: Brookings Institution, 1986.

———. *Decade of Decisions: American Policy toward the Arab–Israeli Conflict*. Berkeley: University of California Press, 1977.

Rabin, Yitzhak. *The Rabin Memoirs*. Boston: Little, Brown, 1979.

Ramberg, Bennett. "Tactical Advantages of Opening Positioning Strategies: Lessons from the Seabed Arms Control Talks, 1967–1970." *Journal of Conflict Resolution* 21, no. 4 (December 1977): 685–700.

Reich, Walter. *A Stranger in My House: Jews and Arabs in the West Bank*. New York: Holt, Rinehart and Winston, 1984.

Report of the United Nations Special Committee on Palestine, September 3, 1947. United Nations Document A/364, Supplement II, Paragraphs 127–160c. New York: UN General Assembly, 1947.

Rosenau, James, ed. *Linkage Politics*. New York: Free Press, 1969.

Rubin, Barry. "Middle East: Search for Peace." *Foreign Affairs* 64, no. 3 (1985): 585–604.

Rubin, Jeffrey, ed. *Dynamics of Third Party Interventions: Kissinger in the Middle East*, New York: Praeger, 1981.

Rubinstein, Alvin Z., ed. *The Arab–Israeli Conflict: Perspectives*. New York: Praeger, 1984.

Russett, Bruce, and Harvey Starr. *World Politics: Menu for Choice*. San Francisco: W. H. Freeman, 1981.

Sachar, Howard M. *The Course of Modern Jewish History*. New York: Dell, 1977.

———. *Diaspora: An Inquiry into the Contemporary Jewish World*. New York: Harper and Row, 1985.

———. *A History of Israel: From the Rise of Zionism to Our Time*. New York: Knopf, 1979.

Safran, Nadav. *Israel: The Embattled Ally*. Cambridge, Mass.: Belknap Press, 1978.

Satloff, Robert B. "Beyond the Peace Process." *Middle East Review* 19, no. 2 (Winter 1986–87): 24–27.

Saunders, Harold H. "Arabs and Israelis: A Political Strategy." *Foreign Affairs* 64, no. 2 (1985): 304–25.

———. "An Israeli–Palestinian Peace." *Foreign Affairs* 61, no. 1 (Fall 1982): 101–21.

———. *The Other Walls: The Politics of the Arab-Israeli Peace Process*. Washington, D.C.: American Enterprise Institute, 1985.

———. "Superpower Stakes in the Middle East" *AEI Foreign Policy and Defense Review* 6, no. 1 (1986): 14–27.

Schelling, Thomas. *The Strategy of Conflict*. New York: Oxford University Press, 1963.

Schiff, Ze'ev. *A History of the Israeli Army (1870–1974)*. San Francisco: Straight Arrow, 1974.

Schiff, Ze'ev, and Ehud Ya'ari. *Israel's Lebanon War*. New York: Simon and Schuster, 1984.

Schiff, Ze'ev, Ehud Ya'ari, and Eitan Haber. *The Year of the Dove*. New York: Bantam, 1979.

Segal, Jerome M. *Creating the Palestinian State: A Strategy for Peace*. Chicago: Lawrence Hill Books, 1989.

Segev, Tom. *The First Israelis*. New York: Free Press, 1986.

Shaked, Haim. "Continuity and Change: An Overview." In *The Arab–Israeli Conflict: Perspectives*, edited by Alvin Z. Rubinstein. New York: Praeger, 1984.

Sharabi, Hisham. "The Arab–Israeli Conflict: The Next Phase." In *Crisis Management and the Superpowers in the Middle East*, edited by Gregory Treverson. Montclair, N.J.: International Institute for Strategic Studies, Gower and Allanheld, Osmon, 1981.

Shazly, Saad el. *The Crossing of the Suez*. San Francisco: American Mideast Research, 1980.

Shimani, Yaacov. *Political Dictionary of the Arab World*. New York: Macmillan, 1987.

Shipler, David K. *Arabs and Jew: Wounded Spirits in a Promised Land*. New York: Penguin Books, 1986.

Sidjanski, Dusan. *Political Decision-Making Processes*. Washington, D.C.: Jossey-Bass, 1973.

Silver, Eric. *Begin: The Haunted Prophet*. New York: Random House, 1984.

Simpson, Michael, ed. *United Nations Resolutions on Palestine and the Arab–Israeli Conflict*. Vol. 1, 1947–74; Vol. 2, 1975–81; Vol. 3, 1982–86. Washington, D.C.: Institute for Palestine Studies.

Smith, David. *Prisoners of God: The Modern Day Conflict of Arab and Jew*. London: Quartet Books, 1987.

Snyder, Glenn, and Paul Diesing. *Conflict among Nations: Bargaining, Decision Making, and System Structure in International Crisis*. Princeton: Princeton University Press, 1976.

Spector, Bertram I. "Negotiation As a Learning Process." *Journal of Conflict Resolution* 21, no. 4 (December 1977): 607–18.

Stinchcombe, Arthur L. "Social Structure and Politics." In *Handbook of Political Science: Macropolitical Theory*, edited by Fred I. Greenstein and Nelson Polsby. Vol. 3. Reading, Mass.: Addison-Wesley, 1975.

Stockman-Shomron, Israel, ed. *Israel, the Middle East, and the Great Powers*. Jerusalem: Shikmona, 1984.

Suedfeld, Peter, Philip F. Tetlock, and Carmenza Ramirez. "War, Peace, and Integrative Complexity: U.N. Speeches on the Middle East Problem, 1947–1976." *Journal of Conflict Resolution* 21, no. 3 (September 1977): 427–42.

Teveth, Shabtai. *Ben-Gurion and the Palestinian Arabs: From Peace to War*. New York: Oxford University Press, 1985.

Thant, U. *View from the UN: The Memoirs of U Thant*. New York: Doubleday, 1978.

Touval, Saadia. *The Peace Brokers: Mediators in the Arab–Israeli Conflict, 1948–1979*. Princeton: Princeton University Press, 1982.

Treverson, Gregory, ed. *Crisis Management and the Superpowers in the Middle East*. Montclair, N.J.: International Institute for Strategic Studies, Gower and Allanheld, Osmun, 1981.

"U.S. Joins U.N. Vote against Israel." *Facts on File* 50 (December 31, 1990): 959–80.

Vance, Cyrus. *Hard Choices: Critical Years in America's Foreign Policy*. New York: Simon and Schuster, 1983.

Viorst, Milton. *Sands of Sorrow: Israel's Journey from Independence*. New York: Harper and Row, 1987.

———. *UNRWA and Peace in the Middle East*. Washington, D.C.: Middle East Institute, 1984.

Wehr, Paul. *Conflict Regulation*. Boulder, Colo.: Westview, 1979.

Weizman, Ezer. *The Battle for Peace*. New York: Bantam, 1981.

Whitehead, Alfred North. "An Appeal to Sanity." *Atlantic Monthly*, March 1939, pp. 309–20.

Zagare, Frank C. "A Game-Theoretic Analysis of the Vietnam Negotiations: Preferences and Strategies, 1968–1973." *Journal of Conflict Resolution* 21, no. 4 (December 1977): 663–84.

Zartman, I. William. "Negotiation As a Joint Decision-Making Process." *Journal of Conflict Resolution* 21, no. 4 (December 1977): 619–38.

———. *Ripe for Resolution: Conflict and Intervention in Africa*. New York: Oxford University Press, 1985.

Ziring, Lawrence. *The Middle East Political Dictionary*. Santa Barbara, Calif.: ABC-CLIO Information Services, 1984.

Index

About the Author

Karen A. Feste, Associate Professor and Associate Dean of the Graduate School of International Studies at the University of Denver, is the author of *The Arab-Israeli Conflict: A Decision-Making* Game (1977) and is specializing on intervention strategy in world affairs.